Equality, Participation and Inclusion 2

- What are the experiences of children and young people?
- How can we think about the challenges they face?
- What systems and practices can support them?
- How can we develop greater equality, participation and inclusion across diverse settings?

This second edition of *Equality, Participation and Inclusion 2: Diverse contexts* is the second of two Readers aimed at people with an interest in issues of equality, participation and inclusion for children and young people. This second Reader focuses in particular upon the diverse experiences and contexts in which children and young people encounter issues of equality, participation and inclusion.

Comprising readings taken from the latest research in journal articles, newly commissioned chapters, as well as several chapters from the first edition that retain particular relevance, this fully updated second edition has broadened its focus to consider a wider range of diverse experiences and contexts, whilst maintaining an emphasis on educational settings.

Drawing on the writing of academics, practitioners, children and young people, this collection is a rich source of information and ideas for students and practitioners who are interested in thinking about how inequality and exclusion are experienced, and how they can be challenged, and will be of particular interest to those working in education, health, youth and community work, youth justice and social services. Families and advocates are also likely to be drawn to the material as much of it reflects on lived experiences and life stories.

Jonathan Rix is Senior Lecturer in inclusion, curriculum and learning at The Open University, UK.

Melanie Nind is Professor of Education at Southampton University, UK.

Kieron Sheehy is Senior Lecturer at the Centre for Childhood Development at The Open University, UK.

Katy Simmons is a Lecturer in inclusive and special education in the Centre for Curriculum and Teaching Studies at The Open University, UK.

John Parry is a Lecturer in early years and inclusion at The Open University, UK.

Rajni Kumrai is a Lecturer in education in the Faculty of Education and Language Studies at The Open University, UK.

Equality Participation and Inclusion 2

Diverse contexts

This Reader, and the companion volume *Equality, Participation and Inclusion 1: Diverse perspectives*, form part of the Open University module *Equality, Participation and Inclusion* (E214). This is a 60-point module, which can be studied on its own or as part of an Open University undergraduate qualification.

Details of this and other Open University modules and qualifications can be obtained from the Student Registration and Enquiry Service, The Open University, PO Box 197, Milton Keynes MK7 6BJ, United Kingdom: tel. +44 (0)845 300 6090, e-mail general-enquiries@open.ac.uk

Alternatively, you may visit the Open University website at http://www.open.ac.uk where you can learn more about the wide range of modules and qualifications offered at all levels by The Open University.

Equality, Participation and Inclusion 2

Diverse contexts
Second edition

Edited by
Jonathan Rix, Melanie Nind,
Kieron Sheehy, Katy Simmons,
John Parry and Rajni Kumrai

LONDON AND NEW YORK

This second edition published 2010
by Routledge
2 Park Square, Milton Park, Abingdon, Oxon OX14 4RN

Simultaneously published in the USA and Canada
by Routledge
711 Third Avenue, New York, NY 10017

Routledge is an imprint of the Taylor & Francis Group, an informa business

Published in association with The Open University, Walton Hall, Milton Keynes,
MK7 6AA, UK

Typeset in Bembo by Glyph International
Printed and bound in Great Britain by
CPI Antony Rowe, Chippenham, Wiltshire

British Library Cataloguing in Publication Data
A catalogue record for this book is available from the British Library

Library of Congress Cataloging-in-Publication Data
Equality, participation and inclusion 2 : diverse contexts /
edited by Jonathan Rix...[et al.]. – 2nd ed.
    p. cm.
1. Inclusive education. 2. Special education. 3. Multicultural education.
I. Rix, Jonathan.
LC1200.E78 2010b
371.9'046—dc22   2010018662

ISBN 13: 978-0-415-58425-8 (hbk)
ISBN 13: 978-0-415-58424-1 (pbk)
ISBN 13: 978-0-203-83977-5 (ebk)

Contents

Acknowledgements

We wish to thank those who have written chapters for this Reader or who have given their permission for us to edit and reprint writing from other publications. Special thanks to Bharti Mistry and Christine Hardwick for their invaluable support in preparing these materials for publication. Grateful acknowledgement is made to the following sources for permission to reproduce material in this book. Every attempt has been made to contact the copyright holders of all articles reproduced in this book. If any requirements for the reproduction of these works remains unfulfilled, please contact the publisher. Those chapters not listed were specially commissioned.

Wiley Blackwell for permission to reprint McConkey, R. (2002) 'Reciprocal working by education, health and social services: lessons for a less-travelled road', *British Journal of Special Education* 29(1). Reproduced by permission of Wiley Blackwell Publishing Ltd.

Wiley Blackwell for permission to reprint Norris, C. and Closs, A. (1999) 'Child and parent relationships with teachers in schools responsible for the education of children with serious medical conditions', *British Journal of Special Education* 26(1). Reproduced by permission of Wiley Blackwell Publishing Ltd. Reprinted with permission of the author.

Wiley Blackwell for permission to reprint Brodie, I. (2000) 'Children's homes and school exclusion: redefining the problem', *Support for Learning* 15(1). Reproduced by permission of Wiley Blackwell Publishing Ltd.

Wiley Blackwell for permission to reprint Visser, J., Cole, T. and Daniels, H. (2002) 'Inclusion for the difficult to include', *Support for Learning* 17(1). Reproduced by permission of Wiley Blackwell Publishing Ltd.

Taylor & Francis Ltd for permission to reprint extracts from Hutton, Eve, '"Back to school" – piloting an occupational therapy service in mainstream schools in the UK', *Reflective Practice*, (2008) 9:4, 461–472. Reprinted by permission of the publisher (Taylor & Francis Ltd, http://www.tandf.co.uk/journals).

Cook, T., Swain, J. and French, S. (2001) 'Voices from segregated schooling: towards an inclusive education system', *Disability and Society* 16(2), 293–310.

Reprinted by permission of the publisher (Taylor & Francis Ltd, http://www.tandf.co.uk/journals).

Pier Professional Ltd for permission to reprint extracts from Ann Workman & Jeremy Pickard, 'Professional Identity in Multi-Disciplinary Teams: The Staff Speak', *Journal of Integrated Care*, Volume 16, Issue 3, June 2008 29–37.

Wiley Blackwell for permission to reprint Hamill, P. and Boyd, B. (2002) 'Equality, fairness and rights – the young person's voice', *British Journal of Special Education* 29(3). Reproduced by permission of Blackwell Publishing Ltd.

Taylor & Francis Ltd for permission to reprint extracts from Fazil, Q., Bywaters, P., Ali, Z., Wallace, L. and Singh, G. (2002), 'Disadvantage and discrimination compounded: the experience of Pakistani and Bangladeshi parents of disabled children in the UK', *Disability and Society* 17(3), 237–53. Reprinted by permission of the publisher (Taylor & Francis Ltd, http://www.tandf.co.uk/journals).

The Scottish Educational Review for kind permission to reprint extracts from Lloyd, G., Stead, J., Jordan, E. and Norris, C. (1999) 'Teachers and Gypsy Travellers', *Scottish Educational Review* 31(1).

The British Psychological Society for permission to reprint Crowley, C., Hallam, S., Harre, R. and Lunt, I. (2001) 'Study support for young peole with same-sex attraction – views and experiences from a pioneering peer support initiative in the north of England', *Educational and Child Psychology* 18(1). Reproduced with permission from Educational and Child Psychology © The British Psychological Society.

National Children's Bureau for kind permission to reprint Catherine Clark, Amrita Ghosh, Emrys Green and Naushin Shariff with support from Louca-Mai Brady, Anthony Ellis and Amanda Henshall (2008). *Media Portrayal of Young People: impact and influences* (a Young Researcher Network project). Reprinted with permission of the authors.

Symposium Journals and the author for kind permission to reprint extracts from Louise Archer (2008), 'The Impossibility of Minority Ethnic Educational 'Success'? An Examination of the Discourses of Teachers and Pupils in British Secondary Schools', *European Educational Research Journal*, 7(1), 89–107. www.symposium-journals.co.uk

http://dx.doi.org/10.2304/eerj.2008.7.1.89.

Sage Publications for kind permission to reprint 'Table II: Model tricholtomy mapping …' originally published in Archer, L. & Francis, B. (2006) *Challenging Classes?: Exploring the Role of Social Class within the Identities and Achievement of British Chinese Pupils*, Sociology, 40(1), 29–49. © 2006 Sage Publications. Reprinted by Permission of SAGE.

Taylor & Francis Ltd and the authors for permission to reprint extracts from Jennifer Spratt, Janet Shucksmith, Kate Philip, And Cate Watson, 'Part Of Who We Are As A School Should Include Responsibility For Well-Being': Links Between The School Environment, Mental Health And Behaviour – *Pastoral Care*, September, (2006) pp 14–21. copyright © National Association for Pastoral Care, reprinted by permission of (Taylor & Francis Ltd, http://www.tandf.co.uk/journals) on behalf of The National Association for Pastoral Care.

Taylor & Francis Ltd for permission to reprint extracts from Yates, Scott, Payne, Malcolm and Dyson, Simon 'Children and young people in hospitals: doing youth work in medical settings', *Journal of Youth Studies*, (2009) 12:1, 77–92. Reprinted by permission of the publisher (Taylor & Francis Ltd, http://www.tandf.co.uk/journals).

Taylor & Francis Ltd for permission to reprint extracts from Alice and Themelis, Spyros (2009) 'Working in the community with young people who offend', *Journal of Youth Studies*, 12:2, 121–137. Reprinted by permission of the publisher (Taylor & Francis Ltd, http://www.tandf.co.uk/journals) and the author.

Disclaimer

Every effort has been made to contact all the copyright holders of material included in this book. If any material has been included without permission, the publishers offer their apologies. We would welcome correspondence from those individuals/companies whom we have been unable to trace and will be happy to make acknowledgement in any future edition of the book.

Chapter 1

Introduction

Another place

John Parry, Jonathan Rix, Rajni Kumrai and Christopher Walsh

The thinking behind this collection

Equality, Participation and Inclusion: Diverse contexts and its partner *Diverse perspectives* are readers for the Open University course Equality, Participation and Inclusion: Learning from Each Other. As second editions both books draw on a greater diversity of perspectives and situations than the first editions. This book contains a compilation of challenging new material as well as several chapters from the first edition that retain particular relevance to the exploration of the issues fundamental to social justice. As a resource the chapters will be of particular interest across the contexts of education, health and social care. Practitioners working with and across these sectors should find the book a rich source of ideas and information. We also believe that families and advocates are likely to be drawn to the material as much of it reflects on real experiences and life stories. Indeed we know that some readers, from whatever background, will identify with the experiences of marginalisation and exclusion in the books and have their own stories to tell. We hope this collection of diverse material will therefore support both reflection and learning from each other. It is intended to develop an understanding of the issues of equality, participation and inclusion for children and young people in diverse contexts and raise questions about future policy and practice.

Between 2000 and 2010 a series of UK government-led policy agendas including Every Child Matters (DfES 2004), Getting it Right for Every child (Scottish Executive 2006), Youth Matters (DfES 2005) and the Children's Plan (DCSF 2007) attempted to shape services for children and young people. With such grand intentions as "improving the outcomes for all children and young people" (Every Child Matters 2004) or making "England the best place in the world for children and young people to grow up" (DCSF 2007), striving for equality, participation and social inclusion appeared central to the policy drive (Milbourne 2009). In reality, what we have witnessed is the emerging gap developed between these policy intentions and the real experiences of young people 'on the margins' (Milbourne 2009; Reay 2008; Sheppard *et al.* 2008). This collection of chapters draws on the latter in order to provide clearer insights into the complexities and tensions surrounding the struggle for social justice. In an ever changing political climate the perspectives of those facing or responding to exclusion will remain, in our view, the more robust and meaningful commentary on the issues.

In editing this book, we have drawn on a number of assumptions and theoretical positions to underpin the diverse contributions and to provide some cohesion to a context in which to explore ideas of equality, participation and inclusion. These assumptions have also informed the choice of material for the collection. The first principle to guide our thinking is that "we make no claim for scientific neutrality, indeed we are explicit that our interest stems from a concern for social justice" (Lloyd, Stead, Jordan and Norris in this edition p. 164). We therefore use the international human rights agenda, in particular the UN Convention on the Rights of the Child (United Nations 1989) as a starting position. This means that we believe the development of inclusive communities, provision and services in which all children can participate is fundamental to the pursuit of equality. In these contexts difference is valued and young people receive the support they require as individuals to participate on their own terms.

We also recognize that participation and inclusion do not mean the same to everyone. The young people who share their perspectives in this book have some views in common but also have different visions about what inclusion means to them. Not only can views of equality, participation and inclusion take different forms but they are also ideas that are continually evolving and developing. This development unfolds as we learn from stories of exclusion and innovative ways of overcoming barriers to participation. The thinking behind this book is to make a contribution to the process of development whilst holding onto fundamental underpinning principles: valuing diversity; tackling discrimination on the basis of difference; and listening to the voice of everyone – as challenging as that may seem.

A second concept that frames the collection is that being inclusive requires social change rather than an individual having to assimilate into any one dominant group. Communities have to look at themselves and ask the question "how do we change so that more people can participate?" Inclusion does not mean joining in on other people's terms but it does mean that every new challenge to our idea of inclusivity is met with a positive response; it means the process of change needs to be valued by everyone and is seen to enrich the experience of all involved. Consequently, although the chapters often focus on individual experiences they are not simply asking us to think about individual solutions. Common threads throughout the book are questioning the social mechanisms that have led to an exclusionary practice, and searching for ways to change oppressive attitudes and organizational structures.

This position emerges from our understanding of the social model of disability (Oliver 1983, 1990). However this collection has developed from the first edition in that it acknowledges that issues relating to equality, participation and inclusion impact beyond one excluded group, across multiple socially constructed groupings. In this book we bring together the experiences of children and young people marginalized because of their ethnicity, gender, class, sexuality, impairments and socio-economic status. We also present views from those who have been excluded because of the ways they have been labelled by those in positions of power or because of their cultural heritage. It is important to emphasize that the compilation of material for the book has not been driven by trying to work through a list of groups who were considered likely to experience exclusion. In some ways we have been restricted to grouping children and young people together because this is the way that research is carried out. However a fundamental position we assume is that young people are multidimensional individuals, a composite of gender, ethnicity, cultural background, sexuality, impairments, physicality, material resources and so on (Benjamin in this edition). Therefore we are concerned here with **all** children and young people, as we listen to their views on their situation and thinking about how their perspectives differ and cross-over.

In these chapters we wanted to acknowledge the ongoing change to the delivery of children and young people's services in the UK that has taken place since 2004, with the emphasis on professionals working across service boundaries and the development of integrated teams. Therefore we have chosen to highlight some support services as examples that have developed within this new culture to make a positive response to equality issues (see Maggie Teague or Ann Workman and Jeremy Pickard in this edition). Such changing cultures challenge all of us to think differently, whether we are a practitioner or young person, parent or advocate. However we believe that collaboration is a central element of inclusive practice because professional boundaries often become another barrier for young people to negotiate. From the perspective of encouraging equality, participation and inclusion, the changes to service delivery should be seen as an opportunity rather than a threat.

When people are prepared to work together and learn from each other, the results are often innovative. In our view it is unlikely that any support addressing the complexities of equality issues will have any significant impact without creative thinking. Professionals must be prepared to look beyond their traditions, their training and their job descriptions and move towards changing the systems and settings that exclude and discriminate against young people. We have included in the book the views of practitioners who have begun such a journey.

Innovative responses to supporting young people experiencing exclusion also depend on listening to their views and using their ideas about how things should change. This is fundamental to participation and the development of more inclusive services. Using children's views should be seen as integral to all levels of providing support: planning; delivery; decision making; and evaluation (11 million 2009). Respecting and acknowledging young people's role in developing their provision is crucial to bind the relationship between "inclusion, sustainability, participation, trust and empowerment" (Katy Simmons *et al.* in this edition p. 67). We have endeavoured to show such respect in this book by keeping the young person's voice at the heart of the narrative.

The chapters

The chapters are organised into four sections that move thematically from making proposals for change to considering supportive responses that have tried to make things happen in a different way. As editors we have also added brief introductory and summary comments to each chapter to highlight issues that seemed significant to us. Our comments are intended to provide some framework for the collection as a whole as they often refer back to key principles of participation and inclusion that underpin the book. They are not meant to be seen as the final word, but more openings into further enquiry.

The first section, "More than one way", provides examples of services responding to young people struggling to become part of a community and in doing so highlights that established boundaries have to be crossed. Roy McConkey sets the scene by showing how professionals who once saw themselves working in isolation can reach out to work collaboratively with new colleagues from different backgrounds. They can also shift the context of their work and respond to the privilege of interacting directly with families and local communities. Moving away from an institutionalized approach is a theme developed by Claire Norris and Alison Closs in their chapter. They talk with children with serious medical conditions and their families who are clear that their inclusion and participation in education services depends on schools connecting with the realities and routines of their home life. The chapters exploring the inclusion of children labelled as looked-after

(Isabelle Brodie) and young people "with emotional and behavioural difficulties" (John Visser, Ted Cole and Harry Daniels) show that professionals cannot simply transform into taking on broader roles. It takes reflection on their practice coupled with an understanding of the issues facing young people who encounter exclusion and marginalization. These commentators also emphasize that a focus on changing the learning environment rather than "fixing" the learner has to be accepted by any supportive staff.

Both Katy Simmons and Eve Hutton describe in their chapters ways of supporting communities that are founded on taking an untraditional approach. For the Occupational Therapists in Eve Hutton's research this means leaving their clinic base, working in schools and collaborating with teachers to improve the learning experience for all the children in the school. The Community Mobilisers in Katy Simmons chapter facilitate communities to develop their own support and solutions to the inequalities they face. Listening to what people have to say is central to the project and runs as a common thread through this section. To find "more than one way" to empower inclusion and participation requires listening to those who are traditionally not heard.

In the second section, "Transitions: Coming together", we look at contexts that are undergoing change as a response to developing inclusion and opening up participation. Cathy Philips and Helen Jenner give voice to the staff of Bangabandhu school as they reflect on their journey as a setting. They highlight how they have developed understandings and practices which have enabled them as a school to respond with confidence to an increasingly diverse population. Establishing shared principles as a prelude to any change is seen as key to the staff valuing the transition process. In Maggie Teague's chapter building trusting relationships with families as well as within the staff team is critical to the participation of whole community in Deri-View Children's Centre. In both Bangabandhu and Deri-View respecting and responding to the views of everyone involved are shown as key to 'coming together' as change takes place. Tina Cook, John Swain and Sally French also emphasise the importance of this principle in their account of the views of young people as they move from a closing special school into mainstream provision. Their chapter illustrates the real complexities and subtleties at work when transitions to more inclusive practice take place. It is important to look back and learn from the past rather than drive relentlessly forwards.

The final chapter in this section, from Ann Workman and Jeremy Pickard, pick up on many of the previous themes but examine these in the context of the response of professional services undergoing change. Their account of fresh collaborations in a newly created multi-disciplinary team again underlines the importance of developing trust and shared goals so that the people involved can share the process of change together. Along with the other chapters in this section their story reveals the tensions and complexities that can pull any move to greater equality and participation in unintended directions.

The chapters in the next section, "On the margins", once again through a range of different settings provide perspectives from a diverse range of young people. It is not our intention to suggest that these young people represent groups who are more on the margins than others, nor do they necessarily "cover all the bases". We have chosen material which we feel represents the voices of young people and those closely involved with them, to try and capture a sense of the overlapping concerns which all young people have, as they seek to establish their identity and maintain agency in their own lives. Our aim is to acknowledge that the ways in which we group young people and how they frequently choose to group themselves creates individual and collective identities which we need to respect and be responsive to. This includes those learners whose behaviour is challenging to the system (Paul Hamill and Brian Boyd), those learners whose behaviour allows their non-participation to go unnoticed (Janet Collins), and those who experience intensive disadvantage and/or discrimination (Qulsom Fazil, Paul Bywaters, Zoebia Ali, Louise Wallace and Gurnam Singh; Gwynedd Lloyd, Joan Stead, Elizabeth Jordan and Claire Norris; Colm Colwey, Susan Hallam, Rom Harre and Ingrid Lunt). As a whole, by bringing these stories together, they contribute to increased understandings of inclusion, more so than they can achieve individually. Together, the chapters in this section demonstrate the experiences of exclusion that can happen when people make assumptions about other people and when they fail to listen and to make adjustments for each other. This seems particularly evident in the final two chapters of this section, in which the fundamental underlying structures of the education system are shown to inhibit the achievement of many young people (Louise Archer) who are further undermined by negative media representation (Catherine Clark, Amrita Ghosh, Emrys Green and Naushin Shariff). In the chapters within this section, however, are also examples of overcoming barriers and new opportunities being identified and taken, when individuals find time for others, facilitating access to much needed support and resources, and find ways to circumvent the embedded, systemic discrimination so many experience.

In the same way that we need to recognize that the diversity of experience has much in common when it comes to issues of inclusion and exclusion, so too do responses across contexts which aim to bring about great equality and participation. Inclusion and exclusion are practices which occur in the moment, in contexts; some of which are more supportive of inclusion than others (Shereen Benjamin, this edition). As was noted in the introduction to the first edition, this makes the call for learning from each other particularly pertinent. The fourth section *Thinking Differently*, provides examples of settings whose practices and interactions facilitate the inclusion of diverse groups of children and young people (Shereen Benjamin) and have moved away from positioning them within exclusionary categories by seeing them as primary resources for learning (Susan Hart). The chapters also encourage us to recognise that each context has an impact on aspects of young people's lives which may previously have been understood as being the concern of other professions (Jennifer Spratt, Janet Shucksmith, Kate Philip and Cate Watson); that frequently we need to have an outsider's perspective to resolve issues and to avoid reinventing the wheel (Scott Yates, Malcolm Payne and Simon Dyson) and that practices rooted in the concerns of young people which help them find their own solutions to challenges in their lives are more likely to be effective for all concerned (Alice Sampson and Spyros Themelis). At the heart of this final section is respect for the child and young person. This section demonstrates that no context or aspect of an individual's life can be seen in isolation if we wish to facilitate their full participation and inclusion either within a single setting, or within the wider community.

The introduction to the first edition of this collection looked forward to what this second edition might contain, concluding that "it may take a lot of stories of doing things differently and starting from a different mindset, to change the dominant narrative, but a paradigm shift is happening." (Nind *et al.* 2003 p. 7). A question you might reflect on as a reader when you have finished this book is the extent to which any shift to more inclusive provision and practice is inherently possible. Since 2003 there have been structural changes to services for children and young people which have allowed more collaboration and innovation in responding to those facing exclusion. Equality, inclusion and participation remain central to the policy agenda but there is a sense that their influence on the delivery of services is being challenged. Perhaps we are closer to the dilemma imagined by Sharon Owen (formerly Rustemier) where "inclusion has come to mean almost everything but the elimination of exclusion" (Rustemier 2002 p. 4). This book aims for a multifarious understanding of the meaning of equality, participation and inclusion for children and young people. For us the struggle against discrimination on the basis of difference is at the heart of that meaning.

References

11 Million (2009) http://www.11million.org.uk/content/all_you_need_to_know/content_54 (accessed on 22 March 2010).

DCSF (2007) *The Children's Plan.* http://www.dcsf.gov.uk/everychildmatters/about/ childrensplan/childrensplan/ (accessed on 22 March 2010).

DfES (2004) *Every Child Matters: Change for Children.* Department for Education and Skills: London.

DfES (2005) *Youth Matters, Green Paper.* Department for Education and Skills: Nottingham.

Every Child Matters (2004) http://www.dcsf.gov.uk/everychildmatters/about/childrensplan/ childrensplan/ (accessed on 22 March 2010).

Milbourne, L. (2009) "Valuing Difference Or Securing Compliance? Working To Involve Young People In Community Settings", *Children & Society*, **23**(5), pp. 347–363.

Nind, M., Simmons, K., Sheehy, K. and Rix, J. (2003) "Introduction" in Nind, M., Sheehy, K. and Simmons, K. (eds) *Inclusive Education: Learners and Learning Contexts.* David Fulton: London/ The Open University: Milton Keynes.

Oliver, M. (1983) *Social Work with Disabled People.* Macmillan: Basingstoke.

Oliver, M. (1990) *The Politics of Disablement.* London, Macmillan.

Reay, D. (2008) "Tony Blair, the promotion of the 'active' educational citizen, and middle-class hegemony", *Oxford Review of Education*, **34**(6), 639–650.

Rustemier, S. (2002) *Social and educational justice: The human rights framework for inclusion.* Centre for Studies on Inclusive Education: Bristol.

Scottish Executive (2006) Getting it right for every child: implementation plan, http:// www.scotland.gov.uk/Publications/2006/06/22092413/1 (accesed on 16 June 2010).

Sheppard, M., MacDonald, P. and Welbourne, P. (2008) "Service users as gatekeepers in Children's Centres". *Child and Family Social Work*, 13, pp. 61–71.

United Nations (1989) *Convention on the Rights of the Child*, http://www2.ohchr.org/english/ law/crc.htm (accessed on 22 March 2010).

More than one way

Reciprocal working by education, health and social services

Lessons for a less-travelled road

Roy McConkey

In this chapter Roy McConkey reflects on some of the themes from work in the 1960s by Ron Gulliford which retain relevance today. He focuses, in particular, on collaboration between practitioners from different professional backgrounds. He invites the reader to reflect on some of the strengths of current practice and to consider the ways in which these initiatives might be taken forward. The chapter closes with a set of strategies that could be used to develop innovative, holistic, inter-agency approaches in the future.

> *'Intellectual disability is a social as well as an educational problem. It is both inefficient and uneconomical to tackle one aspect and ignore the other.'*

Another road

These wise words could have been written by a disabled activist promoting a social model of disability. In fact they were written over 40 years ago by Ron Gulliford and his longstanding colleague A. E. Tansley in their landmark text on the education of slow learning children (Tansley and Gulliford 1960).

It is a tribute to Ron's foresight and incisiveness that these words are still as true today. There is wider acceptance of the first part of the statement but my generation of educationalists, health professionals and social service staff have done little to tackle both the educational and social dimensions of disability in any coherent way. It truly has been a road 'less travelled' as each service system has forged its own highway in trying to reduce the disabling effects of an intellectual impairment and the inevitable social consequences that it brings. Worse still, at times they have worked competitively rather than cooperatively, blaming one another for perceived shortcomings. And perhaps most seriously of all, they have worked in ignorance of one another's values, priorities and achievements. Yet, as Robert Frost reminded us in the poem from which this phrase is taken, the less–travelled road can make all the difference. […]

The social consequences of disability

Let us begin by considering these facts (Emerson *et al*. 2001) about the lives of people with an intellectual disability in Britain today:

- most (91%) attend day centres for people with learning disabilities;
- most (92%) live in congregated settings of five plus persons who are not related to them and with whom they have not chosen to live;
- most (95%) never marry or have a sexual partner;
- most (60%) have few friends whom they see regularly and fewer still have non–disabled friends.

These data stand in marked contrast to the aspirations for greater social inclusion contained in recent Government reviews of learning disability services in these islands (Scottish Executive 2000; Department of Health 2001). […] Educationalists clearly have a major role to play in ameliorating the learning problems young people encounter but, as Tansley and Gulliford (1960) wisely noted and the above data amply demonstrate, the impact of education or therapy on the social consequences of their disabilities has been very limited. In many ways, their life chances in this new century appear little different from those of their counterparts of a decade and more ago.

Similarly our social and community services, preoccupied as they have been with scarce resources and an emphasis on the social care of people who are viewed as being unable to learn and likely to be forever dependent on others, have struggled to overcome the social exclusion of these young people when they leave school. […]

A change of direction

The 'old road' treated intellectual disability – and indeed many other handicapping (as it was then called) conditions – solely as an impairment of the individual which needs to be put right. Traditional folklore invoked explanations of possession by evil spirits that needed to be exorcised while today medical science tries to identify the genes that may account for children's deficiencies and impairments such as autism, speech and language problems. Psychologists and therapists have invented a battery of tests to identify a myriad of deficits in 'problem' children and created many therapeutic approaches – often contradictory in their aims and methods – to remediate these diagnosed faults.

Educationalists too have taken to this deficit view with alacrity, labelling pupils as having attention deficits, dyslexia or poor sensory integration and creating all sorts of remedial programmes aimed at correcting the faults in the child. […]

In recent years, this deficit view of disability has been challenged by developmental psychologists who espouse a transactional view of children's acquisition of social and cognitive skills.

In this view language acquisition, numerical competence and reading skills – to name but three important intellectual functions – will be influenced by the experiences to which young children are exposed, primarily in their daily interactions with more competent humans. Deprive children of these nurturing opportunities and their development invariably suffers. The effects of institutionalisation are well documented, as is the superior performance of children from more affluent families on tests of academic attainment from pre-school years through to A levels.

Likewise, disabled activists have argued that their disabilities are compounded by the denial of opportunities which are readily available to their able-bodied peers. These opportunities include:

- having access to a suitable means of communication if you have hearing impairments or learning disabilities;
- being socially included in family and community events from the pre-school years onwards;
- having the chance for suitable vocational training and employment.

Activists argue that it is the denial of such opportunities, rather than any biological impairment, that subverts their intellectual, social and emotional development.

To my mind, the transactional view of development underpins all our endeavours in the field of special educational needs. It is the learning opportunities that we offer children, both in school and beyond, that will overcome some of the potentially disabling impairments that children are born with or those they acquire through childhood illnesses or accidents. […]

Successes of education

The new road will also take more account of the successes that educationalists have had in facilitating the learning of children whom past generations would have dismissed as ineducable [...] Education has evolved a number of strategies that have proved highly effective in overcoming children's learning disabilities. These include:

- *functional assessments*, which rely on devising means of ascertaining what the children can do in terms of everyday, observable skills rather than relying on assessments of abstract concepts such as intelligence;
- *learning goals*, which entail the identification of clearly stated learning targets that are appropriate to the child's present level of competence and provide the focus for teaching in school and at home;
- *learning methods*, which include teaching strategies such as breaking tasks into small steps, the use of prompts, positive reinforcement and modelling, all of which have proved effective in helping children acquire new skills and in managing challenging behaviours;
- *evaluating progress*, which involves monitoring learners' progress through careful observation and recording these findings to enable even small changes to be identified;
- *accredited learning*, which entails developing new means for accrediting students' learning so that nearly all may leave school having attained some form of externally recognised competencies.

Sad to say, many of these approaches are not widely applied outside of the school and classrooms. In residential homes provided by health or social services, there is growing interest in the concept of care staff providing 'active support' to residents so that they can acquire the skills that will enable them to live more independently and to manage problem behaviours more effectively (Jones *et al.* 1999). But active support is but another name for the learning approaches developed and applied by many teachers in special needs education.

Likewise the increased emphasis on supported employment as an alternative to attending day centres became possible as trainees were given 'systematic instruction' in the skills needed to do the job (Beyer and Kilsby 1997). Once again, teachers would recognise these methods as being closely akin to their practice.

Yet we still have a long road to travel until the majority of adult persons with a learning disability are living in their own accommodation or have part-time paid employment. One can but wonder whether these targets might be more attainable if the skills and strategies of teachers were made more available to staff in social services. This process will need to go beyond extending access for these students to further education, excellent though that development has been. It is my experience in Northern Ireland – and I suspect this is true for many other parts of the United Kingdom – that social service staff in day centres or residences are often ignorant as to what happens in colleges and vice versa. The road to partnership working is largely untrodden but before we get too despondent let us remember that new avenues have opened for joint working.

New avenues

I want to highlight three avenues, starting with early intervention services. Many disabling conditions are identified at birth or within the first 12 months. Yet it has only been in recent years that health and social services have developed support services for families, often offering home-based support to parents and giving guidance on activities that can be used at home to promote the child's development. Many of these schemes also involve educational personnel such as peripatetic or home teachers. Such services consistently receive high ratings from parents for their helpfulness and many epitomise the best attributes of trans-disciplinary working as they focus on common goals for the child and family (Carpenter 2000).

A second avenue that has opened for bringing together professionals from different disciplines is that of statutory assessments and issuing Statements of Special Educational Needs. I realise there is much that is imperfect in the way the system works and the wide variation that exists across the country, yet at the heart is a brave attempt to take a more holistic view of each child's needs. In this, I am echoing the views of a parent quoted by Jones and Swain (2001):

> Education is not the three 'Rs'. To educate our children you have to educate the whole child. It's their health needs, it's their social needs and it's their education, the whole child has to be seen to.

(p. 61)

Likewise the annual review process is another avenue for pooling expertise and setting common agendas.

The third avenue of opportunity is transition planning. Legislation makes it mandatory for the career service and social services to join with educational personnel in developing a transition plan that will take the young person and the family through the final years of his or her schooling into some form of post-school provision in a planned and, hopefully, seamless way. It is perhaps too soon to judge the efficacy of these procedures as their full implementation is still patchy but in other countries there is clear evidence that they do result in wider choices for the young people and families and that new forms of provision have been developed in response to their needs (Phelps and Hanley-Maxwell 1997).

I want to draw two lessons from these new avenues. They have all occurred within the last 20 years; often in response to parental and professional dissatisfaction with what was on offer. Hence it is possible for education, health and social services to work together more closely, albeit within a relationship enforced by legislation.

Thus it is worth pondering on what new avenues for partnership need to be opened. Among those that I would nominate are:

- helping children who have been excluded from schools because of their behaviours;
- managing the risks involved when students use community facilities such as public transport;
- the provision of lifelong learning opportunities.

However, the second lesson to be drawn from these new initiatives comes from the cynic who dismisses many of them as 'window-dressing' and doubts whether joint working really occurs in practice. I fear there is much truth in these claims but this is only a reminder of the lack of bridges on these new roads.

Roads but no bridges

Here are some examples of the lack of bridges that presently beset our services. Health professionals deliver therapeutic programmes in clinics that take little cognisance of the social circumstances faced by families or the practical application of the child's skills into daily life. Such therapy may even be done separately from the education provided by the child's teachers whose work is open to similar criticisms of being isolated from the child's life outside of school. Indeed the world beyond the clinic and classrooms is seen as the domain of social and community services with teachers and therapists having little or no responsibilities or influence.

Such dichotomies of functions are bolstered by the different management and funding structures of education, health and social services. They have become ever more entrenched with the growth of professional training and career structures that emphasise uni-disciplinary pathways.

But perhaps the main justification for the continuing separation of functions follows from the demands already placed on the various professionals by their own systems. Therapists are under pressure to get the waiting lists down; for social workers, the management of families in crisis is a priority; and teachers have recently been preoccupied with a myriad of tasks from the implementation of the National Curriculum to school attainment tests. There is little spare energy or enthusiasm for building bridges across agency boundaries.

Building bridges

Fortunately we have some blueprints for building bridges across service systems. The following paragraphs summarise some of the tested designs. [...]

Individual family plans

In the United States, legislation mandates early intervention services to create plans that embrace the family's needs and not just those of the child. At worst, this at least keeps all the diverse professionals informed about the family's needs and aspirations. At best, it can create the milieu around which joint working unfolds as teachers, therapists and social workers interlink their efforts towards common outcomes.

Out-of-school learning

Schools are limited in the 'real-life' experiences they can offer learners. Hence schools and services need to mobilise and utilise the resources that all communities can offer by way of facilities and personnel to further students' learning. Indeed this is the ethos that underpins the work experience opportunities many schools make for pupils in senior classes. This approach could be extended to other spheres of community life – leisure, public transport, voluntary service and political activity.

Merging staff roles

In the British system we have clearly demarcated the roles of teachers from those of therapists and social workers. Other European countries have developed more integrative training for staff whom they call 'pedagogists' and other countries have experimented with joint training for nurses and social workers. Similar calls have been made in this country for increased collaborative working between teachers and speech and language therapists (Law *et al.* 2001). [...] In all these examples, there is a realisation that the staff will work within a specialism defined by the needs of the people they serve. The British model is predicated on the notion that staff will follow career paths within their own discipline. Perhaps the time has come to rethink this presumption?

Reorganising services

Another radical response to the challenge of building bridges between services might lead us to question the wisdom of administering education services separately from the health and social services offered to children and families. Might there be a case for an integrated child and family service that brings teachers, therapists and social workers under a common management and finance structure? Some local authorities in Scotland and England are making moves in that direction following on from the recent reorganisation into unitary authorities (Walters 2001).

Creating new freeways

The American expression 'freeway' is so much more expressive than the British term 'motorway'. Building a road free of obstacles may seem to be a pipe dream now but 30 years ago, the idea that children with severe mental handicap (as it was then called) could be educated also seemed to most commentators to be a pipe dream. Today, that freeway is well established, so much so that it takes learners into mainstream schools as well as special schools.

I can think of three examples of freeways that might appear in the future to support the development of joined-up services for the benefit of children and families.

The school as a community resource with varied functions

The trend towards using the school as a community resource has already begun, with pre-school playgroups meeting in vacant classrooms or public libraries sharing the building. But this concept could develop much further. Child health and antenatal clinics could take place in the same building. Social workers and community workers might also be based there. These community facilities could be open at evenings and weekends so that opportunities for lifelong learning could be extended to young people and their parents. Such 'one-stop' facilities could be owned by the community they serve, rather than be the property of a health trust or an education authority as happens at present.

Multi-skilled personnel

Providing a common context in which people work will not in itself provide a freeway to joint working among people from different professions. More opportunities are needed for joint training at both a pre-service and in-service level (Law *et al.* 2001). Some of these may take the form of one- or two-day courses on specific topics while others may lead to postgraduate qualifications that recruit students from a range of professions to equip them with the multidisciplinary skills needed to focus on certain client needs, such as early intervention services; adolescent and young adult services; supported employment; or supported living. Training courses of this sort are starting to be offered and I predict we will see many more in the future.

Common management

Shared buildings and shared staffing will invariably lead to common management structures or, conversely, common management is required to produce these two outcomes. Either way, it will not come without courage and pain as the last bastion of a uni-disciplinary service is the power that comes from directing others and allocating money. Even so, there are already local authorities that have merged their education and children's social services and the Government is encouraging health authorities to develop jointly funded initiatives with social services departments for adult persons with learning disabilities (Department of Health 2001). This trend towards merging money and management has the potential to address the cost-effectiveness arguments raised by Ron Gulliford some 40 years ago.

Research and evaluation

If you have journeyed with me thus far, then it is only fair that I confess some doubts about whether these new freeways will take us to where we want to go. Human beings have a wonderful capacity to subvert the best of intentions to their own ends. One safeguard is to have open and objective feedback systems that demonstrate whether or not the goals are being achieved and identify the most effective means of producing them. In short we need to research and evaluate partnership working. There are three broad strategies for doing this.

Developing model projects

The experiences gained in setting up a 'model' project at a local level, by even a small group of innovators, will provide many learning experiences that, if documented and shared, will make it easier to repeat similar operations elsewhere. [...]

Evaluating new styles of services

The literature is replete with many studies investigating the efficacy of various educational and therapeutic interventions for disabling conditions. Far fewer multidisciplinary evaluations of services have been published. We have much to learn about how to obtain funding for such studies, as well as about the skills required by the evaluators and how they might meet the challenges of this new style of research in the measures and methods they use with a diversity of stakeholders.

Longitudinal studies

More ambitiously, we need to follow the progress of children and families over time and across service systems. For example, the data on social inclusion that I presented at the outset could be replicated within each local authority on these islands if schools (or some other body) were charged with following up the young people. [...]

Ironically, these research and evaluation initiatives will probably only occur when there is a culture that values and nurtures partnership working. Evaluation can inform us about how to do better the job we are committed to doing. It will not get us started on making the change.

The end of the road

[...] Our vision today is more clearly stated than ever before. It focuses upon inclusion within society and the right to a full and decent life. In order to achieve this, education must join forces with other services for, as Tansley and Gulliford (1960) asserted, it is both inefficient and uneconomical to be travelling on our own road when there is another one we should be taking that could make all the difference.

References

Beyer, S. and Kilsby, M. (1997) Supported employment in Britain. *Tizard Learning Disability Review*, **2**(2), 6–14.

Carpenter, B. (2000) Sustaining the family: meeting the needs of families of children with disabilities. *British Journal of Special Education*, **27**(3), 135–44.

Department of Health (2001) *Valuing People: a new strategy for learning disability for the 21st century*. London: Department of Health.

Emerson, E., Hatton, C., Felce, D. and Murphy, G. (2001) *Learning Disabilities: the fundamental facts*. London: Foundation for People with Learning Disabilities.

Jones, E., Perry, J. and Lowe, K. (1999) Opportunity and the promotion of activity among adults with severe intellectual disability living in community residences: the impact of training staff in active support. *Journal of Intellectual Disability Research*, **43**, 164–78.

Jones, P. and Swain, J. (2001) Parents reviewing annual reviews. *British Journal of Special Education*, **28**(2), 60–4.

Law, J., Lindsay, G., Peacey, N., Gascoigne, M., Soloff, N., Radford, J. and Band, S. (2001) Facilitating communication between education and health services: the provision for children with speech and language needs. *British Journal of Special Education*, **28**(3), 133–7.

Phelps, L. A. and Hanley-Maxwell, C. (1997) School-to-work transitions for youth with disabilities: a review of outcomes and practices. *Review of Educational Research*, **67**, 197–226.

Scottish Executive (2000) *The Same As You? A review of services for people with learning disabilities*. Edinburgh: Scottish Executive.

Tansley, A. E. and Gulliford, R. (1960) *The Education of Slow Learning Children*. London: Routledge and Kegan Paul.

Walters, B. (2001) Does size matter? Is small beautiful? *British Journal of Special Education*, **28**(1), 35–43.

The metaphor of the journey, used by Roy McConkey in this chapter, is one that recurs in much writing about inclusion. It conveys a sense, which we also find elsewhere, of an unfolding process that encompasses much more than school. This chapter gives directions for a collaborative, holistic way of working that brings together professionals and addresses shared problems. It prompts us, as does the next chapter, to consider what such new ways of working might mean for professionals and for their established ways of working.

Chapter 3

Child and parent relationships with teachers in schools responsible for the education of children with serious medical conditions

Claire Norris and Alison Closs

In this chapter, Claire Norris and Alison Closs describe a small study of the interpersonal relationships between children with chronic and/or deteriorating conditions and their parents and teachers. This was one aspect of a wider study (Closs and Norris 1997) which sought ways of enabling the mainstream education of such children in Scotland.

The research population

Terminology is problematic in areas of overlap between illness and disability (Barnes & Mercer 1996) but prior discussion with families, voluntary organisations, educational and other professionals indicated that *uncertainties* about the future health and abilities of children might be a key issue in educational responses. Therefore the research was limited to concerns about children whose conditions were not 'static' but were fluctuating or deteriorating, both physically and cognitively.

As the experience of illness is both highly individual and subjective, it was not thought advisable to establish a 'hierarchy' of conditions, but to select children whose state of health was of sufficient severity and duration to disrupt significantly (in their own, their parents' and their schools' view) patterns of school attendance and educational progress. Illustrative examples of conditions experienced by the children were cancers including leukaemia; ME (myalgic encephalomyelitis); chronic heart, kidney and other organ malfunctions; cystic fibrosis; muscular dystrophy; rheumatic and mucopolysaccharide conditions; Niemann Pick syndrome; severe asthma; eczema; psoriasis; and some forms of epilepsy. Disabilities which were, debatably, more *static* such as cerebral palsy, visual and hearing impairments were not included, nor were mental health conditions, infectious diseases, injuries or conditions requiring routine surgery. Children who required a series of extended surgical interventions (such as orthopaedic conditions or plastic surgery following burns), however, were included in the general study, although none were profiled.

Many of the issues in education facing these children, and those involved in making educational provision for them, are shared by other groups of children whose education may be constantly disrupted. Nevertheless, children with chronic and deteriorating conditions are likely to experience an identifiable *constellation* of difficulties (including absence and fatigue) in attempting to maintain access to, and progress within, education. The risk of pathologising these children and their families was recognised (Eiser 1993) and it was salutary to be frequently reminded by the children interviewed of the wide range of experiences, interests and aspirations which they *did* share with other children, as well as their dislike of 'difference' and their wish to be 'the same'. Scott, a ten-year-old with Friedrich's ataxia, described his PE lesson:

> ... they usually play things like shots and victories at basketball and I can't do all of that, so sometimes I just get to shout orders or just to shoot for the basket, and I don't like it then because I'm different and people make fun of me ...

Sources of data

In order to understand how school education was experienced by all those involved, 18 authority-based personnel in two demographically contrasting authorities were interviewed: education officers responsible for mainstream schooling and for pupil support services; special education 'support for learning advisers'; access officers; education welfare officers; and educational psychologists. In addition 21 staff from a primary and a secondary school in each of the two authorities: headteachers; class and subject teachers; learning support and guidance staff; and auxiliary assistants; in addition to school doctors and nurses. Eighteen children across Scotland, from 6 to 18 years of age, were profiled, using in-depth interviews, follow-up meetings and telephone conversations with one or both parents and (when informed consent could be obtained and health allowed) with the children themselves. The children can therefore only be viewed as illustrative of a large and extremely heterogeneous population, and the British Paediatric Association (1995) reports that just under 10 per cent of children under the age of 15 have an illness which chronically reduces their functional capacity.

Some children in our sample, despite sometimes extensive absences and poor prognosis, were fully included in their school community but about two thirds of them and their parents felt that they were marginalised or excluded. There was no clear relationship between the severity of the condition or the extent of absence and feelings of inclusion or exclusion. Not surprisingly, we found that good relationships between teachers and pupils and teachers and parents were perceived as fundamental to positive, inclusive educational experiences. There were, however, a number of issues relating to pupils with serious medical conditions, their families and their teachers, which could enhance or impede these relationships.

Teacher–pupil relationship

We recognised the difficulties in maintaining what might be considered 'normal' teacher–pupil relationships with children who were often absent. As one headteacher in the study remarked: 'Schools are busy places, and once a child is not there you tend to forget about them.' Some seriously or terminally ill children continue to attend school as do others with less dramatic but still debilitating and irritating conditions. Yet even when children were attending school regularly, it was found that teacher–pupil relationships could be negatively affected by teacher perceptions of pupils' medical conditions.

Teachers were sometimes unsure whether or not to treat their pupils with medical conditions in the same way as their peers. Some of the parents interviewed, described teachers' 'softness', 'lowered expectations' and 'over-protectiveness' arising from anxiety. One learning support teacher commented that her colleagues had asked about an under-challenged abler pupil with a physically deteriorating condition: 'Should I push him? Should I make him do this?'

A parent described the fearful response of her daughter's reception class teacher on being told that the child had nocturnal epilepsy. The mother volunteered to stay in the class with her daughter and later an auxiliary helper was employed on the insistence of the teacher. This arrangement effectively separated the child physically and socially from her peers since both teacher and auxiliary were happy for the auxiliary to 'care for' the child at the far end of the classroom. The matter was only resolved in the following year when a more confident teacher took over and included the child fully in school activities.

Another teacher described a colleague's refusal to take a pupil with a physically deteriorating condition to school camp, listing the activities in which the boy could *not* participate. The interviewee said that thinking about the boy's condition 'gutted' his colleague, such were his own inhibitions about disability and death; this attitude impeded his constructive responses.

The examples given above show how ignorance, fear and inhibitions about death and illness (Leaman 1995) can impede positive relationships and experiences. In contrast, the class teacher of a child with a recurrence of acute lymphoblastic leukaemia tried to discriminate positively in relation to the boy's behaviour. She described her feelings and responses:

> My relationship with him is different from that with other children, and when I don't know what his prognosis is, it alters the stance I take with him. There are times when he can be a bit naughty and cheeky and a little bit forward, and in other children you would reprimand that behaviour, but with him you don't because you don't want him to have any negative experiences, and you want your relationship with him to be almost like a fun relationship … I'm conscious of the fact that over the next two or three years everything might be over for him, so you want everything to be good for him …

Her responses arose therefore not from fear or ignorance of his condition but from her own wish to give him happiness. Not surprisingly, this led to some peer rejection.

Teachers' capacity to empathise and relate positively with children, whether arising from personal experiences or simply from greater interpersonal skills, enhanced teacher–child relationships and also contributed positively to peer relationships. One girl with Hurler's syndrome described how her class teacher had explained in class circle-time that he (the teacher) had diabetes, got very tired and therefore could understand how she and 'any other child who felt poorly' might not always be able to do perfect work, but that trying hard was the most important thing in life. The class then all discussed the times when they felt tired or unwell and agreed to support each other.

The children in the sample were *in tune* with our professional interviewees on what was effective teaching for them (Cooper & McIntyre 1993). They appreciated well-organised teachers who accepted their difficulties, and who helped them to learn by being clear and going over missed work or offering lesson notes. They liked classes to be orderly and good-humoured, but made a clear distinction between good humour and the kind of cruel, insensitive remarks disguised as 'jokes' which were sometimes made by their peers and even occasionally by their teachers. These children had much to lose if teachers did not model positive acceptance and respect.

Brown and McIntyre (1986) found that teachers describe their work in terms of their pupils' progress and behaviour. Leaman (1995) argued:

> The structure of teaching and learning itself, the notion of a curriculum with its grades and hierarchy, with its ranks and promotions, encourages the idea that life consists of a series of stages and obstacles which must be met and surmounted if one is to be successful.
>
> (p. 22)

If one adds to this the multiple pressures on teachers in the drive towards raising school achievements, it is perhaps not surprising that some come to view pupils with chronic illness, who fall behind in their work, as problematic or even 'bad' pupils, rather than pupils of equal value who require additional support.

Class and guidance teachers were key communication links when children were absent. Packages of homework might enable 'keeping up' but the more personal contact of letters, cards and phone calls, sometimes initiated and less frequently maintained by teachers, facilitated social continuity. Larcombe (1995) noted the importance of social contact with friends and teachers for absent children in preventing the onset of school phobic-type symptoms at the thought of returning to school, also noted by some of the interviewees. Few absent children were visited by teachers, even when their condition was serious and long-standing. Those who were visited, however, were positive. Jenny commented:

> It was kind of embarrassing, I suppose, but I did feel really pleased she came. I mean, I think it showed she cared … and she said they hadn't forgotten me and would be pleased to see me back. I won't forget it.

Parent–teacher relationships

Parents described how some school staff had facilitated their children's education. They appreciated staff who listened to them, understood that their worries about health or educational progress were real, and accepted and used the information that they gave. One mother described how her son's headteacher had not only read leaflets she had brought into school but had also bought a book for the children's library and another for the staff. It seemed, however, from parent and teacher interviews, that schools did not find it easy to accept all parents as knowledgeable about their own children, far less medically authoritative about their condition. A headteacher's comment about one mother was revealing in its implications for other 'non-professional' parents:'Of course, she really does know what she's on about. She's a properly qualified nurse.'

Headteachers have considerable influence on a school's ethos and attitudes towards potentially disadvantaged children. Parents also perceived headteachers, particularly in primary schools, as both establishing, and ensuring the continuity of, supportive systems. Mark's parents had been very agitated about his progress after he developed learning difficulties as a result of treatment for leukaemia. They had tense relations with the school and 'officialdom', although neither teachers nor educational psychologists had been aware that irradiation could cause cognitive impairments in children and had consequently offered no additional help. The arrival of a headteacher, whom they felt to be more knowledgeable and active on their behalf, enabled the school and the family to form better relationships even when Mark's leukaemia recurred. In such tense situations, the skills and attitudes of staff are vital.

Several parents described how medical crises or inappropriate school responses to a medical need had resulted in conflict. Sally, who has Hurler's syndrome, was sent by a new teacher on a school cross-country run in cold weather although she was only supposed to take limited exercise in the gym. Her mother had phoned the headteacher to ask why this had happened and, since she was already angry, added that she was upset that a change of teacher had only been notified to the children the day before the transition, and not to the parents. The headteacher had apologised but had followed up the call with a four-page letter detailing what the school was doing for Sally Her parents felt that the letter was both a defensive action and also a reprimand for their complaint:

> It would have been much better if we could just have sat down together informally for a chat. I'm sure we would all have felt better because really we were not making a general complaint.

Although secondary headteachers were also perceived by parents as being very important, the direct parental contact was often dispersed across guidance, learning support or registration staff. This scattering of contact was confusing and worrying to parents, and a single influential and reliable contact was thought necessary. Rick's mother had expected to be in contact frequently when her son went to secondary school as his condition was deteriorating and he had been bullied at primary school. Her anxiety, however, had abated because she had confidence in Rick's guidance teacher: 'He's really vigilant, he phones regularly and I can go up at any time.'

Any mismatch in values and in aims for children's education between school staff and parents could be exacerbated by issues related to the child's condition. Although rarely made explicit, some teachers seemed to expect families' compliance with school values and practices 'in exchange' for the extra effort it took to meet children's needs. Time spent by parents and school staff getting to understand each other's concerns and in initial shared planning, was fundamental to subsequent positive experiences. A guidance teacher described how she, '… spent two hours at the beginning to *save* 22 later'.

One mother described the last year of her daughter's life when Rae still very much wanted to be in school with her friends despite failing health and the need for piped oxygen. The headteacher and other staff also wanted Rae to be there but were conscious of her physical vulnerability:

> They (the school staff) were cautious. They not only had the home number, they had the office number and the car phone number, I had that for the last 18 months of Rae's life, so the headteacher could get me at any time, and she would let me know if she had concerns about Rae's breathing or if she had bad colour. On the other hand she didn't just phone me always or panic, they were cautious but not excessively.

Not all accounts were so satisfactory. Beth had been absent intermittently for nearly two terms with glandular fever, during which time her mother had regularly sent in medical certificates and requests for homework. Her mother only received one phone call from the guidance teacher and one package of homework, and felt that there should have been more contact and,

> they could have made a wee bit more effort. Compared to what they used to be, I mean, it's gone down hill,

referring to the school in the time of the previous headteacher who

> paid attention to things like that.

The educational welfare officer involved thought that Beth's mother was less able socially to assert her real concerns to the school and described the school's attitude to her family as 'negative'. 'Beth has the odd time off even when she's well', was the guidance teacher's response to the welfare officer's enquiry. The school had made value judgements in relation to its own resource allocation and also failed to refer Beth to the home-visiting teacher service. In Scottish education authorities, unlike England and Wales, the provision of education for children not attending school is a 'permitted action' but not a 'mandatory requirement'. A consultation document (SOEID 1998), however, asked whether this situation should be changed.

For many parents, optimising their child's educational progress and ensuring that they 'kept up' were matters of deep concern. While parents of children who had had periods of acute illness recognised that there were times when education was irrelevant, a poor prognosis in itself was not seen as a reason for not attending school. For some parents, regardless of their children's ability, educational achievement at their own level was a marker of children's existence and in some cases it was also perceived as a compensation for their physical limitations. Attendance, however irregular, at local mainstream schools was seen as 'normalising' and offering the best chance for children to find friendship (Closs and Burnett 1995). Some school staff did not see such parental aims for their children as 'strictly educational' and were critical of the resource implications for schools.

Parents of children with serious medical conditions (especially their mothers) are under multiple pressures, not all of which are readily perceived by school staff or easily communicated by parents. For example, many families in the study faced increased expenditure associated with their child's diet, heating and transport, but did so on a single income because of the need for one parent to be available for care duties. Others were deeply concerned about siblings' well-being. Eiser (1993) suggests that life can never be truly 'normal' for a family with a child with a very serious condition. Nonetheless, many aspire to normality and achieve it to a remarkable degree, and a mother in our study described the process:

> The way I see it, we have two lives, the one that's like everyone else's where we eat and sleep and communicate and see friends and go on holiday, and the other that's tied to this condition with hospital and hospice visits, and lifting, and phoning and waiting for the special this, that and the next thing and waiting for all the professionals … and so on, a real struggle. I suppose what I try to do is to ensure that the second world doesn't take over the first. Sometimes, amazingly, I succeed.

In such circumstances, however, it would be surprising if home–school relationships were not occasionally fraught. Gordon's mother described how she felt when she discovered that the school had not told her how far behind Gordon was in his maths:

> They said he caught up quite quickly, but what's been happening is that he's caught up on what they are doing then, but there's a space left behind and it shows later. I can't be up at the school every day seeing

if that's happening. You just assume that the teacher's doing that … It's his education and I feel time is very important. They don't know how long he's going to be all right this time, the specialist said maybe six to nine months, so we're nearly up to seven months so if he relapses in another couple of months who knows how often or how long he will be off then, so when he's well I want every minute to count for his education and I don't want somebody else being lax about it when I'm doing my damnedest to make sure everything is going right.

Teacher training and information

As Ainscow (1997) has argued, if we are to recognise fully the implications of inclusion, we need to begin by assuming that all children have the right to attend their local school:

> Therefore, the task becomes one of developing the work of the school in response to pupil diversity … this has to include a consideration of overall organisation, curriculum and classroom practice, support for learning and staff development.
>
> (p. 5)

The great majority of children with a medical condition attend mainstream schools and it became clear during the research that schools could indeed 'develop the work of the school in response to pupil diversity'; in this case the specific, and sometimes complicated, needs of the research group. Rae's mother, after her daughter's death, was able to say of the local primary school: 'I have a great admiration for this school. They have done everything they possibly could to help us.'

However, the teachers in our study acknowledged their need for more staff development. Training teachers in the special needs of children with serious medical conditions is a neglected area, both in initial teacher training and in-service courses. Eiser and Town (1987) and Eiser (1990) have noted how poorly trained and ill-informed many teachers are in terms of childhood disease, and how they tend to overestimate the likelihood of medical emergencies arising in school. Leaman (1995) notes that most teachers respond to illness and death as lay people rather than as trained professionals.

Official guidance on duties and good practice in schools in relation to pupils with medical needs issued jointly by the DfEE and DoH (1996a; 1996b) in England and Wales (which have as yet not been matched in Scotland or Ireland) address meeting the medical needs of pupils in school. It is good to record that all 18 pupils profiled in the study were, in their own and their parents' opinions, having their medical needs fully met even though these had sometimes required extended negotiations between parents and community child health officers, and the school. The good practice guide is useful as it is important for a member of a school staff to be trained and willing, for example, to give rectal valium to counteract an epileptic seizure or to use a 'histostab' to reduce anaphylactic responses to acute allergies. However, the general and special needs of many more children would be met more effectively by a general awareness raising of a practical kind, opening up issues and raising questions, developing positive attitudes and laying foundations of good policy and practice on which training in relation to individual children can successfully be based.

Part of the awareness raising could also include the opportunity for teachers to examine their own preconceptions, attitudes and fears about illness and death, which are important factors in relationships between pupils and their teachers. Several teachers in the study described feelings of initial fear and repulsion over a child's illness. Death as a topic for discussion, especially when raised by a child in relation to her or himself, can be so distressing to a badly prepared teacher as to incapacitate him or her:

> When he said he wanted to die because he was so unhappy about what the others had said but that he would be dying anyway, I didn't know what to say … I wanted to cry or to hug him but I think I just said to get on with his work.

Conclusion

There is an urgent need for more initial and in-service staff development to enable the inclusive education of children with serious medical conditions. Above all there would appear to be a need for staff to develop their inter-personal skills, useful in all aspects of their professional and personal lives, but absolutely *essential* when working with children with serious medical conditions and their families.

References

Ainscow, M. (1997) Towards inclusive schooling. *British Journal of Special Education*, **24**(1), 3–6.

Barnes, C. and Mercer, G. (1996) *Exploring the Divide: Illness and Disability*. Leeds: The Disability Press.

British Paediatric Association (1995) *Health Needs of School Age Children*. London: BPA.

Brown, S. and McIntyre, D. (1986) How do teachers think about their craft? In M. Ben Peretz, R. Bromine and R. Halkes (eds) *Advances in Research on Teacher Thinking*. Berwyn, IL: Liss, Swets and Zeitlinger.

Closs, A. and Burnett, A. (1995) Education for children with a poor prognosis: reflections on parental wishes and on an appropriate curriculum. *Child: Care, Health and Development*, **21**(6), 387–94.

Closs, A. and Norris, C. (1997) *Outlook Uncertain: Enabling the Education of Children with Chronic and Deteriorating Conditions* (Research Report). Edinburgh: Moray House Institute of Education.

Cooper, P. and McIntyre, D. (1993) Commonality in teachers' and pupils' perceptions of effective classroom learning. *British Journal of Educational Psychology*, **63**, 381–99.

Department for Education and Employment and Department of Health (1996a) *Circular 14/96, Supporting Pupils with Medical Needs in School*. London: DfEE/DoH.

Department for Education and Employment and Department of Health (1996b) *Supporting Pupils with Medical Needs: a Good Practice Guide*. London: DfEE/DoH.

Eiser, C. (1990) *Chronic Childhood Disease: an Introduction to Psychological Theory and Research*. Cambridge: Cambridge University Press.

Eiser, C. (1993) *Growing Up with a Chronic Disease*. London: Jessica Kingsley Publishers.

Eiser, C. and Town, C. (1987) Teachers' concerns about chronically sick children: implications for paediatricians. *Developmental Medicine and Child Neurology*, **29**, 56–63.

Larcombe, I. (1995) *Reintegration to School after Hospital Treatment*. Aldershot: Avebury.

Leaman, O. (1995) *Death and Loss: Compassionate Approaches in the Classroom*. London: Cassell.

SOEID (1998) *Special Educational Needs in Scotland: a Discussion Paper*. Edinburgh: Scottish Office.

This chapter, like many in this volume, goes beyond school and looks at how inclusive practice can extend to relationships with homes and families. This reaching beyond school demands new responses from professionals. To work effectively in more inclusive ways, teachers are likely to need more broadly based training as well as insight into their own attitudes and perspectives.

Chapter 4

Children's homes and school exclusion

Redefining the problem

Isabelle Brodie

This chapter focuses on one group of children and young people 'on the margins' – those who are 'looked after' by local authorities, often referred to as 'in care'. The author, Isabelle Brodie, argues that we need a more complex understanding of exclusion that goes beyond formal official exclusion from school. She shows a range of routes through which 'looked after' young people come to be out of school in what can be a de-motivating process for all concerned.

The education of children looked after by local authorities ('in care') is currently high on the professional and political agenda. Moreover, there is generally a consensus on the nature and seriousness of the issues which need to be addressed. Few would contradict the view of the House of Commons Health Committee (1998) that 'It is clear that SSDs [Social Services Departments], LEAs and schools are failing to work effectively together to promote educational opportunities for children in their care' (p. lxii).

In the light of the criticisms of numerous reports, the government has now sought to respond to these issues through a range of policy initiatives, most notably through the 'Quality Protects' programme (Department of Health 1998a). Most recently draft guidance has been issued on the education of children 'looked after'. This will eventually replace the current guidance contained in Circular 13/94 (Department for Education 1994) and is generally more comprehensive, seeking to improve information gathering and planning at all levels of policy and practice in the local authority (Department for Education and Employment 1999).

This chapter is concerned with the exclusion from school of children looked after by local authorities. Available evidence suggests that children 'looked after' are more likely to be excluded or not to attend school, but relatively little consideration has taken place of the processes through which children 'looked after' come to be excluded from school, and the ways in which this is managed by the professionals involved.

The discussion will begin by examining the evidence concerning the exclusion from school of children 'looked after'. It will then consider in greater detail the ways in which children 'looked after' come to be excluded or 'out of school', arguing that formal official exclusion is not always the issue and that a more complex understanding of what constitutes exclusion needs to be developed if appropriate professional interventions are to be made. This part of the discussion will draw on evidence from an intensive study of the exclusion from school of a group of young people looked after in residential accommodation in England (Brodie 1999).

Background

In England and Wales on 31 March 1998 there were 53,000 children looked after by local authorities (Department of Health 1999). Of these, just over 35,000 were living in foster care, with a much smaller number – 4,900 – looked after in local authority children's homes. Another 770 lived in privately registered homes. The remainder either remained at home with social work support, or were resident in, for example, secure units. It is important to remember that these statistics refer to the number of children 'looked after' on one day, and do not take account of the larger group which move in and out of the care system during the course of a year. The majority of children looked after in residential accommodation are adolescents, though many local authorities do make provision for younger children. Many young people will be resident in a placement for only a few weeks or months, though many will experience more than one placement during their time 'looked after' (Department of Health 1998b).

There are no nationally collected data on the kind of schools attended by children 'looked after' or on their educational attainment. There is equally a lack of national research data, with most studies that focus on the education of 'looked after' children being local or regional (see Borland et al. 1998). Additionally, much more is known about the educational experiences of children living in residential accommodation than about those in foster care, despite the fact that the latter is a significantly larger group.

The most recent national studies show that most children looked after in residential accommodation who are not disabled are registered in mainstream schools, with some 10 per cent registered in special school provision (Social Services Inspectorate (SSI)/Office for Standards in Education (Ofsted) 1995; see also Department of Health 1998b and Borland et al. 1998). The research evidence suggests, therefore, that children 'looked after' will usually represent only a tiny minority in any one school and may not, in fact, be perceived as a distinct group or expected to present problems (Berridge *et al.* 1997).

The exclusion from school of children looked after by local authorities

In regard to non-attendance and exclusion, the Audit Commission (1994) reported that 40 per cent of 'looked after' children were not in school for reasons other than illness. A joint inspection by the SSI and Ofsted (1995) of residential and foster care in four authorities found that this problem was most concentrated at secondary school, with 25 per cent of the 14 to 16 year-olds in their sample out of school. These findings are reflected in smaller studies. Berridge and Brodie (1998), in a follow-up study of residential care in three local authorities (Berridge 1985), found that of 21 adolescents of school age living in five children's homes, only three were attending school regularly. Of the 18 non-attenders, seven were formally permanently excluded. On the other hand, in the three homes for younger children studied, all the children resident were attending school. A survey in Strathclyde (Lockhart *et al.* 1996, cited in Borland *et al.* 1998) found that one in five children's home residents were not registered at any school, employment or college and almost 40 per cent were absent from school on the day of the survey. Among those of school age, 16 per cent were not registered at any school. It is fair to conclude, then, that non-attendance and exclusion constitute a significant problem for the 'looked after' population.

The educational difficulties of children 'looked after' are not confined to exclusion and non-attendance, but are inevitably linked to other problems. Research into the educational attainment of children 'looked after' has shown that a disproportionate number fail to achieve the standards of their peers. The SSI/Ofsted study found evidence of widespread underachievement. This was most pronounced at secondary school level, where none of the sixty children studied were judged by their teachers to be likely to achieve five subjects at Grades A–C in national examinations at age 16. This compares poorly with the general school population; Biehal *et al.* (1995) found that two-thirds of their sample left care with no qualifications, whereas the proportion in the general population is 16 per cent. Similarly, studies of young people leaving care have found that few obtain any recognised qualifications, a fact which bears negatively on their future employment prospects (Biehal *et al.* 1995).

The educational difficulties experienced by children 'looked after' are generally thought to result from a combination of factors. The experiences of children prior to entering the care system are clearly important. Recent research has emphasised the fact that the group entering residential accommodation presents more complex and challenging problems than in the past (Berridge and Brodie 1998, Department of Health 1998b). These include higher levels of previous emotional, physical and sexual abuse. That said, it has rightly been argued that to plead past experience can be 'an extremely lame and convenient excuse' for the often poor quality of educational experience within the care system (Firth and Horrocks 1996). Depressingly, research continues to highlight the unstimulating educational environment, poor recording of educational information and low priority given to education by carers and social workers (Berridge *et al.* 1997, Department of Health 1998b). Poor planning and lack of liaison and communication between education and social work professionals also continue to stand in the way of the educational welfare of the children concerned.

'Redefining' school exclusion

While existing research evidence is fairly conclusive in showing that children 'looked after' frequently do not attend or are excluded from school, much less is known about how their experience of exclusion – and when and why this occurs – relates to their experience of the care system. The rest of this paper will be devoted to a more detailed discussion of what exclusion means in relation to children looked after in residential care, based on findings from an intensive qualitative study of 17 boys aged 6–16 living in residential accommodation in three local authorities.

Some information about the group studied is necessary. All seventeen had extremely troubled backgrounds. Ten were known to have experienced some kind of abuse or neglect. Other research has shown a strong statistical association between experience of abuse and educational difficulties, including exclusion (Farmer and Pollock 1998, Department of Health 1995). The group also had unusually lengthy histories of care, with 14 of them 'looked after' for a year or more, and seven for four years or more. This is atypical of the care population as a whole, but perhaps provides the opportunity for a better understanding of the relationship between the care system and exclusion.

Eleven of the boys had experienced a previous exclusion from school on either a fixed-term or permanent basis. In three cases, the exclusion had taken place from a special school for children with emotional and behavioural difficulties. Seven of the group had statements of special educational need at the time of their exclusion, and in a further case a statement had been pending. However, while by most standards this group presented significant challenges in respect to their education, this did not make their permanent exclusion from school inevitable.

This research was initiated in response to concerns voiced by residential staff regarding the problem of exclusion. However, during the initial fieldwork for the research, it frequently became apparent that children described as 'excluded' were in fact not attending school for other reasons or had been excluded by informal processes. Staff were not always aware of the precise educational status of the young people in their care and were consequently not always able to respond appropriately. An important question for the research therefore became what was meant by 'exclusion' and how this affected the experiences of the young people and professionals involved.

Legislation makes provision for two types of exclusion: fixed-term, which can take place for up to 45 days across the school year, and permanent. Most research has, understandably, focused on exclusion which corresponds to these statutory definitions. Reference has also been made, however, to 'unofficial' or 'informal' exclusion. Stirling (1992) found that of a sample of 60 children living in seven children's homes, 32 were not attending school. Only two of these were officially excluded. Stirling therefore argued that informal exclusion represented a means by which schools could circumvent reporting exclusions to the local education authority. The Department for Education (1994) also noted, on the basis of anecdotal evidence only, that schools were more likely to exclude informally children 'looked after' on the grounds that they had access to full-time day care. The research was therefore interested to learn more about how formal exclusion, when the official procedures contained in Circular 13/94 were invoked, related to informal exclusion.

An alternative framework

Through in-depth interviews with young people and the professionals involved in the case, including teachers, social workers, carers and others such as educational psychologists, the research identified four ways in which children looked after in residential accommodation were excluded. While the numbers are small, these four 'routes' or 'pathways' are helpful in developing an understanding of how children come to be out of school and how this relates to different patterns of professional response.

Exclusion by non-admission

For three young people in the sample, their 'exclusion' had arisen from the fact that they did not have a school place. All presented serious behavioural problems, but the disruption of their education had also occurred for other reasons, including changes of placement. All the children in this category had arrived at the residential placement without prior arrangements being made for their education. The difficulties which then emerged concerned persuading schools to admit the young people. It was difficult to discern how far these problems were due to the fact that a child was 'looked after'. Care staff in particular felt strongly that the children in their care were stigmatised and examples were given where schools had explicitly refused admission on the grounds that they were 'looked after'. The consequence of this view was that children's homes tended to target schools which had the reputation of being amenable, or those which were undersubscribed and would find it more difficult to refuse admission. However, negotiations tended to be lengthy and the time the young people spent out of school considerable.

In one case, considerable efforts were made to encourage a school to admit a 10-year-old. The headteacher visited the children's home and a part-time timetable was worked out as a starting point. This proved successful and had the merit of ensuring that when the child did start attending the school on a full-time basis, all those involved were aware of the level of support likely to be required.

Exclusion on admission

This group involved young people who were officially or unofficially excluded very quickly after their entry to a school, usually within a few days or a few weeks. Two issues seemed especially important in relation to this group. As with other young people whose educational careers are characterised by transience, these young people had arrived with little information about their backgrounds and previous schooling. This made it difficult for the new school to assess their situation, and made dealing with their behaviour more difficult when problems arose, as they soon did. Furthermore, young people in this group tended to be unprepared for entry to a new school and lacked the knowledge of school systems and culture which would have enabled them to integrate. In some cases, indeed, they had not even wanted to attend the new school.

Nicki's case is a good example of these problems. Nicki was 13 and was living in a private children's home some distance from his own local authority. Scarcely anything seemed to be known about either his educational or care background; he was last known to have attended a junior school for a few weeks aged 8. He began attending the education unit attached to the private children's home, but the local authority withdrew funding for this part of the placement, and a school place had to be found elsewhere. The children's home had weak links with schools in the area, but eventually found a school willing to accept Nicki. He was excluded after only two days after punching another boy during a games lesson.

In these cases, neither the children, carers or schools indicated a strong commitment to the young person attending the school. Indeed exclusion, when it came, was generally welcomed. The lack of information and prior preparation on the part of all those concerned made it unlikely that the placement would succeed, and the episode, however short, appeared only to add to the young person's educational problems.

Graduated exclusion

This group consisted of five adolescents, all of whom had a school place. In accordance with other research findings, exclusion occurred via a fairly lengthy process. In all the cases, exclusion was predicted by at least one – and usually all – of the professionals involved, who felt that the young person could not remain within the school unless significant improvements in his/her behaviour were made.

Teachers and social workers also emphasised that attempts had been made to prevent the exclusion. This contrasts with the category of 'exclusion on admission', above, where such efforts were not perceived to be worthwhile. Thus, for young people who experienced a graduated exclusion, classroom support and consultation with external professionals such as educational psychologists did take place. The children's homes also offered support, usually by removing the young person when requested for 'cooling off' time.

Such support was valued by the school, but obviously further reduced the amount of time spent by the young person in the classroom. Indeed, the exclusion process in these cases was characterised by the progressive isolation of the young person from his/her peers and teachers. While time out did appear helpful in containing the situation, in these cases it sometimes seemed questionable whether this was realistically a long-term measure by which exclusion could be prevented.

Planned exclusion

For two of the young people involved, exclusion was not only anticipated but was also 'planned'. As problems escalated, professionals sought to minimise the consequences of the exclusion by making alternative plans. These were generally intended to reduce the amount of time the young person would be left without education in the event of exclusion taking place. In one case, this involved the negotiation of an alternative care placement with education attached, and in another preparing a report recommending placement at a Pupil Referral Unit.

These cases were characterised by at least one professional taking responsibility for the young person's education and making considerable efforts on their behalf. This links to other research into the care process, particularly as it is experienced by adolescents, which has commented on the fragmented nature of professional involvement and the absence of any one individual to advocate on the young person's behalf (Department of Health 1996). The professionals who performed the active role in cases of planned exclusion also had good informal links with other key individuals, and were supported by colleagues in the young person's school and children's home. Significantly, they also perceived the young person to have the ability to respond positively to education, if this was provided in an appropriate context.

Exclusion from school and professional intervention

The four categories outlined above are unlikely to be exhaustive, but draw attention to the different ways in which 'exclusion' can take place. It is important to point out that when exclusion took place in all these categories, this occurred through both formal and informal mechanisms.

A striking feature in all categories was the unevenness in professionals' understanding of the educational needs of the children concerned and in the action taken. Consequently, while considerable efforts were made on behalf of some young people, other cases were allowed to drift for unacceptably long periods of time, making a return to education increasingly remote. The educational prospects for the children concerned were therefore often a matter of chance.

Within these categories there are, regrettably, many familiar themes concerning continuity of care and the need for careful planning. No matter how committed certain teachers, social workers or residential carers might be to the education of the young person, they were often struggling to deal with a problem which had been allowed to fester for many years and had been subject to the attentions of numerous other professionals.

Overall, however, it seemed that greater differentiation was required in terms of understanding the nature of educational problems presented by young people 'looked after'. The reasons why children are out of school when living in residential accommodation are inadequately described by the term 'exclusion'. Greater attention is required both to the care and educational careers of individuals and also to the context of residential care. Specific types of care placement may have important implications for the 'route' to exclusion that is taken. For example, in this research, children living in private homes were more vulnerable to 'exclusion on admission' due to such factors as the weaker links between the home and local schools.

More generally, however, and as a smaller number of children are looked after in residential accommodation, it is clear that they often present acute problems which will require expert help (Department of Health and Others 1998). While it should not be assumed that children 'looked after' will have difficulties at school, it is essential that the professionals concerned have sufficient information with which to work and know how best to obtain help from others.

Conclusion

Children 'looked after' share many of the characteristics of other children excluded from school, most obviously in terms of their troubled backgrounds at home and at school. Being 'looked after' is, nevertheless, an additional complication which can have significant implications for the way in which the exclusion process unfolds. It is therefore important that research into exclusion, and the development of good practice in this area, takes account of this specific context when seeking to address the problems associated with school exclusion generally.

References

Audit Commission (1994) *Seen but not Heard: Co-ordinating community child health and social services for*
  children in need. London: HMSO.
Berridge, D. (1985) *Children's Homes*. Oxford: Blackwell.
Berridge, D. and Brodie, I. (1998) *Children's Homes Revisited*. London: Jessica Kingsley.
Berridge, D., Brodie, I., Ayre, P., Barrett, D., Henderson, B. and Wenman, H. (1997) *Hello – Is Anybody Listening? The education of young people in residential care*. University of Warwick: Social Care Association.
Biehal, N., Clayden, J., Stein, M. and Wade, J. (1995) *Moving On: Young people and leaving care schemes*. London: HMSO.
Borland, M., Pearson, C., Hill, M., Tisdall, K. and Bloomfield, I. (1998) *Education and Care away from Home*. Edinburgh: Scottish Council for Research in Education.
Brodie, I. (1999) *Redefining School Exclusion: Children's homes and the educational process*. Ph.D. thesis, University of Luton.
Department for Education (1994) *Pupils with Problems* (Circulars 8–13/94). London: DFE.
Department for Education and Employment (1999) *Draft Guidance on the Education of Children Looked After by Local Authorities*. London: DfEE.

Department of Health (1995) *Child Protection: Messages from research*. London: HMSO.

Department of Health (1996) *Focus on Teenagers*. London: HMSO.

Department of Health (1998a) *Quality Protects: Framework for action*. London: Department of Health.

Department of Health (1998b) *Caring for Children Looked After away from Home*. Chichester: Wiley.

Department of Health (1999) *Children Looked After in England, 1998/99*. London: Department of Health.

Department of Health and Others (1998) *The Government's Response to the Children's Safeguards Review* (Cmnd 4105). London: HMSO.

Farmer, E. and Pollock, S. (1998) *Caring for Sexually Abused and Abusing Children away from Home*. Chichester: Wiley.

Firth, H. and Horrocks, C. (1996) No home, no school, no future: Exclusions and children who are 'looked after'. In E. Blyth and J. Milner (eds) *Exclusion from School: Inter-professional issues for policy and practice*. London: Routledge.

House of Commons Health Committee (1998) *Children Looked After by Local Authorities*. Vol. 1. *Report and Proceedings of the Committee*. London: HMSO.

Social Services Inspectorate and Ofsted (1995) *The Education of Children Looked After By Local Authorities*. London: Ofsted.

Stirling, M. (1992) How many pupils are being excluded? *British Journal of Special Education*, **19**, 128–30.

Isabelle Brodie has demonstrated here the importance of recent initiatives aimed at preventing young people in care from falling through the net of potential support. Like other pupils 'on the margins' these young people can be invisible and vulnerable to subtle as well as explicit exclusion; and like others they can also be resilient. The chapter is important because we need to understand exclusion in order to promote inclusion.

Chapter 5

Inclusion for the difficult to include

John Visser, Ted Cole and Harry Daniels

This chapter reports on the findings from a DfEE funded study of mainstream schools' practice in relation to 'pupils with emotional and behavioural difficulties'. The authors outline some key features of schools which cater successfully for many of these pupils. They suggest that schools that foster a culture of caring, sharing and learning are more effective in achieving inclusion for those pupils who are regarded as the most difficult to include.

Introduction

The consultation Special Educational Needs Green Paper (DfEE 1997) and resultant Programme of Action (DfEE 1998) show the current Government's commitment to the increased inclusion of pupils with SEN in mainstream schools. [...] The Government suggests that inclusion should be seen as a 'process' rather than merely as 'placement' of pupils in a mainstream school. However, it is clear in these documents that some pupils are seen as more problematic than most when it comes to the achievement of inclusion. These pupils are generally perceived as those whose special educational needs fall into the area of emotional and behavioural difficulties (EBD). Both documents (DfEE 1997; DfEE 1998) highlighted pupils with EBD as constituting a greater challenge for inclusion than all other areas of SEN.

Pupils with EBD have always presented a challenge to schools and teachers, and yet some schools have a much better record of meeting these pupils' needs without recourse to permanent exclusion or a statement requiring the pupil to be educated in a special school or placed in a Pupil Referral Unit. In 1997 we (the Bimingham EBD research team) were awarded a grant by the DfEE to establish the features to be found in such mainstream schools. The details of this research were published by the DfEE (Daniels *et al.* 1998).

Methodology

The research used a three-phase nested design, where the main purpose of each phase was the clarification and refining of an understanding of good practice and how it is achieved. In Phase One, criteria associated with meeting the needs of pupils with EBD were taken from relevant reports, research and reviews. These criteria were distilled into a draft model whose validity was probed in interviews with key professionals within the field, and included DfEE, Ofsted, SCAA (now QCA), LEAs, social services and staff in schools. A refined model was then examined at a one-day conference with sub-groups using nominal group techniques as well as plenary discussions. The research team used this data to further refine the model.

Phase Two identified, in consultation with others (Ofsted, LEA officers, DfEE), 30 mainstream schools representing a range of social and economic contexts, maintained and grant maintained status and the full range of Key Stage configurations. Each school was visited and the model used as the reference point for interviews with key personnel in the areas of management, special educational needs and pastoral care.

Five primary and five secondary schools were chosen, on the basis of their practice, their willingness to cooperate and their locational spread from the Phase Two group for Phase Three. This last phase examined policy, provision and practice in depth and related this data back to the model which underwent further modification.

Two other studies contributed to the development of the model. The first was a national study of special school provision for pupils with EBD (Cole *et al.* 1998). The second was a study of one LEA's provision and practice in relation to pupils with EBD which has remained confidential to that authority. […]

Non-prescriptive features

The key features of the model described below are not put forward as prescriptive. The research took us into a wide variety of secondary and primary schools, where differing policies, practices and provision were observed. We did not find one dominant approach which, if transplanted to all schools, would meet all the needs of every pupil with EBD. There is not a single, 'one size fits all' approach to the different needs of pupils with EBD. Like MacGilchrist *et al.* (1997), in their work on school improvement, we found no blueprint in terms of systems or particular approaches (such as 'assertive discipline') for the effective inclusion of pupils with EBD in every mainstream school.

Rather, the features we describe provide teachers and schools with a way of examining their policy, practice and provision against some key principles which interact with each other. These interactions are governed by factors intrinsic and extrinsic to the school, and are underpinned by the values, attitudes and beliefs held by teaching staff and governors. The outcomes of these interactions make up the unique features of each school's approach to meeting the needs of its pupils. [...]

Finally we do not think that the features we outline are a surprise. The features we found resonate with much of the literature on effective schooling (for example, Sammons *et al.* 1995). What we do emphasise is that good practice in meeting the needs of pupils with EBD is derivative of good practice in meeting the learning needs of all pupils.

Key features

The key features found in schools which demonstrate inclusive practice in relation to pupils who are difficult to include were:

- effective leadership which generates direction for all staff
- a 'critical mass' of staff committed to inclusive values
- senior management (SMT) who are committed to the development of good quality teaching which matches the learning styles and abilities of pupils including those with EBD
- a willingness and ability to access outside agencies to help develop and sustain inclusive practice.

These features formed the basis for an ongoing dialogue between key staff, in particular the school's leadership, and a critical mass of other staff. This dialogue was based upon values which espoused caring, sharing and learning. These values enabled schools to maintain and sustain the ethos and processes which enable pupils with EBD to be included.

Leadership

Creating, maintaining and sustaining effective leadership is seen by a wide range of sources as a major feature in any discussion of good practice. These sources (for example, Davies 1997; Prince 1997; DfE 1994) often list the features which create effective schools but are less explicit about those which sustain and maintain good practice. The maintenance of good practice lies in ensuring that the structures remain appropriate and meet the needs of all concerned.

To sustain good practice the morale and commitment of staff has to be nurtured and acknowledged. Structures, systems and organisations need maintenance to remain effective. Relationships, values, beliefs and attitudes need sustaining – they are key aspects of inclusion in meeting the needs of pupils with EBD.

We found that these aspects of creating, sustaining and maintaining good practice were found in leadership patterns which sought to consult and seek consensus while giving a 'clear sense of direction'. This sense of direction was built upon a collegiate approach providing consensus, consistency and cohesion. Staff in good practice schools showed an awareness of the need for consensus in arriving at decisions and policies, consistency in their application, and cohesion of purpose of schooling implicit in their policy, practice and provision. These three 'Cs' enabled schools to be more flexible and transparent in meeting the needs of pupils. This is of particular importance for inclusive practice where the valuing of diversity is high on the daily agenda of staff.

Teachers and schools meet the educational needs of pupils with emotional and behavioural difficulties, through the relationships they develop and the organisational strategies they employ (DES 1989; Gleeson 1992; Mortimore *et al.* 1988; Ayers *et al.* 1995; HMI 1987; Smith and Laslett 1993). We found considerable variation between teachers and schools in these relationships. A variety of styles of teaching, ways of motivating pupils and responses to behaviour found challenging were observed. Common strands in these observations were the fostering of a climate of praise, with a high level of expectations in behaviour and academic progress, together with 'understanding' when these were not achieved by individual pupils.

The practice of these staff was enhanced when they had an understanding of EBD, where they were able to differentiate this from general 'naughtiness' and the transient misbehaviour most pupils engage in. The practice exhibited by staff was characterised by attributes and beliefs which showed a professional commitment which engendered a consistency in approach, allowing for flexibility in their skilled responsiveness to an individual pupil's needs. They offered constructive support to colleagues. They had a problem-sharing and solving approach to issues which encouraged an open discussion of classroom management issues. Above all they *believed* in the inclusion of pupils with SEN in their mainstream school.

These effective leaders and staff formed a 'critical mass' in the schools we examined. In some schools this critical mass consisted of a majority of the staff while in others it was a smaller number of staff. These critical mass groups contained those who were perceived as key players in the school. The importance of this 'critical mass' lay in the creation and ownership of the school's behaviour policy. They understood the emotional components of pupils' EBD and the sometimes fractured lives outside school of pupils with EBD. The 'E' in EBD was not swamped by an over-concentration on the 'B'. They also sustained a belief that pupils could alter their behaviour to an extent. Of importance in achieving the 'alteration' was the provision of an orderly, controlled, yet relaxed atmosphere underpinned by a positive whole school behaviour policy. These policies were integral parts of the school's overarching aims. They were linked naturally to the school's mission statement or corporate aims, rather than separately established and bolted to them. They flowed from the aims, values and beliefs espoused by the critical mass of staff. These behaviour policies matched criteria outlined as good practice by a number of sources (see, for example, Clarke and Murray 1996; Ofsted 1993; DES 1989).

These schools' behaviour policies were linked to a concern for educational progress; pupils with EBD were seen as pupils whose special educational needs did not preclude them from needing to, or wanting to, achieve academically. The sample schools had staff with a wide range of classroom management techniques, where teaching and learning was viewed as important, and thus the curriculum being followed and accreditation achieved was given equal status, or at least was not accorded a lower status than that followed by other pupils (see Visser 2000 for an exposition of these factors). The emphasis was upon the learning needs of the pupil being met.

The need for multi-agency work in meeting the often complex range of needs which pupils with EBD have has been advocated over a long period of time and by many authors (Cole *et al.* 1998). However, the evidence suggests that formidable obstacles (a mixture of finance, time and inclination) face schools in achieving or taking part in a multi-agency approach. Even within education (intra-agency approaches) some of the sample schools struggled to achieve the services of support teachers and educational psychologists. Where this was achieved it was largely on the basis of local factors such as personal professional relationships rather than systems and structures which promoted collaboration in identification, assessment and provision for pupils with EBD.

These features and others, such as teacher characteristics, discussed more fully in our report (Daniels *et al.* 1998) were found to varying degrees in all the schools within the study. They were also apparent in an earlier study of provision within special schools (Cole *et al.* 1998). A further analysis of these features gave rise to three descriptive terms which identify common themes in the schools we studied. They were all, to varying degrees, caring, sharing and learning schools.

Caring schools

The schools cared about their pupils. The rhetoric of inclusion was borne out in practice. Pupils were seen as part of a community which the school served; as such they were valued by staff in all their diversity and individuality. Their emotional needs were recognised and addressed, often by staff spending time listening to what pupils had to say. Staff cared by setting achievable high standards in behaviour and learning, while being tolerant and forgiving of lapses by pupils. Caring was not a soft option, misbehaviour was confronted, but it was the 'deed' which was condemned, not the person. These schools did permanently exclude the occasional pupil, but rarely, and always reluctantly. Their systems of rewards and sanctions were applied to meet individual needs whilst upholding widely agreed standards. They understood the need to provide pupils with 'cooling off space' when issues got out of hand, and modelled ways of coping with the strains and stresses of school life.

Sharing schools

These were schools where staff, pupils and parents were able to discuss openly between themselves, and with each other, issues of behaviour. In particular, staff could discuss their concerns over incidents where pupils had been challenging. Staff would collaborate in seeking positive ways forward to enhance their own skills as well as in meeting an individual pupil's needs. They focused on learning and teaching skills rather than upon difficulties perceived as being intrinsic to the child. They acknowledged that the solution to many emotional and behavioural difficulties lay outside of the school's ability to address fully. However, they were equally confident of schools' and teachers' ability to make a significant difference to the lives of their pupils with EBD.

Learning schools

We found that Dennison and Kirk's (1990) model of a do-review-learn-apply cycle was in evidence in all the schools. These were institutions where staff frequently reflected upon their actions, decisions and organisation. Importantly these reflections were taken into account in the planning of their subsequent actions. These were not schools which proceeded in a linear fashion to plan-do-review where the review does not feed back into the planning. There was a genuine circularity to their educational activities, where their reviews were an active part of their planning. Also these actions were not seen as separate entities, where separate incidents or processes were examined as if they had no wider consequence within the institution. Each action by pupil and staff, while seen as important within its own context, was also reviewed to ascertain its wider implications for staff, teachers, pupils, parents and SMT in the context of the whole school. Meeting the needs of pupils with EBD was not seen as separate from meeting the needs of all pupils. What was found to be effective in a given situation was used to inform policy, practice and provision more widely.

Conclusions

The lessons which we believe schools can draw from these findings to become more effective in meeting the needs of pupils with EBD echo the work of Thomas *et al.* (1998) and the Elton Report (DES 1989). Schools need to be communities that are open, positive and diverse, not selective, exclusive or rejecting. They need to ensure they are 'barrier free' for pupils with EBD. The development of a collaborative ethos is a key feature. This entails collaboration within school, between staff and between staff and pupils, as well as with outside agencies. Lastly, schools need to develop a sense of equity in promoting every pupil's rights and responsibilities in all aspects of school life. These lessons from our research are easy to state, but we appreciate from this DfEE study and subsequent research (for example, Cole *et al.* 1999) just how difficult it is for schools to achieve the challenges they pose.

References

Ayers, M., Clark, D. and Murray, A. (1995) *Perspectives on Behaviour: A Practical Guide to Effective Interventions for Teachers.* London: David Fulton.

Clarke, C. and Murray, A. (1996) *Developing a Whole School Behaviour Policy: A Practical Approach.* London: David Fulton.

Cole, T., Daniels, H. and Visser, J. (1999) *Patterns of Educational Provision Maintained by Local Education Authorities for Pupils with Behaviour Problems.* A report for the Nuffield Foundation, The University of Birmingham.

Cole, T., Visser, J. and Upton, G. (1998) *Effective Schooling for Pupils with Emotional and Behavioural Difficulties.* London: David Fulton.

Daniels, H., Visser, L., Cole, T. and De Reybekill, N. (1998) *Emotional and Behavioural Difficulties in Mainstream Schools.* Research report RR90. London: DfEE.

Davies, L. (1997) *Beyond Authoritarian School Management: The Challenge of Transparency.* Ticknall: Education Now.

Dennison, B. and Kirk, B. (1990) *Do Review Learn Apply: A Simple Guide to Experiential Learning.* Oxford: Blackwell.

DES (1989) *Discipline in Schools* (The Elton Report). London: HMSO.

DfE (1994) *The Education of Children with Emotional and Behavioural Difficulties*. Circular (9/94). London: DfE.

DfEE (1997) *Excellence for All Children: Meeting Special Educational Needs*. (Green Paper). London: DfEE.

DfEE (1998) *Programme for Action*. London: DfEE.

Gleeson, D. (1992) School attendance and truancy – a socio-historical account. *Sociological Review*, **40**(3), 437–90.

HMI (1987) *Good Behaviour and Discipline in Schools*. Education Observed Series. London: Routledge.

MacGilchrist, B., Myers, K. and Reed, J. (1997) *The Intelligent School*. London: Paul Chapman.

Mortimore, P., Sammons, L. and Ecob, R. (1988) *School Matters*. Wells: Open Books.

Ofsted (1993) *Achieving Good Behaviour in Schools*. London: HMSO.

Prince, L. P. (1997) The neglected rules of leadership: leadership and dissent. In Coulson, A. and Baddeley, S. (eds) *Trust in the Public Service*. New York: Policy Press.

Sammons, P., Hillman, J. and Mortimore, P. (1995) *Key Characteristics of Effective Schools: A Review of School Effectiveness Research*. Report Commission by Ofsted.

Smith, C. and Laslett, R. (1993) *Effective Classroom Management: A Teacher's Guide*. London: Routledge.

Thomas, G., Walker, D. and Webb, J. (1998) *The Making of the Inclusive School*. London: Routledge.

Visser, J. (2000) *Managing Behaviour in Classrooms*. London: David Fulton.

This chapter shows how inclusive schools extend beyond classroom boundaries. Like other authors in this volume, John Visser, Ted Cole and Harry Daniels see inclusion as a process based on clear principles. It involves professionals in reflection that may challenge their existing assumptions and in willingness to work across existing boundaries. Such new ways of working may well be challenging and difficult.

Part 2

Transitions

Coming together

Chapter 6

'We are the ones we have been waiting for'

The work of community mobilisers in Milton Keynes

Katy Simmons, Anna Laerke, Danny Conway and Martin Woodhead

This chapter reports on an Open University evaluation (MK Children's Fund, 2008) of the Community Mobiliser (CM) service for Milton Keynes Children's Fund. This service has been developed as the basic means of ensuring delivery of the local Children's Fund Plan, offering an effective participatory approach to intervention in areas of disadvantage and potential social exclusion. We hear the views of managers, workers, parents, children and community members and see the value of a participatory approach based on respect for service users and an acknowledgement of their central role in the development of local provision that is relevant to their values and aspirations.

Introduction

> Soup kitchen culture is when you just lay everything out for people. When you serve them services. The Mobiliser doesn't do that. He makes people take responsibility. But that's hard work. There is much that drags you the other way.
>
> (Interview with Agency manager)

> It's simple. They help us get things going or keep them going.
>
> (Parent explaining to another parent what the community mobiliser does)

Community mobilisers work with children and families to develop preventative services across their neighbourhood. Their work involves engaging diverse groups of people of all ages working for a common cause – the well being of children and families. Most of their work involves building people's confidence, skills and qualifications, for example, training up a community group to keep open a school swimming pool that normally shuts during school holidays or running a family Fun Day in a local park.

The CM service had its roots, both ideologically and methodologically, in development practices overseas, where community mobilisers have been widely employed in village-based health and agricultural projects. The fundamental presumption, adopted by the Milton Keynes service, is that long-term sustainable change is only really possible if people recognise the needs addressed as their own, along with the methods used, the actions taken, and the institutional frameworks developed. The aim of the CM service was the prevention of social exclusion through the development of local participation and through the empowerment of local communities. The emphasis has been on long-term, sustainable change, owned by local people, rather than on 'quick wins'.

By 2009, 8 CMs were working on estates, employed as one team, for Milton Keynes Council for Voluntary Organisations (CVO). Each CM had a separate working base at primary schools in their area. In an average week, CMs worked with approximately 1,200 different children and their families, supporting them in articulating their needs, identifying appropriate solutions and developing services. The basic premise of the CM service is that those who use the service are the experts on what they need and want.

It is this underlying philosophy about the understanding of poverty and social exclusion and on approaches to intervention and prevention that makes the CM project so different from many initiatives with disadvantaged communities. Social policies and interventions are frequently based on very particular theories about the way poverty impacts on children's development. They often hinge around single solution approaches, as if solving complex problems was no different from fixing the starter motor on a car or prescribing antibiotics to clear an infection. Deep appreciation and respect often seems to be lacking for the very particular circumstances that shape people's lives, their feelings about themselves, their children, their environment and their future. Taking account of the personal, social and community dimensions is the first step towards harnessing the energies of all involved, towards long-term sustainable solutions.

The efficacy of social action based on the participation of children, families and communities as an alternative to top-down (and all too often simplistic) solutions to complex and changing situations is increasingly compelling. Such principles are underpinned by the UN Convention on the Rights of the Child (1989) especially the emphasis on respecting the interests and perspectives of the individual child as the principal stakeholder. Participatory work requires a more enabling, responsive, flexible way of working, as well as sensitivity to the imbalances of power, especially between the 'expert' and the 'client'.

The vision for the CM service has, from its beginning, embodied all these principles. It involves harnessing the power within members of a community, to enable them to act together on the problems that affect them.

The national context

The Children's Fund, initiated by the New Labour government in 2000, played a key role in larger social, health, education and employment policies aimed to reduce social exclusion and target disadvantage. The Children's Fund aimed to develop services so that children and young people at risk of social exclusion were identified early.

Nationally, the Children's Fund had seven objectives:

- To promote attendance in school by 5–13-year-olds.
- To achieve improved educational performance among 5–13-year-olds.
- To ensure fewer young people aged 10–13 commit crime and fewer children aged 5–13 are victims of crime.
- To reduce child health inequalities.
- To ensure children, young people and their families feel the services are accessible.
- To develop services which are experienced as effective.
- To involve families in building the community's capacity to sustain the programme and thereby create pathways out of poverty.

Guided by various deprivation indicators, local partnerships were charged with identifying areas, communities or groups in need and with allocating funds to support a wide range of services for children and families.

The Children's Fund in Milton Keynes

The Milton Keynes Children's Fund Partnership was set up in 2003/2004 as part of the Third Wave of Children's Fund local initiatives in England. Prior to this locality mapping had been carried out which had identified pockets of deprivation in the city. In addition to seven national objectives, two further objectives were added locally:

- To increase the amount of affordable and accessible play provision for children and young people in the Children's Fund areas.
- To increase and improve informal support for parents of children in the Children's Fund areas. (Milton Keynes Children's Fund, 2010)

Key to the delivery of the Children's Fund work in Milton Keynes was the CM service.

Listening to paid workers

From the start, the managers who established the service explicitly took an anti-stigmatizing approach, based on respect for individual needs and choices and described by one manager as "targeted universalism":

> Someone might choose to get involved in the community mobiliser service … So they choose to do that, it's a natural choice rather than someone saying you're a problem family, as an individual family … Whereas what this is actually saying is here is a series of services that you can use.

Most CMs had extensive experience working with children, young people and families, but only one was professionally specialized in such work. In explaining recruitment criteria, the team leader pointed to what he saw as a fundamental difference between the CM approach and that of other services. He saw a candidate's personality, and his/her ability to communicate with a range of different people as paramount, whilst previous training and work experience were less important in the recruitment process. He explained that a CM with extensive experience in more traditional and long-established agency work might be "already too settled in their ways", and there would be a risk of such a professional perceiving community mobilisation as "narrow agency work under another name".

CMs emphasised the importance of being able to mediate, communicate and "think out of the box" in terms of preventative community intervention. All the CMs characterised him/herself, in some way, as "a people person".

> I've worked very hard at my relationships with people. I'm a very easy-going kind of person, I don't hold grudges, you know, I think that's such an important thing – to be somebody who can talk naturally with people in the community. I don't see myself as an important person, I'm another person that lives and works in Milton Keynes, as important as anyone else [...]
>
> (Community Mobiliser)

The CMs had a highly individualised view of their role, with mobilisers responding to the particular needs of the area where they were based.

They were committed to community participation, empowerment and prevention as a response to the problems of disadvantaged communities. They emphasised the importance of local ownership of initiatives:

> And once they've gone through all that, and it's been achieved, they actually sort of take ownership, because they were part of the whole process. So you're just helping people to achieve what they want rather than just doing it for them.
>
> (Community Mobiliser)

The mobilisers' perceived role was "different" from the role of other agency workers: mobilisers explained the difference:

> It's definitely a different style of approach that we've had. It's quite ... it's a very different way of thinking. In my last job [at a children's charity], they would put on activities for children and families, whereas we are asking the families and children to put on activities for themselves. That's the difference.
>
> (Community Mobiliser)

When asked directly what they thought a mobiliser's role might be, CMs gave answers such as:

> I see myself as a kind of community member who can make changes in that area and support others to do it.
>   Basically it comes out differently every time, but the way I describe it to people is community mobilisers are people who help communities get things going and started. So we support parents and children to talk about and to action some of the things they would really like to do in the areas that they live. [...] That doesn't mean necessarily giving them answers and quick results but it does mean that we, you know, are somebody who is there to listen to their opinion and hopefully support them to action some of those ideas.

The variation in practical approaches can be seen, for instance, in different CMs' description of how they make themselves available to, and communicate with, members of local communities, and their different perceptions of how well they know the people they target:

> I don't go in there saying I'm a community mobiliser because I don't like that approach myself, I don't like saying, well, I'm this and I'm going

to do that. I just go in as I am and if they ask me what to do then I'll tell them, but I don't go in preaching 'I'm this' or 'I've got to get this group going and you're going to part of it'. I hate that in–your–face thing.

All CMs stressed the importance of communication, information and accessibility; all spoke of the crucial importance of 'getting the message across'. Although aspects of this 'message' varied from CM to CM, there were some key notions that are expressed by all CMs. The following statements are typical:

> [My role] is to find out what they want to do. And help them achieve it rather than them tell you 'we'd like this and you do it'. Have them involved in the whole process.
>
> So, we are trying to give them that support, that freedom, and then obviously that opportunity to change their lives for the better. Because no way can you go into the community and say 'I know what you need, you need this and that'.

The very consistent reluctance to – or even inability to – identify service users in terms of social class, education, cultural background or family background, testified to a deep-seated reluctance to stigmatise.

Some mobilisers, in particular experienced workers who had been in post for longer, emphasised the crucial link between sustainability and allowing children and families to identify their own needs.

> So I look for … I look for sustainability. When we put on basketball or football, I look to see for those fathers that would be interested and become coaches themselves.
>
> And once they've gone through all that, and it's been achieved, they actually sort of take ownership, because they were part of the whole process. So you're just helping people to achieve what they want rather than just doing it for them.

They were highly sensitive to the perceptions of local people, some of whom deeply resented the presence of 'people in fleeces with clipboards' who ultimately disappeared, leaving local residents facing continuing challenges.

Listening to parents

> What's changed? Everything's changed! He's changed my life.
>
> (Mother of two)

She's given me a life, basically.

(Mother of five)

She's made a thirty-four-year-old do life guard training – what more can I say?

(Mother of four)

The minute they see him, they rush up, hang on his arm, he lifts them up and they do a headstand – and that's just the mums.

(Group of mothers)

The CM service was highly valued by families who used it. It was seen as de-stigmatising, thereby developing the potential to reach families considered to be 'most excluded'. One mother described her experience of working with her local CM:

> The Mobiliser's approach deals with elements of the cause as well as the effects. If you get labelled, you feel labelled and then you can get stuck in a rut, and – even worse – you distrust anything or anyone that comes along and offers anything. The Mobiliser's softly softly approach is so effective. She isn't forceful, but she listens to the community and individuals very carefully. It is their comments that generate the projects that she supports. The Parent and Toddler group is a superb example. Here was a group of parents with an array of skills, who were very unhappy with the facilities on offer and who – with support – had the ability to do something about it.

Parents described how work with the CM had enabled them to take control over their own lives:

> On a personal level, the Mobiliser has been working with me with the view to me utilising my IT training skills by enrolling on 'Train to be a Trainer' certification. And, more crucially, she has within the past few days introduced me to an organisation who may assist me in achieving my ultimate goal of running my own business.
>
> In summary, I would say that without many of the projects that the Mobiliser has supported, there is no doubt in my mind that parents would not have achieved this on their own. And, more crucially, the self-realisation that parents had the power to achieve despite their circumstances would never have evolved. EMPOWERMENT!

With support from the CM, another parent had written an article for the local community magazine about her children's summer in the local community. One mother of five embarked on a child minder qualification. A single mother of four was encouraged to start an Open University degree to qualify as a Teaching Assistant, when her youngest child started full-time schooling.

Many adults commented that the mobiliser service had helped them break the isolation they had previously experienced:

> I used to take the children to school and walk straight back home again. I used to be at home all day. Now I'm never at home.
>
> (Mother of four)

> I didn't know any of you a year ago – and look at us now!
>
> (Mother of one speaking in a focus group discussion)

Another mother described the difference between her older children and her younger one who has benefited from the presence of a mobiliser:

> I can really see a big difference between my two older ones and my youngest. She's four and has had the Mobiliser, and she's a completely different kind of person, because she's had all these things going on and she's made friends with other kids through the activities the Mobiliser has set up. It has given her social skills. She is much more out-going. It's going to be easier for her to start school she starts now, this September, full time. My older ones, they used to keep themselves to themselves ... they still do.
>
> (Mother of three, grandmother of one)

A number of service users talked about their growing confidence:

> The Mobiliser has given me confidence. I feel more confident than I ever used to be. And I'm quite proud of that. For instance, I don't like phones. I don't like phoning people. I used to never use the phone. I'm still a bit nervous, but now I'll do it.
>
> The Mobiliser was very important to me during a difficult period in my life. I was seeking custody of one my sons, and the Mobiliser helped me out, she supported me. She knew I was nervous about going to the mediation the first time, and she asked, 'do you want me to come with you?', and she did. She didn't go in with me, but she was there, and she brought me back again afterwards.

> One of the important things the Mobiliser has done for me is taking me seriously. She takes me as a real person. She has helped me get on courses. She's even paid for some of them. She is involved in our lives. It isn't just a job. She makes you feel you are wanted. We love her. Our kids love her. Yes, the children do love the Mobiliser.
>
> (Mother)

On a simple level the mobiliser service gave children and families "something to do". Especially during holidays, families on low income found it difficult to keep children from being "bored" and parents from "going mad at home".

> You get new ideas about what to do with your children. It allows all children to have the same experience. Sometimes, you know, when holidays are over and children go back to school, some children will have done lots of things and will say 'I've done this ... or that ...'. Others won't have anything to say because they haven't done anything. But with these activities, everyone has the same and they have something to talk about.
>
> (Local parent)

> 'When he said we were going to a forest, I thought ... why go to a forest?... there'll only be trees [general laughter]. But it was really good. After we did the walk together, we went and did it again ourselves. We never would have done that.'
>
> 'Yes, we did that. That Secret Garden. I've lived here 29 years and I didn't know it existed. So that night I went right back with my husband and just sat there. It was great.'
>
> (Two parents in discussion group)

It is clear that recognition of individual concerns is at the heart of the mobilisers' success:

> The Mobiliser doesn't just ask us [parents] what we want ... he asks the children. You know, he has set up a local action group for the children and they meet at school and he listens to what they say.
>
> (Mother of two)

> He looks out for everyone ... he takes every one at an equal level.
>
> (Mother of one)

> Have you noticed? When he talks to the kids, he bends down – we don't even do that ... we just shout over their heads.
>
> (Mother of three, focus group)

CMs are uniquely well placed and experienced to act as facilitators and instigators of inter-agency collaboration. However, such inter-agency work can be challenging. One employee who has embraced the local mobiliser and the mobiliser role as "an asset to the community" explained that not all agencies and agency workers do so. As he put, "it's about changing a culture ... it's about challenging the soup kitchen culture". The difference in approach between "providing services" and responding to community need is profound and, for some agencies, challenging.

As one parent said, "Don't just provide activities to support low income areas. Develop the areas by listening to the aspirations of the residents".

Listening to young people

The CM initiative has "punched above its weight", in two important respects: through what the mobilisers call their "mediator" role, the service has overcome barriers to inter-agency collaboration; and with their unique non-specialist approach, they have reached a broad base of service users by creating a non-stigmatising environment for service provision.

As far as children were concerned, it was the provision of a service that does not stigmatise its users that had the greatest influence, though 'de-stigmatisation' was not a word children used. Children distinguished between the CMs and other agency workers:

> The Mobiliser is a friendly face for the community to recognise – someone you can relate to, who you know.
>
> (Young person)

> [The mobiliser] is completely different to the others [agency workers]. The others just come in and do their thing. They come in, maybe a couple of hours, on the Estate. [The mobiliser] is quite often here all day, she is flexible and she can listen – whereas the others, they can't listen.
>
> (Young person)

> [The mobiliser] helps out in the community, and our parents get involved. And it's good because children have a say in what they want to happen – like holiday activities and sports and clubs and that.
>
> (Child, aged nine)

When asked what mobilisers do, children typically replied:

> We do fun things with other children and learn about things ... like
> [how to] not talk to strangers. Don't take sweets from strangers.
>
> (Child, aged 10)

> It's all about recognising each other ... on the street, in the shops, you
> recognise people and they're more approachable.
>
> (Young person)

For many children and young people, simply having something worthwhile
to do was an important part of what the mobiliser service offered.

> We help each other, you feel you have achieved something when you
> help with the younger children.
>
> (Child, aged 11)

> I can kick a football now! [The mobiliser] got the footballer from the
> Dons to come and show us ...
>
> (Child, aged 12)

> We made pizza and brownies and my brownies are better than my
> mum's now.
>
> (Child, aged 10)

One boy aged nine had taken part in the interviewing process to appoint
three new community mobilisers.

> Interviewer: how do you think you'll get on with the new Mobiliser?
>
> Boy: I think I'll get on really well. I helped to choose her. She's fun, but
> sensible. Being sensible is really important. You know ... having fun:
> (squeaky voice) 'let's all have fun ...! Wheeee!!!!' Then they are not
> paying attention and ... Bang! (he collapses onto desk) ... too late. Yes.
> Being sensible is really important ... You know, I got 4 letters. They
> started 'Dear colleague' (he laughs) I know who the new Mobilisers are.
> I know what they'll spend the money on. I know who's going to be
> where. And I know how much money they will spend on things.

When asked what the mobiliser service "is about", a group of young people
from the Lakes Estate had this to say, in an extract from an interview that is

fully recorded in the full report:

> Young Person 1: Providing opportunities for youngsters ... get fit ...
>
> YP2: Get fit the cheap way – gyms are expensive.
>
> YP3: And you have to be of a certain age as well.
>
> Interviewer: Is there one thing that the Mobiliser has done which has really made a difference?
>
> YP2: What she's done is a MIRACLE.
>
> YP3: She's made me a better person ...
>
> YP1: Yeah, and not only has she helped us, sort of mentally, but then we can pass that on down to the kids ... like a chain reaction.
>
> YP2: Things have just grown and grown ... how long have we been doing this?
>
> YP1: We started last summer ... we weren't in charge then ... we were under [the Mobiliser] ... but now we are in charge.
>
> YP: Must have been six half-terms [holidays] now ...
>
> Interviewer: You said it has grown?
>
> YP2: Yes, last time we had something like a hundred kids coming to our activities and of those there would be about 90 kids off the Estate ... you can't really ask for more ... than 90 kids coming to do sports and fun activities ... it gives them something to do ... instead of going round causing trouble.
>
> YP1: We started off with about ten to fifteen kids ...
>
> Interviewer: And am I right in thinking that you planned these activities?
>
> YP1: Yeah, we take responsibility for our services.
>
> YP2: We organise it and plan what areas need improving, and we meet up and finalise it and then we advertise it and we end up with one hundred, two hundred kids ...
>
> Interviewer: Have you learned anything in particular from that whole process of planning?
>
> YP1: We're learning some stuff that didn't work last time, some things that need improving ... so we're all learning different things, like.

YP2: Like, for the first time this term we've done arts and crafts, and it worked really well, so we'll probably do it again.

YP3: And team work ... before we worked more on our own, but we learned some great management skills, and it obviously paid off.

YP1: I haven't been involved in anything like this before ... it's just so well organised ... and when I started, the team just took me in straight away ... I didn't feel any pressure ... I just went straight in ... I started this year, and I've learned a lot from it already.

These young people, supported by their local CM, had brought about considerable positive changes in their local community in terms of the accessibility, safety and pleasantness of public spaces, and in terms of out-of-school sports activities for children who would otherwise have had very little to do "other than hanging about making trouble", as one of the children put it.

Perhaps the most remarkable aspect of the Lakes Estate project is its potential for longer term sustainability. In terms of individual students' lives, the impact of this programme is likely to reach well beyond the student years. The initiative has enabled these young people to pursue interests and careers which they readily acknowledge would most likely have been out of their reach otherwise. The CM has, as one put it, started 'a chain reaction'. By passing on their skills and experience to younger recruits, and by acting as 'role models' for the children they work with, the students speaking here appear to have succeeded in developing enough momentum and interest to secure the service's long-term sustainability.

What made a difference?

During the evaluation, the following aspects of the CM service emerged as the most highly valued by adult service users:

- Training and education opportunities which have led to improved social and parenting skills, to better quality of life for individuals and families, and to improved future employment prospects.
- Development of mutually supportive community networks and pathways out of individual/family isolation.
- Increased communication between local residents which has led to increased confidence and improved access to sources of information.
- The experience of being taken seriously and not "spoken down to" as "just a mum in a deprived neighbourhood".

- "Having something to do": opportunities for both adults and children to get involved in all stages of activity planning. Affordable holiday activities for children and opportunities for adults to meet other adults.
- Empowerment.

The children and young people identified as important the following outcomes of the mobiliser service:

- Feeling safe as a means to becoming more involved and familiar with one's neighbourhood and local community. Or: becoming streetwise.
- Having access to and use of safe, clean places outside school.
- Having fun through regular, reliable activities/clubs and planned one-off events.
- Learning new skills and being proud.
- Getting to know and make friends with new people.
- Being listened to and treated with respect.

Both young people and adults saw a distinct difference between the CM service and other agencies that worked in their localities. The CM service did not come with ready-made answers, but rather engaged with local people to identify the questions that really mattered to them.

Overview

The greatest strength of the CM service is its direct engagement with local people and its readiness to adapt to changing local need:

> They can really glue … they are massive agents for change and communities … boy do these communities need change … I think it is about challenging the status quo for people … reaching out to people who need it, who really need it …
>
> (Interviewee)

The community mobiliser service is now established as an innovative way of supporting communities to engage directly with the issues that affect them most. It is long-term work and there are no "quick fixes". The mobilisers do not "deliver solutions" but rather work alongside communities to bring about sustainable change:

> They are brokers for things … they light a little touch paper and things happen … they don't necessarily do all of it themselves, but they start off

... so, for example, the local action group, that was very much kicked off by the community mobilisers ... But it is now almost a sustainable and self-running thing, so yeah, they still need guidance but it's them doing a lot of it ...

(Interviewee)

The service is actively working to promote the participation of families and children in their communities, creating opportunities for self development in families previously at risk of social exclusion.

Those who work with people on the ground – service providers and service evaluators – know that inclusion is crucial to sustainability. They experience in practice how complex are the interrelationships between inclusion, sustainability, participation, trust and empowerment. Perhaps most importantly, practitioners also know that genuine inclusion takes a great deal of time. The CM philosophy of working alongside communities, helping them identify solutions to problems that concern them both individually and as part of a neighbourhood, provides a new model for genuinely inclusive practice.

References

Milton Keynes Children's Fund (2010) "About the Children's Fund", http://www.mkweb. co.uk/mkchildrensfund/DisplayArticle.asp?ID=31560 (accessed on January 15 2010).
Milton Keynes Children's Fund (2008) "External Evaluation of Mk Children's Fund", http://www.mkweb.co.uk/mkchildrensfund/home.asp (accessed on 3 March 2010).

Activism can take many forms. It can function at micro and macro levels. Many of us have the ideas and commitment to generate considerable change within our communities, but lack the connections and confidence to initiate that change. Frequently it takes someone from outside our immediate environment to provide us with the spark and initial support we need; we, of course, have to be alert to the opportunity and be ready to listen to each other.

Chapter 7

'Back to school'

Piloting an occupational therapy service in mainstream schools in the UK

Eve Hutton

Occupational therapists are traditionally employed within the UK healthcare system to work with individual children and families. This chapter predominantly shares the experiences of two occupational therapists who were asked to provide their support in mainstream schools rather than through their usual clinic-based approach. The impact of this new direction on the therapists is explored through the retrospective accounts of their time in the schools and their reflections following the project. The author describes how working in partnership with the teachers and shifting the focus from supporting individual children influenced the therapists' view of their service.

Background

[…] OTs work with children to promote their engagement in a range of daily occupations, including self-care, play and school-based activities. OTs who work in children's services in the UK are employed mainly in the healthcare rather than the education sector; this contrasts with the situation in other countries, including the USA, where the majority of child OTs work within, and are employed directly by, the school system. The reasons for this lie in the historical separation of health, education and social care in the UK system (Ham, 2004).

Only a relatively small number of OTs out of the total employed in the UK healthcare system choose to work with children and families and, as a consequence, historically demand has outweighed supply […] Local occupational therapy services, in line with other specialist therapy provision, responded to these pressures by tightening referral criteria (Crace, 2005). This has narrowed the gateway for children and families, so that only children at the most severe end of the disability spectrum benefit from OT support. The strategy may have brought waiting lists under more manageable control, but this has been achieved at the price of applying a reductionist framework to the clinical practice of children's occupational therapy, ironically at a time when the profession is attempting to redefine its contribution to health and well-being and when UK government policy, in line with global trends, is adopting a more radical health promotion agenda (Kronenberg, Algado & Pollard, 2005; Department of Health, 2006).

Occupational Therapy into Schools (OTIS)

In 2004 a service review was undertaken by an occupational therapy service in the south east of England [...] The review highlighted the limits of the existing service; which prioritized the needs of some children while limiting access to the service for others. With this in mind the team decided to pilot a model of service delivery based on the principles of educational inclusion and early intervention. The project was named Occupational Therapy into Schools (OTIS) and was informed by a similar model previously piloted successfully in pre-school settings in the area.

In consultation with the local education authority two schools were identified, both in areas of social deprivation. The index of multiple deprivation (IMD) scores of the wards in which the schools were located were 48.15 and 35.47, respectively (Office of the Deputy Prime Minister, 2004). These schools had a higher than average proportion of children with identified additional needs [...]

The aim of making occupational therapy services for children more accessible was achieved by therapists basing themselves within school and working closely with teachers, assistants, children and families. The two therapists were each allocated an individual school and visited the school regularly over a period of two terms, spending the equivalent of two days a week there. This enabled them to establish working relationships with the staff. They were able to create learning opportunities for teachers, where they could share their occupational therapy knowledge and skills, in the context of a classroom or teaching session (Lave & Wenger, 1991).

The interventions were tailored to the needs of the schools. The therapists, children and teaching staff identified goals for the project – these goals, although differing in some respects, had a shared focus on increasing the engagement and participation of children in a range of school-based occupations such as writing, colouring and cutting, using cutlery at meal times and participation in physical education and playtime games (see Table 7.1).

It is important to emphasize that both the OTIS approach (working inclusively, across the whole school) and the OTIS methods (delivering

Table 7.1 Examples of the type of goals negotiated at the outset of the project

Goals at school 1	Goals at school 2
Beam and Fizzy groups established	Work with school council to identify area of change in school environment
Increase understanding of motor control and sensory development	Workshops with PD children to explore and improve their school experience
Introduce staff to strategies which will encourage children's participation	Provide new resource box on scissor skill development and training
Practical creative workshops for children and their families	Parent advice sheets on motor skills and link with classroom skills

occupational therapy interventions through partnership with school staff) of working presented a novel challenge to the two therapists who piloted the service. Both therapists were experienced and had a wide range of clinical experience in community settings, but both had worked exclusively with individual children and their families, referred specifically for occupational therapy intervention.

The evaluation of OTIS

The evaluation was designed to explore the impact of the presence of the therapists in the school on the knowledge and skills of the teaching staff. [...] However, it is helpful to note here the positive response of the schools. One headteacher described the project as 'Incredibly motivating – one of the best things we have done'. A head of early years said of her interactions with the therapists that she 'had learnt more in two terms than I ever did at college, or in my 26 years of teaching'. And a teaching assistant observed that as a result of the project the school 'have seen benefits, in terms of improved handwriting, more relaxed sitting and fidgeting has become less of a problem in the classroom'.

As the project concluded I felt that there was a further aspect to the evaluation of OTIS. This was the impact of the project on the learning and professional development of the therapists themselves, arising directly out of the challenges they had faced when working with new approaches and methods in an unfamiliar environment. [...]

Methodology

The account below is based on data collected during the single in-depth interview I carried out at the conclusion of the project [...] I used a thematic approach, and I checked this interpretation with the therapists to confirm the validity of my interpretation and analysis, incorporating their ideas and comments (Silverman, 1997). [...]

The first phase describes the therapists' experiences of doubt about their competence and anxiety about the reactions the teachers would have as they based themselves within schools. This was followed by a second phase as the therapists considered their professional knowledge and frameworks and how adequately they met the demands of working inclusively in schools. This led to the final phase, a period of experimentation, where new ideas and ways of working were explored, resulting in changes in the therapists' attitudes to working in schools and a re-evaluation of their approach to their role as child OTs.

An uncertain situation

Piloting a new therapy service in schools provided both challenges and opportunities. The first phase of the project lasted approximately two weeks and involved spending time in the school getting to know the staff and observing classroom and playground activities prior to formulating, with the school, a set of negotiated goals.

> Initially it was very daunting being part of a new 'team' and working fully within a different organisation, even with previous experience of visiting and working in schools. I did have a real fear of not being able to deliver. As a single representative of a professional service, there was no escape if it failed!
>
> (OT1)

> What was challenging was having none of the familiar back-ups and systems of support, like being able to go into the office and talking through with other colleagues. I needed these people to like us not just work with us!
>
> (OT2) [...]

Both therapists found working with the school team without a clearly defined role or specific expectation difficult.

> I hated it, I felt very deskilled. I was concerned that I would have nothing to say and that I didn't know what I was doing. I was used to assessing and treating individual children and coming up with results

according to our frame of reference – now I had to make what I knew
relevant and appropriate to a busy teacher with other pressures. I knew
I would have to learn a new language.

(OT2)

It was important for both therapists to have the support of one another as
they negotiated their way through unfamiliar professional and personal
terrain. Both therapists met with each other regularly and discussed
day-to-day issues on the phone.

> Both of us needed reassurance that the direction we were taking was the
> right one. The pace of disseminating information to the teachers was
> slow, so it was good to talk to a colleague who spoke the same language.
> I felt reassured that she also felt isolated and we laughed a lot, as a way
> of coping.
>
> (OT2)

Although challenging, the therapists realized that being at school offered
opportunities to observe and engage with children and families in their local
community. The contrast of working inclusively across the whole school, as
compared with assessing children on an individual basis in a clinic, was
identified.

> I felt it was easier to picture the children we work with and consider their
> whole life experience as the school community has regular exposure and
> involvement. As therapists we do see children in their homes as well as
> schools but our visits, especially to the over fives, are very limited. The
> school, on the other hand, is a constant in these children's lives.
>
> (OT1)

> I saw children in the classroom, at play, during PE and break times. I
> learned who dropped the children off and collected them from school.
> I saw them on good days and bad. I felt I got to know them and what
> was important to them. There were pressures on some children from
> deprived backgrounds that made me re-evaluate occupational therapy
> goals.
>
> (OT2)

In the past therapists would visit schools and make recommendations to
teachers, formulated as individualized therapy programmes – the therapists,

having spent time in the school, now realized how unrealistic some of their expectations had been in devising these programmes, and also how hard it was for teachers to implement therapy programmes without support.

> [Prior to this project] we were seen as being critical of and criticising teaching staff, this was because we offered strategies but didn't back these up with support to the teachers in how to implement them. Also the child didn't understand what was happening either; we hadn't taken the time to explain to them the purpose of the programmes.

In order to integrate fully with the school team the therapists worked closely alongside all the team, from teaching staff to dinner ladies – trying to understand the reality of school life.

One therapist mentioned that:

> It took wiping down tables and acknowledging a good job done before I felt accepted by the team.
>
> (OT2)

> New initiatives seemed to arrive in the school on a daily basis and I didn't want to be just another new initiative. People need to have what they are doing acknowledged before wanting to move on – if you show you are interested in the 'story so far' then they might be interested in the next chapter.
>
> (OT2)

Applying and evaluating existing knowledge in practice

The second phase of the project involved the goal setting for each individual school (see Table 7.1). Once these were agreed the therapists had to consider the means by which they could achieve these goals, drawing initially upon their existing knowledge and experiences. Goals in each school differed, however, the therapists described very similar approaches in how they adapted and modified their intervention to meet the specific needs of teachers.

> I drew upon all of the knowledge bases that I would use normally, neuro-developmental, sensory integration, but mainly I considered basic child development – physical and psychosocial – and I tried to place the

children in the school within a social model of disability at the core, which was hard as the school environment does not really allow this model to flourish, even with the ethos of inclusion.

(OT1)

I took a very developmental approach and drew on solution–focused approaches to problem solving. I would try to engage the teachers in a conversation around, for example, why they wanted children to 'sit still', leading them to realize that developmentally some children may not be able to sit still and listen at the same time – in this way teachers began to accept and understand developmental approaches.

(OT2)

The therapists began to appreciate the differences between their own and the teaching staff's knowledge base, especially around the subject of the sensory and motor development of children and their understanding of disability and difference. The therapists had assumed that the teachers possessed a basic level of knowledge in relation to the above. Spending time in the school made them re-evaluate this.

Sometimes we assume other professionals working with children share the same knowledge as we do and know what we know. We have to be careful to understand their objectives and realize that it sometimes takes more than a quick explanation for some of the stuff we know to make sense to teachers. Later on in the project I could see the 'lights going on' for some of the staff, but I was reminded that it took years of working for me to integrate this knowledge so why would I think that others should get this in 5 minutes?

(OT2)

I found that teaching staff's knowledge base is wide but completely different to our own, with very little exposure or training in difference, disability and additional needs.

(OT1)

The challenge for the therapists was how to share their knowledge and skills with teachers.

We wanted to see a shift in how teaching staff see the children – to gain a greater understanding of why a child does something. That it is not always about behaviour.

(OT2)

In delivering therapy interventions the therapists had to think about how to communicate with teachers and teaching assistants and explain the purpose of therapy to the children. Therapists used similar communication skills to those they would use in a clinic setting, but adapted and modified these.

> I used the communication skills that I employ at all times in my professional role. However, they were 'maxed up' to ensure that my place within the school was strong. I was constantly conscious of ensuring that my approach was non-judgemental, empathic and supportive at all times. Exhausting!
>
> (OT1)

There was a conscious decision by the therapists to avoid jargon and medical language when they spoke with children, teachers and families.

> I needed to be clear in my communication and the skills that I modelled, that they were accessible to all the school staff and that they could be continued without the input of a therapist . The skills and knowledge I used remained the same, but it was my presentation of these that I adapted.
>
> (OT1)

> Jargon tends to be used because it's quick in the right setting, We [OTs] know what we mean by 'core stability'. In the school I needed to take time and use day-to-day examples to describe what I meant, I used my own experience as a parent and drew on this, a more human approach less medicalized.
>
> (OT2)

Both therapists were surprised at how they were perceived by teachers and teaching staff prior to the start of the project.

> I think I assumed before the OTIS project that I never gave off the air of expert/powerful one! And I was quite shocked to hear that that was how we were perceived. I think before the project began I was conscious that the only way to work successfully within the school was to become a team member of the school. This was quite scary as naturally our time in the school was short and I wasn't there full time – I thought it would be hard to 'break in' and feel accepted as part of the team.

The therapists experimented with different ways of working, for example organizing workshops for teachers and teaching assistants while a class was running as normal. The therapists also developed resources and educational materials for parents that were accessible to families from disadvantaged backgrounds.

> I decided to take the approach of not too much new stuff at once.
> I often thought of a dancing analogy to describe what I was doing – I'm a terrible dancer, but if someone takes it slowly with a tune I know and shoes I'm comfortable in then I might do OK. If I'm in high heels with an unfamiliar tune expect me to fall flat on my face – I'll also decide I never wanted to dance anyway! This guided a lot of what I did, especially with the parents. Most of the parents and teachers were doing the best they could in difficult circumstances.
>
> (OT2)

Re-evaluation

The concluding phase involved the therapists learning from their experience in order to consider the implications on their practice and the future direction of the service. The schools evaluated the service very positively, however, the therapists identified areas that could be usefully developed and expanded upon.

> I have come away thinking a lot about the social model of disability and how as a service we could engage more with this and support schools to consider their actions within this.
>
> (OT1)

The therapists had re-evaluated their approach to children with disabilities and to the staff in the school who worked with them.

> As OTs we pride ourselves on our holistic approach, yet I feel that I failed many disabled children by not understanding their life on a day-to-day basis within the classroom. I feel that teaching staff need to be educated and supported more. There needs to be a three-way negotiation with the child, the therapist and the teacher about what happens to the child during the day.
>
> (OT1)

The therapists wanted to re-evaluate and change not only their own practice but also the structure of the service.

However valuable it was to see children at school, this may be because this is where they are when we are at work — the danger with this approach is that we may get caught up in meeting the schools goals.

(OT2)

I believe there is still a place for clinic based services, particularly for assessment. However I feel that the way we support the children we work for in schools needs to be evaluated particularly for those who are disabled or socially disadvantaged. We need to ensure there is true equity within the service and that we consider the culture of the environments that the children are within.

(OT1)

Since the project has ended I spend time with a child in class rather than carrying out formal assessments — I use functional observations and talk to the key people who work with the child, I feel more confident with this approach even though I don't have standardized scores to include in a report. I believe now that the child's context and environment are more important than what they can achieve with a therapist in a separate room. It's back to the basics, team working, not splinter skills and clinics. I feel more comfortable with this approach, I still use my clinical knowledge to guide my thinking but I make sure that I share this with others in a universal language.

(OT2)

The lead OT wanted these experiences to be shared with the whole team. She commented that the project had:

Underscored my conviction that school-based work is valuable. I will ask staff to reflect carefully on their use of programmes for schools without an underpinning explanation from us and engagement from the school to ensure cooperation. Also, I will ask staff to reflect on how to develop plans to support schools in using equipment inclusively, working creatively with the class timetable.

(Lead OT)

Discussion

This pilot offered an opportunity to explore the learning and professional development of the therapists involved in delivering a new service. This was at a time when there are competing views about what values should inform an occupational therapy service to children and families. The piloting of this new service was, in the words of the lead occupational therapist, about exploring 'A vision of the future of the OT service, based on inclusive practice and partnership with schools'.

The therapists applied their skills and shared their knowledge of children's occupational participation with teachers and teaching assistants. They adapted and modified the information they shared and learnt first hand about the need to 'learn a new language', avoiding jargon, and the importance of using examples from their own experiences to illustrate and explain what they were doing.

The therapists acknowledged assumptions that they had previously made about the teachers' knowledge of children's sensory and motor development. They learnt that it took 'more than a quick explanation' for teachers to understand complex ideas and concepts related to a child's developing occupational competence.

The therapists learnt how to devise learning opportunities for teachers in class that made the information they were imparting relevant to the teacher. They did this by demonstrating a new strategy or technique as part of an activity or in relation to a specific child. For example, running sessions on the development of handwriting skills as part of a handwriting lesson. By working in partnership they realized that they could have a greater impact on children's occupational engagement, in comparison with working as they had done previously.

If the UK government wants to achieve the goals they have identified for children then teachers and therapists will need to find ways of working more closely together. This depends on creating opportunities for a greater appreciation of the respective knowledge bases that underpin the practice of teachers and therapists. This account of knowledge sharing and transfer of skills is an example of the development of a 'community of learning', generating collective learning in a shared domain (Wenger, 1998). The teaching staff and children benefited from the presence of OTs within the school and the therapists learnt from their engagement in this project.

In addition to the learning and development that has taken place, the project has been a potential 'catalyst for change' (Ghaye, 2005). The project has challenged the acceptability of providing an occupational therapy service which focuses on disability and opened up the possibility of adopting a wider health promotion and early intervention approach. The therapists discovered that they could be truly inclusive and child-centred – the opportunity to work within the school enabled them to experience first hand the everyday influences on a child's life. One of the goals of reflective practice, according to Morley (2007), is to 'assist practitioners to bring their practice more in line with their espoused values'. It is appropriate, therefore, to conclude with a statement from the lead occupational therapist involved in OTIS:

> Our core values [as OTs] were reinforced as this project showed us how we could revert to being truly inclusive and reach an important client group that our clinic-based services often do not reach. [...]

Acknowledgements

Thanks are due to the three therapists involved in the occupational therapy into schools project, Wendy Clarke, Lesley Perry and Marian Niarac – their accounts and experiences form the basis of this article. Thanks are also due to the teachers, teaching assistants and children in the two schools who participated in the pilot project. [...]

References

Crace, J. (2005) 'Not so much a choice, more a battle of wills. Some of the white paper's promises ring hollow to the families of children with special needs'. The *Guardian, 8 November*, http://www.guardian.co.uk/politics/2005/Nov/08/schools.education (accessed on 20 October 2008).

Department of Health (2006) *Our health, our care, our say: A new direction for community services*, http://www.dh.gov.uk/en/Publicationsandstatistics/Publications/ PublicationsPolicyAndGuidance/DH_4127453 (accessed on 8 August 2007).

Ghaye, T. (2005) *Developing the reflective healthcare team*. Oxford, UK: Blackwell.

Ham, C. (2004) *Health policy in Britain, the politics and organisation of the National Health Service* (5th ed.). Basingstoke: Palgrave Macmillan.

Kronenberg, F., Algado, S. and Pollard, N. (2005) *Occupational therapy without borders*. London: Churchill Livingstone.

Lave, J. and Wenger, E. (1991) *Situated learning*. New York: Cambridge University Press.

Morley, C. (2007) Engaging practitioners with critical reflection: issues and dilemmas. *Reflective Practice*, **8**(1), 61–74.

Office of the Deputy Prime Minister (ODPM) (2004) *Indices of deprivation*. London: ODPM.

Silverman, D. (Ed.). (1997) *Qualitative research: Theory, method and practice*. London: Sage.

Wenger, E. (1998) *Communities of practice: Learning, meaning and identity*. Cambridge: Cambridge University Press.

This chapter highlights that moving to more inclusive practice often challenges professionals to re-define their role. The therapists involved responded creatively to their unfamiliar situation and discovered that there were 'other ways' of supporting children's participation. Sharing their knowledge and skills with teachers and parents through group work and training became the focus. This required the therapists to modify how they communicated their advice and to think carefully about how best to develop other people's understanding. It was particularly interesting that the therapists realized the importance of considering factors in the child's environment when deciding on support rather than concentrating on individual skills. Significantly the impact of working more inclusively had a positive effect on everyone: the children; the schools; the teachers; and the therapists themselves.

Chapter 8

Inclusion at Bangabandhu Primary School

Cathy Phillips and Helen Jenner

In this chapter, Cathy Phillips (headteacher, Bangabandhu Primary School) and Helen Jenner (Inclusion Officer with Tower Hamlets Local Education Authority) consider the central role that inclusive practice has played in developing the work of the school. They show how inclusive practice at Bangabandhu is based on a set of guiding principles. Those principles are characterised by respect for individual difference and openness to change. The article shows how definitions of good practice constantly change, led by responses to the diversity of the school's community. The authors do not claim to have every answer to the challenges the school has faced. However, they show how inclusive practice, supported by shared principles, can respond not only to individual circumstances but also to the concerns of whole communities.

History

Bangabandhu Primary School is situated in the east of Bethnal Green in the London Borough of Tower Hamlets. We are a community school and welcome children of all abilities, cultures, ethnic groups, political status and special needs. Sixty pupils a year join our two-form entry school and we have two nursery classes. The surrounding area is a mix of medium and high rise council flats with small areas of privately owned terraced houses. It is an area of considerable deprivation, with the majority of the school population being affected by substandard housing, overcrowding, unemployment or a lack of safe places to play.

Bangabandhu opened in January 1989 in temporary accommodation following an unprecedented rise in the size of the Bangladeshi community. Our name means 'Friend of Bengal' and is taken from the honorary title given to Sheik Mujibur Rahman, who helped found Bangladesh in 1971.

In 1991 we moved into our attractive, purpose-built building. It was described as barrier-free but this did not prove to be the case. Our first wheelchair users found that the level of the playground was 90 cm lower than the classroom floor and ramps had to be built to classroom doors. Fire doors did not open automatically and the toilets 'for the disabled' were too small. The vast majority of the initial school intake was Bangladeshi. Some children had been without a school place for several years. The Bangladeshi parents, as new arrivals, had least access to the education system. The parents were also very concerned, in a climate of racism, for the safety of their children and wanted a school in their immediate neighbourhood. Our initial roll was almost exclusively bilingual, with children who had not attended school before or who had had extensive breaks in their education.

We worked very hard in the initial year to let the wider public know of our existence. The school is in an out-of-the-way location and was perceived by many as a private Asian school. We were able to increase our profile when we moved in to our new building. We leafleted the neighbourhood and invited everyone to open evenings to see the school.
As the local community discovered the school and its reputation increased, the intake became more mixed in cultural and class terms and is now more representative of the wider community.

Many of the children enter the school with low levels of basic skills and there are still a number of children who join throughout the school from overseas or take extended leave with families abroad. Our school population is now approximately 65 per cent Bangladeshi, 15 per cent English, Scottish and Welsh, and the other 20 per cent come from a range of nationalities with Somali, Turkish and African Caribbean being the next most prominent groups.

Equal opportunities

As a new school we have made equal opportunities central to our practice. Antiracist teaching is an integral part of our provision and has a central place in the curriculum. From the start, we aimed to provide resources and a curriculum that reflected the nationalities and cultures within the school and a workforce that reflected the community.
We have appointed support staff and, where possible, teachers who reflect the school population. Signs appear in both English and Bengali, and letters home are translated.

Teaching, assemblies and celebrations are planned with the diversity of our community in mind. We are predominantly a Muslim school and we ensure we are knowledgeable about what this means for our pupils, their families and many of our staff. We recognise, however, that for our pupils to have equal access to all that society has to offer, they need to know that Britain developed as a Christian society, many of its institutions shaped by Christianity.

Equal opportunities are at the heart of inclusion. We see equal opportunities as not about treating everyone the same but rather about meeting people's individual needs and celebrating individual strengths. Equality does not mean uniformity. It is about acknowledging and valuing the differences between individuals.

We recognise there is great tension between the government's standards agenda and their policy on inclusion. This tension has put great pressure on the school. We are concerned with social as well as academic progress. We want to foster young people who will be tolerant and able to make informed choices. We recognise that inclusion will weaken our performance in the league tables but are prepared to defend this position despite pressures to abandon an inclusive approach, narrow the curriculum and target resources at those children who will ensure that our position in the league tables improves.

Children with special educational needs

Once we moved to our new building, a teacher from a local special school approached us. She felt that many of her pupils were wrongly placed and would move to mainstream secondary schools. She wanted them to come to us on a part-time basis. Inclusion for pupils with significant special educational needs was, therefore, a gradual process for us. A few children became part-time pupils, several then moving to us full-time. We began to have pupils directed to us because of the suitability of the premises and the welcome and acceptance that pupils experienced. We also had a number of children from our own school population who were diagnosed with progressive conditions that would result in physical impairment. We also began to see a rise in the number of children on the autistic spectrum.

Our initial reaction was to look for experts 'out there' who would tell us how to meet these new needs. We actively sought any advice we could get from doctors, specialist teachers, physiotherapists, occupational and speech therapists. We also experienced at times feelings of frustration, disappointment and a lack of support. We came to realise that every child is an individual and that a label of cerebral palsy or autism did not necessarily tell you what that child needed next in the classroom with their learning or social skills. We are developing our own expertise with help wherever we can get it and will continue on this path. We have formed a productive partnership with Stephen Hawking School, a local special school.

We have had children on roll who are registered blind, with TAR syndrome (the child had no arms and poorly formed legs), 3 M syndrome, ataxia telangiectasia, cerebral palsy, spina bifida, brittle bone disease, autism, Down's syndrome and many other conditions. We knew nothing about some of these conditions until the children turned up and in some cases the diagnosis is so rare that little is known even in the medical world. We have learned that it is the individual child who is at the centre of our planning. For example, two children from a one-parent family were suddenly diagnosed with a serious degenerative condition. One child needed a teaching assistant as soon as possible as his movements were becoming more and more unstable. His mother was Turkish with limited English. We found a Turkish teaching assistant (TA) by advertising in the Turkish press in north London. Not all situations have been resolved so easily.

|Adopting an inclusive approach requires us to recognise that we are always learning and that we may make mistakes. Ensuring that a school is thriving, making progress and raising achievement involves accepting challenges and taking risks at times.|This risk taking is hard for everyone but particularly for new and inexperienced staff. It is important to listen to staff expressing their anxieties and concerns. We want people who constantly challenge themselves but we need to have the confidence to be able to say when we need help, be it training, more resources or whatever. In adopting an inclusive approach, staff learn that when something is not working then they have to change something, in the class, in their own approach or in the environment. They should not expect the child to change.

Induction of new children is a vital step in ensuring success. Photographs are introduced before the child arrives. A parent or teacher talks to the class about what the child can and cannot do, what they like and what they do not. We find that children who do not look the same physically do not then get stared at or asked inappropriate questions from curious children. If parents and staff have seen photographs displayed, they too do not react inappropriately. One of the most positive outcomes of inclusion is improved behaviour in the school generally and a high degree of disapproval if a term of abuse is used in the playground about physical characteristics or learning capabilities. Children who have had difficulties in schools with a less inclusive approach have transferred with success, though we have not eradicated name calling altogether.

Inclusion is a process. We will never get there completely but we can try! At first there was segregation in special schools, secondly, integration which said 'Yes, you can come to our school but you have got to fit in with us' and finally inclusion where we say 'Yes, please come and we as adults, pupils and our institution as a whole, will adapt as best we can in order to meet your needs'. This may mean adapting our attitudes and thinking, the curriculum, classroom organisation, furniture and equipment and the building.

The SEN Code of Practice allows inequality. Children with similar degrees of need do not necessarily all get a statement of special educational need: a statement can depend on the attitude and persistence of parents and the range of supporting evidence they can produce. The process of getting a statement can in itself lead to a focus on the need to change the child rather than the need to adapt and develop school provision. Inclusion should lead to greater equality, with resources shared more appropriately and children with more significant need being given an opportunity for greater independence, where possible.

Support staff

As we began to expand our special need provision, the number of support staff increased considerably. Some staff were general classroom assistants, others were special needs assistants, later to be called learning support assistants. There were different job descriptions and rates of pay for the two groups. In 1998 we made the decision to treat all assistants the same, to rename them as teaching assistants and ensure they had the same job description and the higher rate of pay. We were delighted when this happened nationally and welcomed the move from the DfES to increase the number and status of TAs. In recent years the school has been able to employ TAs directly and we have been able to create a management and career structure for them. While we want TAs to develop specialisms and interests, we also want all support staff to work with a range of children so that expectations are kept high, that there is variety of experience for staff, and all children feel that they have access to extra support at times. It is also important that teachers work with the full range of children in their class and do not become reliant on TAs taking responsibility for certain children. We also try and avoid children becoming dependent on one TA or vice versa, both errors we have made along the way. We also aim to employ the majority of TAs full-time. Training opportunities are offered such as the Open University STAC course and City and Guilds qualifications.

The Index for Inclusion

When our LEA asked us to pilot the Index for Inclusion in 1999, we found it a very useful tool for school development planning. Our initial focus was the role of the TA. Our main project focused on interviews with TAs and some teachers and pupils on the TA role. We discovered that our assistants had a high sense of job satisfaction and found the work rewarding. They needed improved opportunities for communication with teachers, more training and more time to prepare resources. Teachers recognised the vital work that TAs did and the contribution they made to children's progress. They also wanted more time to meet with their TA to plan and share information, and recognised the management issues involved with working with more than one adult in the class.

We changed assembly arrangements so that teachers and assistants could spend that time three times a week talking and planning together. Many TAs are also employed before the start and after the finish of the school day to allow more time to talk. Cover is provided for conferences with the SENCO and other professionals when needed. Ensuring there is enough time to talk, however, continues to be an area of concern.

Parental involvement

We had to work hard as a new school to gain parents' trust. We developed a number of social activities including our annual International Evening when parents and children contribute food from their country, wear traditional dress and listen to music from a range of places. Our last evening saw food from England, Scotland, Wales, Bangladesh, Israel, India, Japan, Morocco and Turkey. We hold a Mela in the summer term, similar to a summer fête, and have a range of stalls and events.

We have welcome meetings at the beginning of the school year when staff working in each year group are released at the beginning of the day to meet parents to talk about the year ahead and general expectations. Once a term we hold parent/teacher consultations where staff and parents can talk about children's progress and targets. We release class teachers for a day to allow those parents who would be reluctant or unable to come in the evening an opportunity to talk to the teacher. We also offer evening appointments for those parents who are working. A friendly reminder on the phone ensures that those who forget can still take advantage of this important meeting.

Parents and carers are also invited in to regular class assemblies when their child's class show and talk about some of the work they have done. Some classes have 'author's breakfasts', when family members are asked to join their children with refreshments to share their written work for the term.

A toddler group meets once a week with a toy library and is aimed at parents who will be sending their children to the nursery. It is very popular and mums, childminders, grandmothers and sometimes dads, have been regular visitors. A bilingual TA runs the group and ensures that newcomers feel welcome.

The appointment of a bilingual receptionist has made it much easier for many parents to approach the school.

Parents have generally been very positive about our inclusion policies. The messages to parents are strong but happen through practice – seeing how children are included in class assemblies, outings and shows, for example.

The curriculum

We believe that a broad and balanced curriculum is essential for inclusion to be successful. An emphasis on sport and the performing and creative arts allows all children to participate more fully in the life of the school and opens up ways of communicating that do not always rely on the spoken or written word. Although we understand the importance of the core subjects in the curriculum, these subjects alone are not enough.

The proximity of central London offers a wealth of resources, and visits to museums, galleries and theatres are a regular part of the school curriculum. We welcome visitors to the school and have long-standing partnerships with the Guildhall School of Music and Drama and the Barbican Education Centre. We currently employ a dance company who are working with a range of children including those with physical and learning disabilities. Yoga is taught to two year-groups who are benefiting in terms of health and behaviour.

Artists in residence undertake a range of projects with the children. Children's confidence, speaking and listening skills and enthusiasm are all promoted and we see a growth in their literacy skills as a result.

Our behaviour policy

We believe that everyone at school is important and to be valued, is here for a purpose and has a positive contribution to make. We expect each individual to respect others, their families, cultures and beliefs. We aim to encourage self-discipline and keep rules to a minimum: rules are in place to support and maintain our ethos of care for each other, the community and the environment. We try and make our rules explicit, apply them equitably and ensure they are for the good of all.

We have a very strong policy on bullying and it is an item each term in school assemblies and in circle time. We try and ensure that everyone has a shared view on the definition of bullying in its widest sense in order to minimise its occurrence.

We see it as everyone's responsibility to ensure our policy is followed. Adults should at all times observe the same rules they expect of children.

As members of staff we aim to be courteous and fair. This means keeping calm, listening carefully, being consistent in our dealings with others and using humour, praise and rewards wherever possible rather than sanctions, though these do, of course, have to be used at times. We have introduced a variety of strategies to support the inclusion of vulnerable or disaffected children including conflict resolution procedures, circle time, 'circle of friends' and playground management training for staff.

Children with emotional and behavioural difficulties usually present the most difficulties for staff. These children can cause the most stress, make us feel we have lost control, and can challenge our own emotional weaknesses. To better meet these needs, we are aiming at becoming a more emotionally literate school and put a strong emphasis on the emotional development of children and on raising their self-esteem. We still have work to do in this area.

A holistic approach

Additional teachers have been a feature of Tower Hamlets for several decades, with funding for pupils from minority ethnic backgrounds coming initially from the Home Office under Section 11 and then from the DfES. In the past, children might have received support under a range of different headings and may have worked with a SENCO, a Section 11 teacher and a TA within the space of a few days.

Now class teachers, together with their support teacher, meet termly to discuss the needs of each child and focus support appropriately. Decisions about support are based on the child's needs and on staff skills. We also employ two part-time workers, one who works with families with attendance problems and the other with those who have emotional or behavioural difficulties that prevent effective learning. We are also fortunate in being able to employ two part-time specialist teachers: one who works with children with speech and language delays and difficulties, the other with children with specific learning difficulties in literacy. We have also employed a speech therapist one day a week.

Teaching

Adaptability and flexibility lead to successful inclusion. We believe we need to look at the individual child and constantly evaluate what is in their best interests and those of the other children. An autistic child generally benefits from one-to-one tuition outside the classroom for part of the day because they find the normal classroom too busy to cope with all day. A child with Asperger's Syndrome is not made to join in an activity that he cannot understand and see as having no relevance to him such as competitive sport, but would be expected to join in physical activity to develop skills and keep himself fit. A child may spend all their time in the mainstream classroom but work for much of the day on an individual programme, fitting into general classroom activities whenever possible.

We discuss with individual children, and their parents, what they find difficult and devise with them strategies to help them cope or alternative activities. We also include them in the target-setting process for their individual education plans. This way, the teacher and TA gain much greater insight into the child's situation.

We believe all children at Bangabandhu have the same entitlement to the curriculum. If, however, a child is not benefiting from what is on offer to the class, withdrawal for some sessions or parallel individual or group sessions can be offered as long as there is greater educational value to the child than staying with the whole class. The aim will always be for the child or group to rejoin the class when ready – a timescale is set for this.

The LEA is committed to provide additional facilities at Bangabandhu following the closure of the special school, mentioned earlier. Our new resources will include two class bases, a practical area, a sensory room, a therapy room, a soft play room and an extended ICT suite. We currently have a number of children with complex needs who are in the mainstream classes. We hope future pupils will also spend most of their time there and that these new resources will expand our provision for all our children. The sensory room and soft play areas, for example, will be used by a range of children, not just those with complex needs.

Resources

Funding has been a difficult issue for us over the years, as it is for most schools. We have found it easier to manage the many issues around finance and inclusion now more of the school finance is delegated. We have a large budget and we need to look at it as a whole to ensure that our resources are distributed fairly. We have had to develop a relationship with the LEA that ensures access to the level of resources we feel we need and have had to learn to make realistic demands. It is important to review spending regularly and to be flexible. We are also able to be more pro-active now that we have more control and try to use resources for early intervention rather than wait until a child's difficulties become more severe.

We constantly look for appropriate resources that will support our teaching. These include specialist PE equipment that can be used by all children but is particularly accessible if you have restricted movement or poor sight. We are always looking for new ICT hardware and software that can support the curriculum and make it more accessible. We carefully consider topics taught to make them relevant but also to open up the world to those whose circumstances leave them with very limited horizons. Working on an opera project based on *The Rake's Progress* was a great success with children and parents because we were sensitive to Muslim sensibilities in adapting the story.

Principles

Inclusion is about equal opportunities. We recognise that we have embarked on a process that may never be finished but aim to become more inclusive year by year. We believe in the need to build an inclusive society and that developing an inclusive approach to all aspects of school life can act as a pathway towards inclusion in the wider community.

We have established some basic principles. We consider all the children in our immediate neighbourhood have a right to attend our school. Every child has the same right of access and is entitled to appropriate support to meet their individual needs whatever their race, culture, faith, gender, sexuality, physical or learning impairment. We accept staff on the same basis.

Children with a language other than English, physical, learning or sensory disabilities, emotional or behavioural difficulties, have a right to the support they need in our classrooms. We recognise that all children have a right to learn and play together and that no one should be excluded because of their ethnicity or disability – this is discrimination. Our school community is open, positive and diverse and our school is accessible to staff, parents and carers with disabilities.

We understand that we have to challenge our thinking at all times – are we asking this child to fit into our routine or our preconceived ideas of what is best? Or are we really trying to adjust what we offer in order that every child feels secure, understands what is required of them and feels valued for what they are, not what we would like them to be? We believe that children do better, socially and academically, in inclusive settings and that any teaching or caring that happens in a segregated school can take place in an inclusive school. Inclusion supports school improvement and effectiveness.

Inclusion is a process that has the potential to develop friendship, respect and understanding. All children, with or without disabilities, benefit from inclusion. By aiming to meet the full range of needs in an ordinary setting, we can improve the learning environment for everyone – teachers and parents as well as children. The teaching and learning and social development that are right for inclusion are right for all children.

We recognise we have entered a process that involves changing and challenging systems and structures, adapting the curriculum, the buildings, language, images and role models. We also recognise that inclusion is not a single issue but involves a wide range of options and depends on a range of factors that include the individual, the setting and available resources.

What we have learned

We have come to some conclusions as we have worked towards being an inclusive school. We have learned that:

1   inclusion is a step on from integration;
2   a child does not benefit from having an individual at his/her side at all times – independence for that child is of prime importance;
3   a child who does need full-time support should work with more than one TA within a day;
4   a more flexible use of TAs is more productive than trying to ensure that each child with a statement of special educational need has his/her agreed level of support;
5   the needs of children at School Action (Code of Practice) and a full statement are often very similar, the only difference being the stage their paperwork is at;
6   outside agencies need to work with us in a planned way;
7   the class teacher has the central role in providing for the child;
8   all staff need training;
9   the specialist teacher has a key role.

Our aim has been to move gradually away from the position that we started with, where each child has a clearly defined entitlement to certain resources, to one where we in the school determine what resources are appropriate and how they are deployed.

Where next?

Our main priorities for the future are to:

•   ensure that all our children are independent learners. We are concerned that as there are often several adults in the class, children can easily resort to their help rather than develop their own persistence and problem solving skills;

- ensure that staff expertise is known more fully and used effectively and that staff are encouraged to draw on and share their knowledge and skills to support learning;
- improve the welcome new staff receive when they start at the school. We want to ensure that new staff feel included and that their experience and observations are valued;
- improve the quality of communication between parents and the school. We have felt that parental involvement is a strength of the school but there is room for improvement and we want to develop further strategies to ensure all parents/carers feel valued, involved and confident in offering their concerns and contributions to the growth of the school.

Bangabandhu is, we feel, an exciting and challenging place where adults and children alike develop their skills, attitudes, learning and knowledge through a broad-based curriculum while developing strong links with the community. It requires everyone to work hard to maintain and develop this ethos. Ofsted recognised what had been achieved:

> Bangabandhu is a successful and effective school. Pupils with a wide range of attainment, including a high percentage of pupils for whom English is an additional language and a high percentage with special educational needs, achieve well and make good progress.

> Through excellent teamwork, excellent relationships and learning are maintained, reflecting the school's clearly stated aims.

> (Ofsted, June 2000)

We earned these comments because we embraced inclusion wholeheartedly when the school opened and before the word was in general usage. Inclusion is central to the life of the school.

> This chapter gives us the flavour of an inclusive school. As in some of our other chapters based in schools, we get a sense of work in progress. While no one claims to have right answers, the process of change is valued and encouraged and the goal is clear. The chapter shows us how important it is to establish clear principles, as a prelude to developing good and effective practice.

Chapter 9

A personal perspective

Developing a partnership approach at Deri View Primary School and Acorn Integrated Children's Centre

Maggie Teague

Maggie Teague became the head teacher of Deri View Primary School and the Acorn Integrated Children's Centre in September 2005. This chapter offers her perspective upon how they have become accepted as a key resource for the whole community. Maggie describes how parents and children, primarily from the local housing estate and from low socio-economic backgrounds, have been encouraged to work together with the setting to establish a culture of acceptance and an ethos of inclusion for all. However, when Maggie first started working in this area of Abergavenny, as a deputy head teacher in one of the schools which was subsequently closed to make way for the new school and centre, she found that relationships between parents and staff were very different.

Starting out at Deri View and the Acorn Centre

Having grown up in a working class environment in Ireland where education was hugely valued it was a shock to find myself working in a community where education had a very low status. The head teacher of the village school where I grew up was treated with great respect. He was our route to a better lifestyle and a 'better job' which my parents so much wanted for their beloved children. From the day we first started school we knew that we had to work hard and do our best. My mother in particular was determined that her children would not leave school at the age of 14 as she had and that we would have a profession.

Over the years I held this belief firmly in my mind and in all my teaching posts I strived to provide the kind of education that would improve life chances for all my pupils. In 2001 I accepted the post of head teacher of a small school in a Community First area which was later to be amalgamated with other schools to become Deri View Primary School and Acorn Integrated Children's Centre. I was briefed before I started that the school was in a difficult area suffering from high unemployment, substance misuse, petty crime and vandalism. However, I was confident that I could make a difference for the children. After all, I was an experienced teacher, I had taught in a number of different countries and my reputation as a 'good teacher' was well established. I naively assumed that the parents in this community like most parents I had encountered in my career wanted the best for their children and that that meant a high standard of education. However, it wasn't long before I realised that I was very wrong and that education came very low on the list of priorities for families of children in the school. Their day-to-day existence was the priority and many of them were unable or unwilling to engage with education at all. I soon realised that if I applied the 'old fashioned', 'teacher knows best' attitude I would get nowhere.

Few parents showed any interest in what was happening in school. Pupil attendance was very poor and many parents felt that their child should not be disciplined or 'forced' to work in school. On average less than 25 per cent of parents attended parent–teacher consultation meetings, homework was rarely completed, many parents showed a disinterest at best and were positively hostile towards staff at worst. As long as the children were happy to come to school most parents were happy too. Their expectations were low and their ability to support or motivate their children to learn was lacking.

As a staff team we started to look for ways to improve the quality of education and thus the life chances of the children we taught. We had to radically rethink our approach to the parents and find ways to understand and engage them in education. We made an effort to build up relationships with the parents at the classroom doors. We talked and laughed with them, listened to their problems and frequently gave them positive feedback on their children. The parents became more relaxed in our company and started to listen when we talked about their children's work. Many told us that they hadn't done very well in school and wished their children could do better. I began to realise that these parents did want more for their children but didn't know how to go about it. It was our job then to give them the skills to do this. There were many single mothers amongst the parent group and I often told them of my mother's determination for me to be more successful in school than she had been. As a head teacher I seemed very far removed from them but I found they could relate more easily to the story of my mother who left school at the age of 14 and had six children. I hoped by this example to inspire them to believe in the opportunities for their children.

Family learning: empowering parents and children

We began looking for ways to encourage parents to help their children with reading and writing. The first step seemed to be Family Learning programmes to improve children's and parents' basic literacy skills, but it was not to succeed. In the programme introduction the tutor informed the parents that they had been invited to take part because their children weren't doing well in school. The parents were angry at this as it contravened everything the staff had been telling them about their child's ability and progress in school. The group were suddenly deflated; weeks of relationship building was set back, simply because we had failed to work in advance with the tutor to tailor the tone of the introduction appropriately.

It was time to take a completely different approach to family learning and to inclusion. A colleague and I visited children's centres in London to look at their work with families and the strategies they used to engage the hardest to reach. We learned a lot from those visits, not least that we had to completely change our approach to parents if we were to be successful in getting them into school. We realised that little things like the teacher standing at the classroom door at the beginning and end of the day were acting as a deterrent. We were keeping the parents outside and showing them that the classroom was our domain. We began opening the doors at the beginning and end of the day and inviting the parents in to collect their children. In this way they had to come into the classroom to collect their child and whilst there we were able to start building up relationships. Teachers started to show parents the children's work. 'You must see the story he wrote today', 'she has just moved up a level on the reading scheme – have you got the time to hear her read her new book?' Gradually parents became more relaxed in our company and much more confident in asking questions. They began to realise that we wanted the best for their children and very slowly we saw a change in their attitude to school. There was an improvement in attendance to parent–teacher meetings and there were more parents willing to help.

The basic skills tutor for the Local Education Authority (LEA) came back suggesting that we set up another family learning course; but I was reluctant to lose the ground we had gained in our relationships with parents by introducing a formal 'unfriendly' programme of learning. One of my colleagues, the reception class teacher at the time, had very good relationships with the parents of her pupils; she was friendly, creative and innovative in her approach, well liked by the parent group, and more importantly she was motivated and determined to change things for the children and community. She told the parents that the basic skills tutor would give her money to buy much needed maths equipment (the school budget was always in deficit) if she could get 12 parents to attend six meetings in school.

A group of parents agreed to help and that was the beginning of the 'Keeping up with the Children Course' that was designed and planned from week to week. At each meeting the teacher talked about how well the children had settled in her class and what they needed to practice at home. The parents made games and resources that they took home to use with their children and each week they talked about how both they and the child had enjoyed doing this. We provided tea and chocolate biscuits each week and although this seemed a little thing it was very important. We provided a free pack for parents at the end of the course which included information on the curriculum, a children's book, writing paper and pencils; all new good quality resources. We asked everywhere for funding for this – the library service, local bookshops, the basic skills tutor, local businesses and other professionals who seemed to have more money in their budgets than we did. The first course was a huge success and this was followed by a number of Family Learning courses, led by that same teacher and all built on the skills and knowledge gained in previous courses.

Partnership approaches

It became clear to us that the key to the success of family learning courses was the excellent interpersonal skills of the teacher and like-minded colleagues who joined her over the years.

Many of the parents who were cajoled into joining that first course are now in employment and their children are very successful in school. The basic skills tutor paid for supply cover and provided a children's tutor on request, but all of the work with parents was carried out by school staff. We learned that the work must be tailored to the individual needs of the parent group but the funding can be accessed in more than one way. We developed a very good working relationship with the basic skills tutor. She offered adult tuition and interested parents completed accredited courses in literacy.

At the same time we began developing relationships with professionals who were starting out in the community. A Sure Start co-ordinator had just been appointed and when I was approached by an officer from the LEA to provide office space for her I jumped at the chance, despite the fact that it meant moving the school library into a space in the hall. The language and play co-ordinator was appointed for the LEA and later we adapted a store cupboard to make an office for her. By having these professionals working in the same building we had access to good quality family support on our doorsteps. If we had concerns about any pupils we consulted our colleagues who were very willing to go out into the home to offer support and guidance. These colleagues started to encourage parents to get involved in school projects and show an interest in their children's education. Parents began to learn how they could be involved.

Some parents wouldn't attend family learning courses but would come to school to help out with events or activities. There were those who didn't seem to care about education who suddenly became engaged when we started work on a school garden. One dad planted trees in the garden, one mum who had never shown any interest in education volunteered to help the children dig the vegetable patch, saying, 'I love gardening – I'm good at that!'

Over the years we have introduced many different initiatives to help engage and support the parent group, many of which have made a real difference to the families living in the community around the school and centre.

We applied for a lottery grant to run a breakfast club and after-school club, providing low cost good quality childcare which meant that parents could look for part-time work – which made a difference to their aspirations. These clubs are run by school staff who can answer parents' queries about their child in school, continuing the open door policy at the beginning and end of the day.

The nursery staff instigated home visits so that they could get to know the child in the family before they started school. These visits are carried out by the head of early years and her staff after a meeting with the health visitor, based in the Acorn Centre. She has a bank of knowledge about the families in the community and shares her expertise with staff. This prepares staff for the home visits and helps make this a successful experience for parents and children. Parents were suspicious of the visits at first but now welcome the staff to their homes and enjoy talking about their child starting school.

We run 'Getting Ready for School' workshops each summer when the parents of new reception class pupils are invited to six meetings in school. These include a pottery workshop, a Forest School workshop and a literacy workshop, largely run by reception class staff, and involve parents and children working together. In this way parents are given opportunities to gain an insight into the life and work of the school and more importantly to get to know the reception class teachers before their child starts school.

We gained funding for a home–school liaison officer who provides follow on support for families no longer eligible for Flying Start or Sure Start support. This member of staff works with parents in the home, accompanies them to family learning courses, provides transport for medical appointments when necessary and often acts as a go between with other professionals. This has made a big difference to the confidence and engagement with the hardest to reach families. It has had a positive impact on pupil attendance, behaviour, self esteem and achievement.

A pupil mentor has been trained to work with parents and children who are having difficulties in school. This has proved to be invaluable in managing the behaviour of the most challenging children in school. Parents now accept that we have a discipline policy which is applied fairly and firmly with all pupils. They no longer feel that we are criticising them when we ask them to come to talk about their child's behaviour. This has had a positive impact on pupil wellbeing and the school ethos.

Regular events are held in school; the PTA organises 'fun' activities for families as well as fundraising activities. It is important to provide as many opportunities as possible to get parents to attend school functions and it should not always be about raising money. Curriculum meetings with tea and cakes are held to encourage parents to learn about their children's work. Class teachers organise community events to talk about the curriculum and to celebrate the children's work. We provide financial support for children from less affluent families so that they take part in educational trips and visits. Staff recognise that many children never leave their home town. They work hard to provide a wide range of learning experiences for them, keeping the cost of these trips down. They have become very innovative in finding ways to organise free trips, get funding subsidies and support from as many different places as possible.

Increasingly, the staff are finding ways of including children and families and raising the self esteem and capacity of the community around us. The music co-ordinator organises reduced price music lessons and free hire of instruments to children whose parents cannot afford it. There are children in the school orchestra from families who have never played an instrument and it is a great pleasure to see how proud their parents are when they see them play.

Reflections and insights

In the 12 years that I have worked in a Community First area I have seen huge changes in the aspirations and the confidence of the community. People are beginning to engage with a range of professionals and are taking opportunities to improve their own and their children's qualifications. There are many young mothers who now want to be involved in school in the early years, who are trying hard to support their children with their school work. I have learned a lot about working in partnership with the community to raise standards in education. It is not a straightforward process. In many ways it is far removed from the traditional definition of education that many teachers still adhere to; but I can guarantee that it is a very exciting and rewarding approach.

In both the school and the centre we have had a great deal of success in partnership work and in including the parents as part of the team. We have had setbacks along the way but we have overcome obstacles and continued to move forward in our work. Although we have moved a long way, so parents are no longer suspicious and are more willing to engage with staff, our job is not yet done. Success in working in partnership with the community requires resilience and motivation on the part of the staff. From the beginning I have had the co-operation and support of colleagues who share my vision of equality in education for all of the children in the school community. Without their relentless enthusiasm, creative thinking, hard work and commitment Deri View and the Acorn Centre would not afford the reputation that it does.

Maggie Teague describes a transformation which can arise from a focus on a community, working with parents, children and staff in partnership. This is not just a matter of family learning, but it is about organisational learning too. Policy ideas such as extended schools and integrated working may come and go, but underlying them is a more enduring message, a recognition that we need to develop a shared vision, understanding and commitment to making participation a reality.

Chapter 10

Voices from segregated schooling
Towards an inclusive education system

Tina Cook, John Swain and Sally French

This chapter looks at 'inclusion' from the viewpoint of disabled people who have experienced segregated education. The authors review the literature in this area and then explore the views of pupils who are in the process of transferring from a special to a mainstream school. These perspectives are often absent from discussions of inclusion. However, the authors argue that voices from experiences of segregation should be central in constructing an inclusive education system.

Introduction

A local education authority (LEA) we shall call Romantown has begun reorganising its special educational needs provision under a policy flag of 'inclusion'. The changing policy and associated changes in provision and practice are, at least in general terms, being undertaken in numerous local authorities around Britain. One aspect of Romantown's reorganisation involved the closure of an all-age school we shall call Adamston, for pupils with physical disabilities, a school which first opened in the 1920s. The pupils from this school have been placed (in September 1999) in a range of provision, particularly in mainstream schools with 'additionally resourced centres' and newly-opened special schools for pupils with learning difficulties. (The reorganised system did not include a school for pupils with physical disabilities.) We explored the pupils' views about their education, and the changes they were experiencing, in a project in which a photograph album of pupils' memories of Adamston was created.

In this chapter we have three related aims:

(1) to present an analysis of the judgements disabled people bring to bear on their education, from experiences of segregated schooling, through a review of the literature;

(2) to explore the views and experiences of Adamston pupils prior to the closure of their school under the policy of inclusion;

(3) to examine the contribution of disabled adults' and pupils' views in moves towards inclusion. In attempting to realise our aims, our overall argument became that moves towards inclusion must be founded on the participative involvement of disabled people (adults and pupils) in changing education.

Whilst the judgements, views and experiences of both the adults and pupils were different and diverse, gathered from stories about residential and non-residential schooling situated in socially, historically and geographically disparate communities, it became clear that there were common themes that linked their stories. They were predominantly about being what James and Prout (1990: 6) term 'passive subjects of structural determinations' and not being actively involved in the construction of their own lives. The themes that linked them together are around perspectives of both feeling and being excluded from decision-making processes that fundamentally affected their lives, and the imperative for disabled people to participate in debates about their experiences and processes of change which shape and transform their experiences.

In attempting to realise our aims, our overall argument is that moves towards inclusion must be founded on the participative involvement of disabled people (adults and pupils) in changing education.

Inside stories: histories of segregated schooling

In general terms, much of the research on disability, including disabled children, has ignored the views and experiences of disabled people themselves. Non-disabled people have researched disability and given their perspectives. Histories of segregated schooling are, for the most part, the official histories of non-disabled people and professionals, documenting such things as changing numbers, and types of schools and official rationales for changing policies. Furthermore, research into disability has focused primarily on medical and psychological issues, rather than on the disabling environment. These critiques have led to a growing literature on the problematic nature of disability research (Barnes and Mercer 1997). In relation to research with disabled children, Robinson and Stalker state:

> While there is a well established body of knowledge about the way parents experience life with a disabled child, children's own accounts of their lives are largely missing, their voices have not been heard.
>
> (1998: 7)

Shakespeare and Watson (1998) make the point that children can have profound experiences of life, including disability, and yet they have not been consulted or taken seriously by academic or professional 'experts'. A recent exception is the 'Life of a Disabled Child' project, which has focused on disabled children's perspectives and experiences as social actors within a disabling environment (Priestley 1999).

The literature on disabled people's experiences of segregated education is not extensive and comes mainly from disabled adults reflecting on their childhood experiences. In reviewing what disabled adults and children say about their education it becomes apparent that their experiences are varied and their views are diverse. Themes do emerge, however, in terms of what is seen to be important about their education. These themes, of educational standards, personal and social liberation and education as an experience in itself, will be explored first.

Educational standards

Educational standards have consistently been important for disabled people. Segregated schools are judged by insiders in terms of what is taught, how it is taught and the effectiveness of the teaching they experience. The educational standards experienced by disabled people in segregated schools have generally been low (Barnes, 1991). [...] Many special schools placed a huge emphasis on practical tasks like cleaning and gardening. Henry, a man with learning difficulties, recalled:

> We used to play games, learning to read and write, spelling and how to clean places up – how to wash windows, how to clean anything you can mention.
>
> (Potts and Fido 1991: 68)

In addition to low educational standards, physically impaired people frequently complain about the amount of time spent in various forms of therapy. Phil Friend, who features in Davies's book, states:

> ... looking back from the age of nine to sixteen, the primary concern of that school was to 'therup' me. It was nothing to do with education really.
>
> (Davies 1992: 37)

Similarly, deaf people complain that their education was eroded by an obsessive emphasis on the ability to lip read and to talk (Craddock 1991).

These views are supported by Alderson and Goodey who state:

> Too many therapists in a school can divert the school's main remit away
> from education so that learning is fitted around therapy and students risk
> being further disabled academically.
>
> (1998: 154)

Poor educational standards in special schools, though common, were,
however, never universal. Selective schools for visually impaired, hearing
impaired and physically impaired children, who were judged to be academically able, have existed for many years, preparing their pupils for university
or entry to some professions. Disabled people who have attended such
schools sometimes express satisfaction with the education they have
received.

Personal and social liberation

The experience of education also has meaning in the broader terms of how
it impacts on the lifestyles and quality of life of disabled people. Disabled
people may judge the education they receive in terms of empowerment–
disempowerment and oppression–liberation. Some disabled people find that
they receive a superior education and have a more favourable lifestyle than
their non-disabled siblings and peers by virtue of being excluded. Martha, a
Malaysian woman with a visual impairment we interviewed, was separated
from a poor and neglectful family at the age of 5 and sent to a special
residential school. She said:

> I got a better education than any of them (brothers and sisters) and much
> better health care too. We had regular inoculations and regular medical
> checks and dental checks.
>
> (Swain and French 2000)

Martha subsequently went to university and qualified as a teacher, which
none of her siblings achieved. [...]
   A recurrent theme in the accounts given by disabled adults is the
confidence they gained by attending segregated schools. John O'Shaughnessy,
a man interviewed by Willmot and Saul, said:

> I remember my very first day at Uffculme as a very shy 14-year-old lad
> who had spent half of his life at home, ill with asthma and wrapped in

cotton wool ... I left Uffculme two years later an 11½ stone, self-confident young man ready to face the working world.

(1998: 168–9)

The positive social effects of being with similarly disabled people can even emerge within highly abusive institutions:

> Attending special school at the age of nine was, in many ways, a great relief. Despite the crocodile walks, the bells, the long separations from home and the physical punishment, it was an enormous joy to be with other partially sighted children and to be in an environment where limited sight was simply not an issue. I discovered that many other children shared my world and, despite the harshness of institutional life, I felt relaxed, made lots of friends, became more confident and thrived socially. For the first time in my life I was a standard product and it felt very good.
>
> (French 1993: 71)

[...] Although some disabled people have found that the experience of special education gave them self-confidence, others have found the opposite to be the case (Leicester 1999). Eve, a visually impaired woman, said:

> There was too much discipline. They were ever so strict. They used to run people down all the time and make you feel that you were useless. They used to make you feel that you were there as a punishment rather than to learn anything. They didn't understand children at all, never mind their sight. They used to expect you to do what they wanted and they used to get really cross if you couldn't see something, or you couldn't clean your shoes properly, or do anything they wanted you to do; what confidence I had they took it all away.
>
> (French 1996: 33)

Education as an experience in itself

A major theme throughout the literature documenting disabled people's experiences of segregated education is the quality of the experience in its own right. As for non-disabled people, one way of judging experiences is in terms, for instance, of enjoyment and happiness or boredom and unhappiness. John O'Shaughnessy, who went to an 'open air' school, said of his experiences: 'In later years my thoughts drift back to the happiest two years of my childhood' (Willmot and Saul 1998: 169). However, regardless of impairment, accounts of physical, sexual, psychological and emotional abuse are commonly disclosed by disabled adults, especially those who went to residential schools. Harriet, who attended a school for visually impaired girls in the 1950s and 1960s, recalled the physical abuse:

> We went to bed at five o'clock in the evening and we didn't get up until seven o'clock in the morning but we weren't allowed to get out of bed to go to the toilet. I was very unsettled because I'd gone to foster parents at the age of three and then to school at the age of five, and one night I wet the bed. The prefect on duty realised what had happened and she tried to cover up for me, she got me out of bed and put me in the bath, but one of the matrons came along. She picked me up out of the bath, just as I was soaking wet, and gave me the hiding of my life … I yelled and screamed, it terrified me.
>
> (French 1996: 31)

[…] It should not be assumed, however, that all insider experiences of segregated schools are negative in terms of the quality of the experiences themselves. Some of the people interviewed by Willmot and Saul (1998), speaking about their experiences in 'open air' schools, suggested that even though the regimes of these schools were institutional and harsh, they regarded their time there as a highly positive experience, including in terms of the basic necessities of life such as food. […] A strong and recurrent theme in the accounts of disabled people who have attended residential schools is the distress at being separated from their families, particularly when very young. Chris, a young man we interviewed (French and Swain 1997), recalled being very unhappy and crying every Monday morning as he waited for the bus to take him back to school where he was a weekly boarder. He was much happier when transferred to a 'special' unit in a mainstream school. […]

Many disabled adults have found that the experience of segregated education interfered with, or even ruined, their family relationships. Richard Wood, who is physically impaired, said:

> I think it destroyed my family life, absolutely, I don't know my family … I never looked forward to going home in the school holidays … I never felt I belonged there … within two or three days I couldn't wait to get back to school because I really wanted to see my mates.
>
> (Rae 1996: 25–6)

Detachment from the entire home community is also a common experience of disabled people both during school holidays and when they leave school. Lorraine Gradwell, a physically impaired woman, recalled her isolation during school holidays:

> I didn't have any contact. There was one little girl who sometimes came to play. I think that was because her mum knew mine and it was a bit of a duty for her. We played together, but I couldn't really understand why she was coming.
>
> (Rae 1996: 7)

Even children who live at home and attend a special unit in a mainstream school can find themselves isolated from their peers in their immediate home environment. Peter, a young visually impaired man we interviewed (see French and Swain 1997), said: 'It's hard because my friends are up there … I find it hard to mix with them round here because I don't go to their school and I don't know them.'

We turn next to the voices of pupils in a day special school for pupils with physical disabilities. They are also voices from segregation, but speak from and of some very different experiences. Their experiences are particularly pertinent to our analysis as their school has been closed under a policy of 'inclusion'.

The pupil project

This analysis is based on a project conducted with pupils at Adamston School during July in the half-term before it closed. The project involved the planning for and production of a book of photographs by the pupils of things they wanted to remember about their school. We hoped to involve pupils in discussions about Adamston, their experiences there, and their thoughts and feelings about the closure of the school and their future.

We worked with two groups: three primary-aged pupils and four secondary pupils, who participated on a voluntary basis and whose parents were aware of their participation.

[…] At the time of the interviews, the secondary pupils who were placed in new schools had all made visits to those schools, but all three primary aged pupils maintained that they had not seen their future school. The research project was carried out at the school over three sessions.

Session one involved pupils in the planning of the project. They decided what they were going to photograph and why the picture was important to them. A demonstration was provided in two ways:

- one of the researchers showed pictures of herself at work and explained why she had taken the photos;
- an instamatic camera was used with each group to allow the pupils to take trial photos.

The project was planned by each pupil drawing and noting (with the assistance of the researchers) possible pictures for the book. The session was tape-recorded and the tapes were transcribed.

Session two was the photo taking session. Each pupil was given a disposable camera to take photographs for inclusion in the book. The photos were taken in pairs: one for possible inclusion in the school memories book and the other for each pupil to have his or her own personal record of the school.

Session three involved pupils in selecting photos for and making both their own personal records and the school memories book. Each photo chosen for the school book was accompanied by a caption, which was discussed and agreed by each group. The school book, then, had two sections: one put together by the primary group; the other by the secondary group. This session was also tape-recorded and the tapes were transcribed.

We chose to use this method to try and elicit pupils' views about their school and its closure for the following reasons:

- taking photographs was something the pupils would enjoy and that would engage their interest;
- some of the pupils were young and some had learning difficulties, which could have made it difficult for them to develop abstract conversations and concepts using direct interview techniques (Lewis and Lindsay 2000). The concrete nature of the task could help focus their attention and discussion;
- the pupils would work on this in a group, and through talking about their experiences together we hoped the pupils would be more comfortable and more expansive;
- it would allow us to return to the topic at a future date with an obvious starting/reference point.

It was clear that all the pupils were engaged in and enthusiastic about the project. […] Whilst this approach had a number of strengths in terms of the collection of data, there were a number of difficulties.

All the children in this small sample were able to communicate verbally. Children using augmentative communication aides or with whom participation in standard communication would be difficult, were not included.

We were acutely aware of not being able to listen to these children at this point, and hope to work with them in the future. [...]

There were ethical problems, including questions of informed consent. Though the pupils did seem enthusiastic, it was not clear whether the enthusiasm was directed at the project or was motivated by the opportunity to be absent from regular classes.

Though the views of a small number of pupils could be explored in depth we had no control over the explanations provided by teachers. We did find that we had to devote some time to explanations at the start of session one. There were limitations, too, in sampling. By asking the staff to recommend pupils we were unsure as to whether there was any selection of pupils other than on a voluntary basis. We were aware that there were other children who could have different views about Adamston and its closure, who were not put forward by the staff.

Given the hierarchy of adult/child interactions and the focus we gave our work compared with the immediate interests of the pupils, our awareness of directing their thoughts and contributions was necessarily heightened. We tried not to use direct questions, but allowed the pupils to develop conversations around the photographs.

Deciding what was pertinent within the data was complex and we tried to avoid 'lazy interpretation', as described by Alderson and Goodey (1996), that concentrates on inconsequential responses furnished by the children. It was not always easy, however, to spot the 'consequential' responses and there were times within our first trawl of the data when children's responses were ignored as irrelevant, but later thought to be extremely pertinent. The basis for choosing relevance tended to be when the children insisted on having discussions, sometimes along *with* the researchers, but sometimes *despite* them.

We found too that pupils' thoughts and feelings about their future placements and the reorganisation were not easily addressed. The immediate focus for the project was the immediate context for the pupils, that is the closure of their school, their memories of the school and what they valued. The more abstract questions about their future had to be raised by the researchers.

Views from Adamston

Perhaps inevitably the pupils' discussions covered a wide range of topics. However, three broad themes did recur:

- education as an experience in itself;
- inclusion as belonging;
- feelings of exclusion.

Education as an experience in itself

Their experiences were predominantly positive and related almost wholly to the quality of the experiences themselves, rather than to any educational standards or aims. The teachers who featured in the books, for instance, were said to be 'cool' or a 'good laugh', rather than because they were skilled at teaching. The school was valued as 'the best' because it was 'different'.

> *Pupil*: This school's much better. I wish it had never closed.
>
> *Pupil*: There's something different about this school.
>
> *Researcher*: So what's different about this school?
>
> *Pupils*: Lots of things. Horses. Sports Hall. The teachers are different. They're funny.

When asked what they would miss, 'friends' was the first answer and most pupils had predominantly taken photographs of their friends. They appeared to have very strong friendship bonds with each other across both gender and age range.

Amongst the secondary pupils there was the general camaraderie of leg pulling and teasing, often around 'snogging', 'skipping lessons together behind the sports hall', the 'disgusting nature of school dinners' ('I'd rather eat horse muck'), people being 'boring farts', and their mutual purported dislike of anything that suggested work, e.g. 'Maths. French. IT.'

The primary pupils demonstrated their strong friendships in a much more straightforward manner. 'I like knocking about with my friends. I like C. I really like knocking about with him because he's a real sort of friend.' They showed confidence in their friendships. When one child stated that 'my favourite things I like doing is playing with my friends', another's immediate response was 'he must mean me'.

There was evidence within both the secondary and primary pupils' talk of mutual understanding and recognition of the needs of others for greater amounts of help at certain times. For example, all the secondary children were keen to place a photograph of S, a wheelchair user, in their album. When deciding on the caption one suggestion was:

> *Pupil*: Every week S's class goes out [said with a trace of envy in his voice].
>
> *Pupil*: Yes, but that's not really their problem because at the weekend they can't get out so they have to go out with the teacher. They can't get out with their parents because their wheelchairs are too heavy.

The relationships with the staff in all areas of the school were consistently highly valued by all seven pupils. It was cited as the aspect of the school they would praise most highly. They described them as 'funny', 'mental', 'dead crazy', 'excellent', but also as 'kind' and 'helpful', not only towards them but towards their friends.

> *Researcher*: Why do you want a picture of J [staff member] in this book?
>
> *Pupil*: Because she's nice and she helps, she helped M anyway.
>
> *Pupil*: She helped me and all.

The pupils had a lot to say about their shared history. Some children had taken photographs of the nursery because they said that was where they had originally met their friends; it was their history. A number of the pupils appeared to be fascinated by the fact that the Teachers' Centre had once been the school, and so wanted to include a photograph of that in their book. Another source of evidence of shared history came from discussions around performances and outings they had made. The primary school pupils described a band they had formed. They had played to the school and remembered how it had made them feel.

> *Pupil*: We get together as a group and we practise and then we put on a show for everyone.
>
> *Pupil*: Even the physios.
>
> *Pupil*: And it's great because we're all excited.
>
> *Pupil*: Do you feel all good inside when you've done something?

This led to a number of 'feeling good' and 'do you remember' conversations among the pupils that were about doing things together and being part of something within school.

Inclusion as belonging

Some judgements of Adamston were embedded in the pupils' expression of loss at the closure of the school. Some expressions of the loss of the community were poignant. One pupil told us: 'The thing is the school is closing. And the thing is when you leave a school you can come back to see it, but we can't come back and see it.' Another, talking about the book of photographs, stated: 'So like you know when I go to my new school I'll be able to take this and show them who my old teacher was. And I won't know how I'll be able to see my old teacher, and I wanted to be able to see this.' The central theme seemed to be pupils' feelings of inclusion in the Adamston community in the sense of belonging.

The school had a small residential unit (referred to as 'resi'), which provided the secondary pupils the opportunity for overnight stays. This, it seemed, was consistently highly valued and would be missed.

> *Pupil*: Resi is going to be a really big one for me. It's absolutely excellent. It's probably one of the best things about the school.
>
> *Researcher*: What do you like about resi?
>
> *Pupil*: You don't have to be at home being bored. All your friends are there … your own room.

The school had riding stables and many of the children found it hard to imagine leaving the horses.

> *Pupil*: Well I do really want to see them again and I will see them again but I know I'll not see them at school, but I can sometimes come and visit them can't I? Or even there might be some at my other school … cos this is one of the things I want to do … I've got loads of photos of Sparky [horse] here.

The pupils struggled to understand loss. A primary pupil who had been known to one researcher when she was young, but whom she had not seen for four years, appeared to use this experience as a springboard to try and develop her understanding about loss and connections. Despite the researcher inexpertly trying to return the conversation to the topic of Adamston, the pupil repeatedly asked questions and made statements about having known the researcher. This can be seen as an exploration of her own previous experience of history, loss and change.

> *Pupil*: It's really sad that I'm going.
>
> *Researcher*: Do you think you'll enjoy your new school though?
>
> *Pupil*: Well, here I will come back and see them.
>
> *Researcher*: But they are not going to be here are they?
>
> *Pupil*: Yes they are [said in a questioning voice but also assertive].
>
> *Researcher*: Who is?

Pupil: You know Mrs T? She'll still be here … I've got [lists children] in already. Have you known me for ages?

Researcher: I knew you when you were little, yes. But I haven't seen you for a long time. Your mum used to bring you to the hydrotherapy pool at the Centre.

Pupil: Did you used to work there?

Researcher: Yes. And then you went to AW Nursery.

Pupil: Did you come and see me there?

Researcher: Yes, I saw you there as well.

Pupil: So did you used to come to my house?

Researcher: No, I don't know where you live.

Pupil: It's in [region of the city].

Researcher: I would go past it but I didn't come to your house.

Pupil: Do you know [gives her address]? It's got a red door. Do you know the one? You go past the fence, my next door neighbour's fence, and my house is in the middle. […]

Pupil: You know when you were at the Centre, what did we used to call you?

Researcher: T, you've always called me that.

Pupil: Didn't we call you 'Mrs' something?

Researcher: No, we've always called ourselves by name at the Centre.

This pupil had clearly set an agenda here and was determined to direct the conversation. Her insistence demonstrated the importance for her of teasing out history, renewed contacts and change.

The primary pupils repeatedly talked about using the photographs they had taken as a link between the past and the future

Researcher: Why do you want to keep these [particular photographs]?

Pupil A: They have all my memories in … and I want to take some of my friends in secondary … because they have been my friends for quite a long time.

Pupil B: Physios. I want to take a picture of them in this school and then in my new school.

The older pupils offered their thoughts on leaving the school less readily than the primary children, but when they did, their conversations included both anger and sadness. In a conversation about why the school might be closing, one pupil suggested the governors were to blame.

> *Researcher*: So you think the governors have closed the school?
>
> *Pupil*: Yes.
>
> *Researcher*: Why do you think they wanted to do that?
>
> *Pupil A*: Because they opened their big mouths.
>
> *Pupil B*: It's not fair. It's not fair on anyone. It's not fair on us.
>
> *Researcher*: In what way?
>
> *Pupil*: Because there's a lot of people here that need help, physios … and it's not fair on them.

Feelings of exclusion

In separate interviews, their parents had reported what they considered evidence of anxious behaviour, one parent reporting that her child had restarted having fits during this unsettled time. Teachers too reported incidents of unsettled behaviour within the school such as a certain amount of disinterest and disaffection within the classroom that was uncommon in that environment. The central theme embedded in pupils' anxieties seemed to be feelings of exclusion from Adamston, their school.

There was evidence within the interviews that pupils were feeling anxious. Most had worries about their new placement. When asked if they were feeling they were going to be all right in their new school, they offered a mixed response ranging from definite 'no' and 'yes', to 'probably' and 'don't know' replies. With secondary school pupils replies were often tinged with teenage bravado and it was not always possible to engage in conversations with them about their thoughts on their new schools.

All the pupils, both primary and secondary, said how they would miss their friends, especially as they did not live in the same neighbourhoods and Adamston was the main point of contact. One primary pupil, whilst acknowledging he was going to miss his friends, was pragmatic about this and was making arrangements to go and stay with them. He also said:

> *Pupil*: It's quite a big move and I'm a little bit frightened and it's going to be funny at first but I think I'll get into it.

Secondary pupils reported:

> *Researcher*: You went to (mainstream) again on Tuesday?
>
> *Pupil A*: Got more homework.
>
> *Pupil B*: It was rubbish.
>
> *Researcher*: Why was it? Why do you say that?
>
> *Pupil B*: Because it's not like Adams, it's not a special school. Plus it's boring. All the teachers are boring.
>
> *Researcher*: Why do you want to go to a special school?
>
> *Pupil B*: Because I've got (medical conditions) and I'm incontinent.
>
> *Researcher*: And you don't think they can cope with that in a mainstream school?
>
> *Pupil B*: No [An emphatic 'no' which ended this discussion].

Others worried about practical details that had not yet been resolved, such as transport. Many pupils took photographs of the Adamston bus drivers and the buses. They associated them with 'great trips out' and 'getting out of lessons'. The bus photographs prompted a discussion with a primary pupil who, whilst looking at all his photographs of the bus, stated that his new school was not near his home and he did not know how he would get to his new school.

One primary pupil, who had not been placed in the local school attended by his sibling, despite it having an additionally resourced centre for children with physical disabilities, worried both about the travel across the city and the size of the classes. He reported that he had seen his younger sibling in a large class and didn't know how he himself would manage, but he was pragmatic about it: 'they decide what's best for us and I'm willing to take a chance … I'm willing to do it.' He could not tell us why such choices had been made and he himself had not been involved in the decision making. A secondary child referred to this non involvement in decision making.

> *Pupil*: Well most of the kids here have to go to mainstream. I'm going to Daleview (special school). That's the only school I can go to.
>
> *Researcher*: Why are you going to Daleview? Did you decide you wanted to go to Daleview?
>
> *Pupil*: No I got a letter. From the Civic Centre.
>
> *Researcher*: So they decided?

Pupil: Well, yes. And my mam. The first time my mam went to visit the school they wouldn't let us go.

Some of the secondary pupils felt the closure had not been fair, on either themselves or others and felt quite angry about it. Others could engage with their new school, to a certain extent, and were beginning to make visits, but demonstrated mixed emotions and loyalties.

Researcher: And what do you think of the [new] school generally? Do you like going there?

Pupil A: Yes, but this school's better …

Pupil B: This school's much better … in Harpers Lee you get shouted at all the time.

Researcher: Did you get shouted at when you went?

Pupil A: No.

Pupil B: We were late so we got shouted at.

Including insider voices from segregated settings

One way of interpreting the views of disabled people presented here is in terms of the pros and cons, or arguments for and arguments against, segregated schooling. This has been the dominant discourse since the 1944 Education Act, if not since the inception of mass schooling. Given that there has been no significant decrease in the number of disabled pupils placed in segregated schooling over the past 30 years, this debate is at best sterile and, at worst, maintains the status quo.

There is another way of understanding these views and experiences, however, which looks towards inclusive education. Listening to the insider voices from the wide variety of experiences in segregated settings, from historical contexts and Adamston, we are struck first and foremost by the variety itself. They speak of abuse, but also of belonging. If there is a dominant common story, it is of subjugation in a context of unequal power relations between disabled and non-disabled people. Historically, it is a story of disabled children being subjected to various forms of abuse. At Adamston, it is a story of disabled children being subjected to the loss of their community, originally created by non-disabled people through a policy of segregation and then terminated by non-disabled people in the name of inclusion.

Adamston was a small community which provided social, emotional and psychological security for these young people. It is not at all surprising that young people want to hold on to the community they are part of. The re-organisation–closure of their school and placement in the new system–has been done to these young people. They (even more than their parents) have been powerless. The idea that pupils could or should be involved in policy-making or even decisions about their placement in the re-organised education system did not arise for the pupils themselves or anyone else involved. They were completely excluded from the consultation process and did not attend their annual reviews at which decisions about their placement in the re-organised system were discussed. Only once did a pupil appear at her own annual review. She burst into the room asking: 'What are you saying about me?' The meeting immediately stopped and she was gently ejected. The decision at the meeting was that this 14-year-old should attend a mainstream school. No account has been taken of these disabled pupil's views in the planning of inclusive settings. No account has been taken of what these young people valued about their education, how their views might affect processes of change, or what they would look for, and need, to feel included, in a so-called inclusive setting. Similarly, no account has been taken of disabled adults' views, their experiences, their culture.

From the evidence in this paper, insider voices from segregated schooling have much to say about inclusion and the process of changing towards an inclusive system, whether they are the voices of disabled adults who speak from experiences of abuse or they are the voices of disabled young people who speak from experiences of belonging in a long-established community. We shall pin-point just four specific messages.

1   There are positive personal and social effects for disabled people from being with similarly disabled people. Inclusion cannot be realised through the denial of disability.
2   Inclusion has a powerful psychological dimension of belonging. Whilst being included, in educational policy terms, is about having access to ostensible universal standards of education, the confidence that comes from social inclusion is the context for such access.
3   Moving pupils around the system of schooling, especially outside their own neighbourhoods, has dramatic and traumatic consequences for the lives of individuals.
4   Young disabled people can tell us what inclusion means for them.

Most important, however, is the general message that moves towards a more inclusive education system must begin with the inclusion of the voices of disabled children and adults. Insider voices from segregated schooling should inform the processes of change from a segregated to an inclusive education system, if 'inclusion' is not to perpetuate the subjugation of disabled people in other settings.

References

Alderson, P. and Goodey, C. (1996) Research with disabled children: how useful is child-centred ethics? *Children & Society*, **10**, 106–16.

Alderson, P. and Goodey, C. (1998) *Enabling Education: experiences in ordinary and special schools*. London: Tufnell Press.

Barnes, C. (1991) *Disabled People in Britain and Discrimination: a case for antidiscrimination legislation*. London: C. Hurst and Co.

Barnes, C. and Mercer, G. (eds) (1997) *Doing Disability Research*. Leeds: the Disability Press.

Craddock, E. (1991) Life at secondary school. In G. Taylor and J. Bishop (eds) *Being Deaf: the experience of deafness*. London: Pinter Publishers.

Davies, C. (1993) *Lifetimes: a mutual biography of disabled people*. Farnham, Surrey: Understanding Disabilities Educational Trust.

French, S. (1993) Can you see the rainbow?: the roots of denial. In J. Swain, V. Finkelstein, S. French and M. Oliver (eds) *Disabling Barriers – Enabling Environments*, pp. 69–77. London: Sage.

French, S. (1996) Out of sight, out of mind: the experience of and effects of a 'special' residential school. In J. Morris (ed.) *Encounters with Strangers: feminism and disability*, pp. 17–47. London: the Women's Press.

James, A. and Prout, A. (1990) Contemporary issues in the sociological study of childhood. In A. James and A. Prout (eds) *Constructing and Reconstructing Childhood*. London: Falmer Press.

Leicester, M. (1999) *Disability Voice: towards an enabling education*. London: Jessica Kingsley.

Lewis, A. and Lindsay, G. (eds) (2000) *Researching Children's Perspectives*. Buckingham: Open University Press.

Potts, M. and Fido, R. (1991) *A Fit Person to be Removed: personal accounts of life in a mental deficiency institution*. Plymouth: Northcote House.

Priestley, M. (1999) Discourse and identity: disabled children in mainstream high schools. In M. Corker and S. French (eds) *Disability Discourse*, pp. 92–102. Buckingham: Open University Press.

Rae, A. (1996) *Survivors from the Special School System*. Bolton Data for Inclusion, Data No. 2. Bolton: Bolton Institute.

Robinson, C. and Stalker, K. (1998) Introduction. In C. Robinson and K. Stalker (eds) *Growing Up with Disability*, pp. 7–12. London: Jessica Kingsley Publications.

Shakespeare, T. and Watson, N. (1998) Theoretical perspectives on research with disabled children. In C. Robinson and K. Stalker (eds) *Growing Up with Disability*, pp. 13–28. London: Jessica Kingsley.

Swain, J. and French, S. (2000) Towards an affirmative model of disability. *Disability and Society*, **15**, 569–82.

Willmot, F. and Saul, P. (1998) *A Breath of Fresh Air: Birmingham's open-air schools 1911–1970*. Chichester: Phillimore.

Cook, Swain and French's work reveals the importance of inclusion for pupils, both socially and also in the decision-making processes within the school. As with other chapters in this book the importance of listening to pupils is highlighted. This is essential if exclusionary and subjugating practices are not to be transferred into new settings.

Chapter 11

Professional identity in multi-disciplinary teams

The staff speak

Ann Workman and Jeremy Pickard

This chapter focuses on the setting up of a multi-disciplinary team which brought together social workers, community nursing staff and housing officers as a mainstream service. The views of the staff involved in this process are considered as well as the impact on the services they provided. Reservations about the change concerning staff reductions and diluting professional roles are described to demonstrate that many staff viewed multi-disciplinary work sceptically. Three years on, the staff group reflect on their experience and how their confidence in integrated working has grown.

Background

[...] The need for inter-professional working has been steadily ascending the policy agenda for two decades. Initially activity was confined to small *ad hoc* teams in the fields of mental health and learning disability, but the model is now seen as necessary for a range of client groups and settings. In particular, the 2006 White Paper *Our Health, Our Care, Our Say* stated (para 5.32) that:

> *By 2008 we expect all PCTs and local authorities to have established joint health and social care managed networks and/or teams to support those people with long-term conditions who have the most complex needs.*

The sheer organisational mechanics of establishing such teams will constitute a formidable challenge, but there is an additional – and less visible – issue that needs to be addressed, that of professional identity (Elston & Holloway, 2001; Freeman *et al.* 2000).

In such circumstances it becomes imperative to learn the lessons from the relatively small number of teams that have been established for some time. [...] On 21 June 2007 the Tremeduna Team in Sedgefield, County Durham, celebrated its third birthday as an integrated multidisciplinary locality team, and this article brings the story up to date.

The Sedgefield locality teams evolved from collaboration between Durham County Council (the council with social services responsibilities), Sedgefield Primary Care Trust (the then body responsible for community-based health provision) and Sedgefield Borough Council (the district council with housing responsibilities). [...] After 18 months of planning, the Tremeduna Team came into existence, followed by the four other teams that now serve the district. [...]

It is important to understand that integrated locality teams in Sedgefield are not additional to mainstream services – they are the mainstream. There are no district nurses or care managers in Sedgefield who work outside the locality teams.

Integration of housing was managed rather differently, in that the work of housing officers was initially divided into two elements: housing support, which was transferred to the locality teams, and responding to homelessness, which remained with the Borough Council. It was always envisaged that eventually both functions should be undertaken in the integrated teams, and this has subsequently occurred.

The teams, then, inherited two-and-a-half existing professional roles. In addition, two new ones were created: the community partnership managers (to manage the locality teams), and business support officers (to provide a range of services to the teams and to the public).

[...] While most of the running costs of integrated teams are met from a single budget (and allocated on an agreed 'fair shares' formula to the parent organisations) the single major expense – salaries – remains separate; staff are paid by their respective employers, rather than from a single pot. [...]

The human resource work stream was concerned that we would end up with professional staff in one team on different pay and conditions. Retirement ages, lieu time arrangements and so on varied across the three organisations, and it was felt that they would gradually become subversive of team cohesion. There was little that could be done about the contractual matters unless or until the political will existed to move all staff to a single employer. We did, however, try to harmonise the procedures underpinning employment practice, adopting the principle (accepted by the unions) of 'most beneficial rules apply to all'. In addition we hoped that this would make the line manager's job slightly easier.

Anticipation

[...] Faced with structural change, even three years ago, there was a healthy scepticism among the front-line staff about its efficacy – after all, they had all been employed by a succession of varied organisations over the previous ten years. Understandably, therefore, front-line staff sometimes regarded proposals to re-organise as an irrelevance or a distraction. [...]

In response to these concerns the design team made two very explicit promises. Integration would not mean a reduction in the number of nurses or social workers. There would be no requirement or expectation that social workers would undertake 'nursing' tasks or vice versa.

In addition a third undertaking was made in the course of implementing the changes. Clinical supervision would be available outside the line management arrangements.

It is worth reflecting on what the need for these undertakings tells us about the sensitivities of the staff involved.

Staff reductions

This seems to be a pretty universal fear as a response to change, although the extent to which it is based on previous experience is arguable; there are many more social workers and community nurses now than there were 30 years ago, frequent re-organisations notwithstanding. Perhaps the apprehension is more understandable in social work than in health. At the time there was much less growth in social care expenditure than in health, and the public are less inclined to rush to the barricades in support of social workers than of nurses. Having said that, it is true that district nurses were, perhaps, less confident of their own indispensability than other branches of healthcare. They had received far less national attention than other elements of the NHS, and had seen various elements of their role being shared with newer 'sexier' specialisms (palliative care, intermediate care, long-term conditions, etc.).

Role dilution

One occasionally reads accounts of integrated working that seem to welcome the emergence of 'hybrid' roles. Indeed, there are elements of health and social care where such roles would be immensely valuable – a personal carer who could take vital signs or dress a wound, for example – but there is very limited scope for such change between social work and nursing. Nurses have sustained, direct and practical involvement with patients and provide a universal service. Social workers are enablers of care, have brief interventions and assess for eligibility. There is limited overlap of the respective knowledge bases. Giving an undertaking not to promote overlapping roles was no hardship.

Clinical supervision

Early discussions in the human resource work stream anticipated a balance of expertise among CPMs (two social workers, two nurses and one housing specialist). However, personnel procedures required either appointment on individual merit or creation of three roles (CPM [nurse], CPM [SW], CPM [housing]). The latter approach would have been destructive of the whole principle of a unified management, and so the lesser of two evils was adopted and CPMs were appointed against a single job description. This was just as well, as applications were overwhelmingly dominated by applicants qualified in social work (although one nurse was successful). [...]

So nursing staff were, it turns out, right to fear that the knowledge base of the CPMs would not be adequate to provide clinical supervision to all the nurses; the one nurse-qualified CPM would have been stretched exceedingly thin, if she had had to support all the nurses. Fortunately the PCT's nursing strategy already called for creation of a 'modern matron' role to support district nurses, and this was adapted to offer clinical supervision to the nursing staff. There is also a professional lead for social care. A formal distinction was made between line management, which was to stay firmly with the CPM, and professional support from outside.

Implementation

Tremeduna, the pathfinder integrated locality team, went live on 21 June 2004. It consisted of 9.3 wte (whole time equivalent) nursing staff, two wte qualified social workers and one wte social work assistant, one housing support officer, one CPM and three business support officers. Staff were in a single location, used a single assessment process and a single client recording system, took referrals via a single point of contact, and were to be assessed on a single set of performance measures.

Within the following year the other four teams came on line.

What did this do to professional identity? Were the promises made during the design stage fulfilled?

Experience

Nurses

The story is complicated by the fact that Tremeduna was the pathfinder for single assessment as well as integration. Prior to integration the design team were anxious that nurses did not 'blame' integration for the anticipated increase in record keeping that would have been needed anyway as a result of the single assessment process. This was exacerbated by the fact that Tremeduna was moving to an IT-based system – alien territory for many nurses.

The nursing staff in Tremeduna had previously been in three small nursing teams across the patch, each led by a sister. They worked independently of each other and each small team 'consumed its own smoke'. Inevitably, the nurses' workload was not equitable.

The administrative support to the nursing staff prior to integration was two hours a week for filing. Messages were left on answering machines and referrals were received 'from all over the place'. An immediate impact of the move to integration was, therefore, removal of the necessity to review messages and 'interpret' referrals.

Answering machines are, of course, incapable of responding to messages. As the business support officers became more confident in their new roles, they began to solve customer problems as well as simply record them. Thus a message that would have appeared on an answering machine 'Mrs X says she has run out of her dressings' has increasingly turned into a note that reads 'Mrs X ran out of her dressings so I have arranged for some more to be dropped off from the pharmacy tomorrow'.

The community partnership manager (social work trained) offered the nurses one-to-one supervision, notwithstanding the fact that they were to be clinically supported outside the team. The nurses initially viewed this with some bewilderment: 'how could a social worker with no clinical expertise supervise nurses?' However, the reality has been that nurses in the Tremeduna team have come to engage very positively with the one-to-one sessions, using them to discuss personal development, training, team business and any pressures, rather than clinical issues.

On balance, nurses have accepted the additional burden of IT-based record keeping in return for the increased efficiency of referrals and information sharing. [...]

The following comments are quoted directly from the nursing staff in the Tremeduna Team.

> *I have worked for the NHS for over 28 years. I have been through many changes in that time – at least eight in the first 18 years. This is the first change that has actually made a difference to me as a community nurse; my job satisfaction has improved.*
>
> *I feel we have a much improved understanding of each other's roles.*
>
> *The sharing of information between staff is crucial to providing a good service to patients/clients.*

> *One number and single point of access has led to reduced confusion to patients.*
> *I have much improved job satisfaction as the sharing of knowledge and*
> *expertise between staff in the integrated team is tremendous, the speed with which*
> *this happens is key.*
>
> *I have worked for the NHS for a long time. I was coming up to retirement age*
> *when we integrated and I viewed it as just another change. However integration*
> *has led to me feeling the most fulfilled I have ever felt in my career.*

Social workers

Before integration the social care staff were placed in a large social work team covering the whole patch. They felt that they would miss peer support from fellow social workers. The reality has been that the integrated team has become that support mechanism. Regardless of which background staff come from, they support each other. Social care staff can still have real debates with their health colleagues, but all staff now know where everyone else is coming from.

One of the differences mentioned above under professional identity is the length of involvement with customers. Since the 1990 *Community Care Act* the social work task has been to establish a relationship, undertake an assessment, implement a care package, review it once and then move on. Durham Social Services, like many, set up a separate review team to revisit cases, and relied on care providers to alert them to any change in the customers' needs (to 'trigger a re-assessment' in the jargon). [...]

One of the spin-offs of the integrated teams (not anticipated) was that district nurses act as an informal reviewing mechanism on behalf of the local authority. The district nurses may pick up a change or deterioration in a client/patient when they visit, and they are able to ensure that things are actioned quickly. This may mean a response from the integrated team, and then a referral through the system or, if not urgent, a referral through 'the normal route'. In practice the 'normal route' in an integrated team – or at least the natural one – is a quick word with the original social worker when you get back to the office.

The social work staff in the Tremeduna Team report the following.

> *There are huge benefits by the integrated team being co-located. This means*
> *that we can communicate easily with other professionals who are involved in*
> *people's care.*
>
> *It is now much easier to do our jobs.*
>
> *We don't always have to agree, everyone within the team has a view, we take*
> *all into consideration, any decisions taken are those which are the best for the client.*

This is a much more streamlined approach for the client.

In terms of promoting independence of clients integration allows a swifter and more coordinated response.

Hospital discharges can be supported in a more timely and in a much more informed way.

Housing support officer

Prior to integration housing staff were based in the Borough Council offices, the same building as the social care staff. Even with this close proximity it was difficult to reach a common understanding of each other's priorities and problems. In particular, the need to respond to the urgent – homelessness – often drove out the important – housing support.

> *In my previous role within the Borough Council I became involved in things which I felt were not my responsibility but that of social care or health – integration has made me realise that whatever the issue for the client/patient is we are all responsible.*
> *I feel I can think out of the box.*
> *I can be more creative.*
> *I feel forward-thinking leadership has made a difference.*

Business support officer

Prior to integration, staff from the three partner organisations had different levels of administrative support. Social workers had some, district nurses very little and the housing support officer none. The business support officer was always seen as new role, albeit one with clear origins in administration. [...]

In practice, the problem-solving element has grown significantly – for example restarting care packages, chasing up agencies when carers do not turn up or are late, or when transport doesn't turn up for day care, or when equipment needs to be organised. All this was anticipated, and has freed professional time. In addition, business support officers have come to play an important part in sustaining staff morale; it is really valuable for pressured social workers or nurses to have somebody back at base who can be relied upon to sympathise.

These comments are quoted directly from business support staff at Tremeduna.

> *I have worked most of my life in administration and until I started as a business support officer on the Tremeduna Team I can honestly say I had never felt true job satisfaction.*

> *Although stressful and upsetting at times, this job is so rewarding both from helping patients/clients with day-to-day queries to assisting community nurses, social workers and housing officer ... so that they can get on with their main priorities – the care of their patients/clients.*
>
> *It is a role that I would like to develop much more for both myself and the community we serve.*

Community partnership manager

The community partnership manager role was intended to offer 'visible' line management to staff from health, social care and housing. Prior to integration in Sedgefield, each of the partner organisations had a range of management roles, some of which meant that the manager was quite removed from front-line staff [...] The current role has improved the operational links with the social care staff. The housing support officer and business support officers are all line-managed and supervised by the CPM. [...]

CPM experience of integration has been:

- a huge learning curve taking on board district nurses and housing staff and the issues that affect them to ensure good-quality line-management, which actually makes a difference to them;
- finding that although HR procedures were integrated in the design of the model, they were not 'signed-off' by all three partners, and unfortunately have not been implemented;
- dealing with three sets of procedures has not been too much of a problem, but it would have been a huge achievement to have integrated procedures
- some disappointment that organisational change (PCT) has had a great impact on the development and re-design of future services;
- pride in the outcomes for the people we serve and the achievements of the team.

Conclusions

Broadly speaking, the perceived threat to professional identity did not materialise; existing roles have been strengthened rather than undermined. To some extent this outcome was rendered more likely by decisions made at the design stage, but it also results from the way that the team has been managed and the response of the staff involved.

The benefits of integration arise from improved information flows, understanding and co-operation, as well as a shared perception of preferred outcomes, and from the introduction of new roles. No dilution or undermining of existing roles is necessary.

We will leave the last word with the professionals involved. The points below summarise the views of the Tremeduna team, and have been checked with them.

- All staff are more understanding of and knowledgeable about each other's roles.
- Nurses value hugely the IT system and the benefits that it brings – which was not the case before integration.
- Single assessment process has been a steep learning curve for all of us, but now everyone is contributing and it is adding to the richness of the assessment.
- Housing support officer involvement is also a success. We now have one on each team – each area has different pressures – homelessness, evictions and young people.
- A flexible joint approach is taken to all referrals (social care, health or housing) and this leads to a much better service to the patient/client.
- We have been able to encourage innovation.
- Staff support each other no matter which organisation they came from – everyone helps everyone else out.
- There is shared ownership of what we do. [...]

Individual case studies highlighting the benefits of integration

Mr A

Mr A had benefited from the involvement of community nursing services prior to integration. He had a range of health needs, the most dominant of which is his unstable diabetes. Mr A suffered a whole range of problems connected to his diabetic condition. The nursing service was visiting regularly. Between August 2004 and June 2007 there were 200 entries in the client's case notes (the notes that are completed following any telephone calls, meetings, discussions, etc.).

In June Mr A's health deteriorated and he was admitted to hospital.

Mr A was adamant that he wished to remain independent, but acknowledged that his property was unsuitable. With the assistance of the team (social care, health and housing staff from Tremeduna) Mr A was able to move into his new bungalow directly from the hospital ward.

What integration enabled

- Health, social care and housing could work closely with Mr A to ensure that his needs were at the centre of their planning.
- The housing officer was quickly able to look at the application for re-housing, complete all relevant forms, look at available properties and support Mr A, all from the initial joint visit to the ward.
- Due to the detailed medical knowledge and involvement of community nursing staff, information on medical points was accurate.
- Social care staff could gain a true and accurate picture of Mr A's needs so that the care package could be comprehensive and could meet his needs.
- District nursing staff had been struggling to promote Mr A's independence and his wish to remain at home because of the risks connected with his property and the care input needed.
- Hospital staff were somewhat surprised that a multi-disciplinary assessment was undertaken on the ward, and that not only nursing and social care services were discussed and actioned, but that Mr A's application for re-housing was completed at this assessment and an offer of a suitable property was made quickly.

Mr A – a speculation

We cannot know for sure how Mr A's case would have proceeded prior to integration. However we believe that it might have gone like this:

- District nurses would have remained involved with Mr A.
- A separate referral would have gone to social care with regard to a care package; the social worker would have gone out with no previous history or information about the client.
- Staff in the acute hospital might have considered Mr A's housing needs, but even if a referral had been made to the Borough Council there is absolutely no way that we could have achieved what we did in the integrated team.
- Co-location, sharing of ideas and discussion of options and solutions to the problems meant that there was genuine agreement on the preferred outcome and a focused effort to achieve it.
- Although all the staff might have contacted each other from their separate organisations, we would have had a number of referrals, leading to a number of separate assessments, decisions made in isolation, the client being confused, delays and perhaps a transfer from the acute hospital not to a new home but to long-term care. [...]

References

Elston, S. and Holloway, I. (2001) The impact of recent primary care reforms in the UK on interprofessional working in primary care centres. *Journal of Interprofessional Care*, **15**(1), 19–27.

Freeman, M., Miller, C. and Ross, N. (2000) The impact of individual philosophies of teamwork on multiprofessional practice and the implications for education. *Journal of Interprofessional Care*, **14**(3), 237–47.

Professionals can be very protective of their role and identities but in the Tremeduna team the staff did not allow their insecurities to become a barrier to a more joined up approach. Despite initial scepticism, the staff found that their practice had developed and that the overall service had improved. Collaboration encouraged people to take on new ideas, come up with innovative solutions and keep a focus on the requirements of the person receiving support. This suggests that multi-disciplinary working can lead to support which is not stuck in an established way of doing things and which can adapt to a whole range of situations. Such teamwork is essential to an inclusive approach to supporting participation.

Part 3

On the margins

Chapter 12

Interviews with young people about behavioural support

Equality, fairness and rights

Paul Hamill and Brian Boyd

This chapter presents findings from a year long research project undertaken by researchers from the University of Strathclyde. Eleven comprehensive schools in Scotland were involved and the aim of the study was to evaluate the effectiveness of in-school support systems for young people who display challenging behaviour. Pupil support bases had been set up in most of the schools aimed at reducing exclusion rates and these were examined from the perspective of all stakeholders – teachers, parents, young people and key interagency personnel. The chapter focuses on the views of the young people who, although often perceived as disruptive, disaffected, and troubled, articulated clear messages for all professionals. Their perspectives provide insights into inclusive practice which have continued resonance beyond the time of the original research.

Children's rights in the Scottish context

Article 12 of the *United Nations Convention on the Rights of the Child* (UN 1990) asserts that the child has the right to express his or her opinion in all matters affecting him/her. This theme has, in recent years, gained prominence in Scotland. The *Children (Scotland) Act* (Scottish Office 1995) emphasised that children have participation rights in relation to the decision–making process which affect them as individuals. These participation rights have now been extended by the *Standards in Schools (Scotland) Act* (SEED 2000a) to cover rights in relation to school development and education authority plans which impact upon the young person's quality of life. This focus upon taking into account children's views is now high on the social and educational agenda. Promoting the participation of young people in decision making has been an evolving process in Scotland and this can best be illustrated by considering briefly the Scottish context and in particular some practice which has impacted upon the process.

In 1978, an organisation entitled 'Who Cares? Scotland' was established to give a voice to young people who were being looked after by local authorities. This development highlighted the importance of giving this group of vulnerable young people a voice in relation to issues that are relevant in their lives and it was widely recognised as a major step forward.

In 1995, a national initiative entitled 'Connect Youth' was launched, aimed at creating a network whereby young people could exchange ideas and good practice which would promote their right to be heard. This initiative played a part in the development of the Scottish Youth Parliament established in 1999, which aims to promote equality for all young people and to encourage them to play their role in influencing change. The Scottish Alliance for Children's Rights took this a step forward in 2000 when they produced 'A Proposal for a Commissioner for Children in Scotland'. The commissioner would be an independent voice in relation to children's issues.

There is clear evidence therefore to suggest that positive developments are emerging within the Scottish context. However, we still have a long way to go and many young people remain silent and are not in a position to influence the policies and practice that shape their lives. This is particularly true in relation to young people who are disadvantaged and disaffected. This was summed up by the Scottish Office in 1998 as follows:

> In families in danger of being socially excluded the scope for children's needs to be overlooked is even greater.

> (para. 2)

One group of young people who are often excluded from Scottish schools are those whose behaviour can be challenging or disruptive. According to Hamill and Boyd (2000), these young people have:

> difficulty in developing social competence, adjusting to social contexts and in learning to follow normal and accepted behaviour patterns.

> (p. 24)

In short they have special educational needs and, like all young people, they also have the right to participate actively in decisions about their education and welfare. These rights are clearly articulated in *A Manual of Good Practice in Special Educational Needs* (SOEID 1999) which is currently one of the benchmarks of good practice in Scotland.

Inclusive education

Young people whose special needs arise because they have social, emotional and behavioural difficulties are often excluded from the mainstream school, or from classes within the mainstream school, because their behaviour is deemed to be challenging and disruptive. The body of research literature in relation to inclusive education has grown considerably in the past few years, yet, although voices promoting inclusion are now heard increasingly and the arguments for inclusion appear to be overwhelming, inclusion for these young people is still not a reality (Thomas *et al.* 1998; Allan 1999; Mittler 2000).

Advocates of inclusion argue that it is vitally important therefore to establish first and foremost the young person's right to be included. It is only when this has been achieved that effective channels of communication can be set up to enable him/her to exercise the right to express a view in relation to the decision-making process. At present, few of these young people see themselves as having any real say, particularly in relation to one of the biggest decisions impacting upon their lives, namely, the decision to exclude them from school.

In Scotland, as elsewhere in the United Kingdom, the issue of social inclusion is a dominant theme particularly in the educational context. The most recent legislation in Scotland, the *Standards in Schools (Scotland) Act* (SEED 2000a), confirms the intention to create within Scottish education a presumption of inclusion and this principle has been clearly set within the legislation. In accordance with this belief, there has evolved in Scotland a strong focus on ensuring that young people who are disaffected are not excluded from our mainstream schools. This is of course easier said than done, as it often involves changing deep-rooted negative attitudes and expectations. Some professionals still see exclusion as a natural response to what they perceive as disruptive behaviour. Cullingford (1999) sums this up when he says:

> the number of exclusions from school increases each year and one explanation is that exclusions are seen as an inevitable response to difficult and disruptive pupils who come to school already disaffected.
>
> (p. 94)

Cooper (1993) reminds us that it is not easy to define problem behaviour as it results from a:

> complex interaction between contextual factors and aspects which the individual brings to the situation.
>
> (p. 9)

This complexity poses real challenges for those who want to create supportive, inclusive environments where the voices of these young people can be heard. They often appear as defiant rebels but all too often this persona masks a vulnerable, unhappy individual who finds it difficult to communicate his/her feelings, let alone exercise the right to participate in the decision-making process (Campion 1992; Chazan *et al.* 1998; Pomeroy 2000).

In 1999, the Scottish Executive Education Department (SEED) published the *New Community Schools Prospectus* which focused upon the intractable problems many excluded young people face. These relate mainly to poverty, under-achievement and indiscipline. One of the recurring themes in the prospectus is the need to reduce pupil disaffections, tackle social exclusion and raise attainment. Emphasis is placed upon inter-professional collaboration and working in partnership with young people where they are no longer perceived as silent partners. These themes were echoed in the Beattie Report (SEED 2000b), which explored issues relating to implementing inclusiveness and realising potential. Once again the need to maximise the participation of all young people in mainstream schools was highlighted and the need to remove attitudinal barriers was given prominence.

If we are serious about ensuring young people exercise their right to express themselves in relation to matters that have a significant impact on their lives we must ensure this applies to all young people; including those who are disruptive. It is not enough to give a young person a voice; we must also be prepared to listen and act upon what they say. However, we must also take time to ensure we understand what it means to experience social, emotional and behavioural difficulties.

Young people with social, emotional and behavioural difficulties

In Scotland, the label 'social, emotional and behavioural difficulties' is applied to a wide range of young people whose needs lie on a broad spectrum, from those who are occasionally disruptive and whose difficulties are short-term to those whose behaviour is extremely challenging or who have serious psychological problems. Defining this group of young people is a difficult task as the complexity and diversity of need make a simple definition impossible. It is clear, however, that one common factor is that these young people become disaffected and are at great risk of underachieving both educationally and in relation to their own personal development.

This adversely affects not only their own education but also that of their peers. Social, emotional and behavioural difficulties manifest themselves in different ways. Some young people are aggressive and sometimes violent, while others are isolated, withdrawn and introverted. While it is important to recognise that every individual is unique it should also be recognised that there are characteristics that are present to varying degrees in all young people who display 'challenging behaviours'. These characteristics, which are outlined in Part 3, Section 6 of the Scottish Consultative Committee on the Curriculum report entitled *Special Educational Needs Within the 5–14 Curriculum – Support for Learning* (SCCC 1994: 2) include low self-esteem, difficulties with learning and poor interpersonal skills. [...]

The research

Throughout 1999–2000, a research study undertaken by researchers in the University of Strathclyde evaluated provision for young people with social, emotional and behavioural difficulties (SEBD) in mainstream comprehensive schools. The main focus of the research was to throw some light upon the effectiveness of the in-school pupil support bases in reducing rates of exclusion. [...]

The researchers included all the significant individuals, specifically young people, parents, teachers and other professionals, and a range of research techniques were employed including semi-structured interviews, observation schedules, questionnaires, support analysis grids and documentary evidence. An ethnographic case study approach was used to explore how the strategy had evolved and the focus was upon how individual pupils, their families and schools interact. The overall study was set within an action research context which provided an opportunity for collaboration between the researchers and those professionals who work with and support young people within a realistic and sometimes challenging context. Emphasis was placed at all times upon the cycle of feedback linking the researchers, the school communities, parents, other professionals and the young people. The overall aim was to transform environments through the process of critical enquiry. We hoped that the transformative power of such an approach would empower those who work with young people and shape the eventual research outcomes. The bulk of the data was qualitative and, in relation to its analysis, the researchers adopted the descriptive narrative approach outlined by Strauss and Corbin (1990). Consequently the material was analysed in a way that accurately described and reconstructed it into a recognisable reality. This allowed all of the significant players a voice but blended their ideas into a series of themes expressed and shared by a number of individuals. This involved interpreting the data in a way that ensured that the voices of all participants were heard but which, at the same time, brought together related issues within the evidence. The research team were particularly keen to ensure that the voices of the young people were heard. This report therefore focuses on the perceptions of the young people involved in the study.

The sample

In partnership with the behaviour support staff in the 11 comprehensive schools, a group of young people with SEBD was identified for interview. Each individual had been excluded from school on more than one occasion and frequently accessed the pupil support base due to disruptive behaviour. The purpose of the interview was explained to the young people and both their permission and that of their parents was obtained prior to interview. The young people formed focus groups composed of four or five individuals and a total of 45 young people were involved. All of the young people were in the age range 14–16 years and were currently in the final year(s) of compulsory schooling. There were 34 boys and 11 girls in the sample.

A semi-structured interview schedule was used, focusing upon the young person's perceptions of learning and teaching, the curriculum, behavioural issues, the pupil support base and exclusion.

The interview methodology was underpinned by the work of Rogers (1980, quoted in McIntyre and Cooper 1996). He suggests a range of approaches in order to facilitate the interview process, particularly in relation to young people. These include empathy, unconditional positive regard, congruence and repeat probing. McIntyre and Cooper also set out a series of steps to be followed when interviewing young people, including defining relationships, negotiating access, selecting techniques and enacting appropriate relationships. The Strathclyde research team adhered closely to this model.

Emerging issues

At the heart of this research study was a concern for human rights, equal opportunities and social justice. The qualitative nature of the research enabled the researchers to understand more fully how the use of pupil support bases as an inclusive strategy impacted upon the in-school experience of these young people. [...] Methods of data collection reflected the qualitative nature of the research and, within this context, the semi-structured interview schedule was used to elicit extremely rich data from the young people. It was surprising how consistent all of the young people were in relation to the views expressed, and the issues selected for discussion reveal a very high level of conformity.

Curriculum

The research literature in relation to young people whose behaviour can be challenging consistently points to how an inappropriate curriculum can exacerbate behavioural difficulties (Fogell and Long 1997; Cole *et al.* 1998; Montgomery 1998; Porter 2000). This theme was echoed repeatedly by all of the young people in the sample:

> The teacher told me to get on with the work. I couldn't do it but he just said I should be able to. He asked me questions and I didn't know the answer. I ended up swearing at him and he then threw me out and told me to go to the Pupil Support Base.
>
> Mrs X treats me like a person. She knows I am a bit slower and she makes the worksheets interesting and fun. Other teachers find the most boring page and tell you to copy it then I get fed up and start messing about.

There was a widespread view expressed by the young people that the curriculum on offer was often inaccessible to them as it did not meet their needs. When they were unable to respond to the curriculum, they felt that they were perceived as being to blame whereas, in reality, the inappropriate curriculum was a potential source of behavioural difficulties. Thus the perceptions of these young people confirm the research findings as summarised by Porter (2000):

> a relevant curriculum is both a preventative and interventive measure in relation to disruptive behaviour.
>
> (p. 118)

Exclusion – equality, fairness and rights

All of the young people interviewed agreed that, in certain circumstances, exclusion was an effective strategy. They readily discussed occasions when they had been excluded and the extent to which they felt it had been an appropriate strategy:

> I got excluded for shouting and arguing with the teacher and for fighting with X. I know I did wrong and I can accept that I should have been excluded.

However, the young people did not always perceive the process to be fair and they consistently used words like 'equal', 'fair', 'respect' and 'rights' to elaborate upon this theme:

> I only argue with teachers who don't treat me fairly. I like teachers who respect you and don't just automatically blame you. Mr X treats everyone equally but Mrs Y doesn't.

Being treated disrespectfully by teachers was clearly seen as a provocation to disruptive behaviour (Tattum 1982; Olsen and Cooper 2001). Conversely, when these young people felt they were treated with genuine positive regard they were less likely to be challenging (Charles 1996; Cooper *et al.* 2000).

The young people saw themselves as victims who were picked upon and made scapegoats:

> If everyone in the class is carrying on the teacher always picks on me and puts me out. It's not fair. I always get the blame and it's not right.

This view was often linked to the young person's perception that, in the eyes of some teachers, they had a reputation. Once this had been established it seemed almost impossible for the young person to shed this image which, in their opinion, negatively influenced some teachers' attitudes and expectations:

> I'm in fourth year now and I definitely have a reputation. Some teachers just automatically think of me when something bad happens.

One crucial factor which often emerges in the research literature as a measure of how inclusive a school community is, is the extent to which everyone is valued and treated equally (Thomas *et al.* 1998). Again this was a recurring theme which the young people raised. They often expressed views that revealed that the theory of equality did not always translate into practice:

> A lot of teachers do try and treat everyone equally but it's not true that all pupils in this school are equally valued. Some teachers convey a sense that they don't like pupils and treat you as if you are not worth bothering about.

Thus the young people conveyed to the researchers a very clear view that the decision to exclude is a very complex issue. The work of Cullingford (1999) reinforces the view expressed by these young people and confirms the validity of their personal experience of being excluded. They are the individuals who experience exclusion at first hand and although on occasions they accept the decision, more often than not they feel that their view is disregarded as invalid.

Learning difficulties

Thirty out of the 45 young people interviewed emphasised the connection between learning difficulties and misbehaviour in class. This relationship has been well documented in the literature (Cooper 1993; Hewett 1998; Garner 1999; Pomeroy 2000). However, this group of young people felt that some teachers had not yet grasped the importance of making the link between learning and behavioural difficulties. There was a feeling that teachers varied in relation to the efforts they made to support young people who experienced learning difficulties and this could lead to disruptive behaviour:

> I was in English and I couldn't read the worksheet. I asked the teacher for help and she just ignored me so I just asked my pal for help and the teacher gave me a row. I shouted out and she said she was not having me in her class.

These young people consistently made the point that, in most classes, all pupils are expected to tackle the same work. They did not see a lot of evidence of differentiation in action and this posed a problem for them:

> I hate it when I am in a group and I can't do the work. It's really embarrassing and I feel terrible. If people laugh at me I lose my temper and then I am sent to the Support Base because of my behaviour.

However, the young people were keen to emphasise that many teachers are extremely helpful and supportive:

> Mr X knows I am dyslexic. He doesn't shout at me – he explains things and helps me get it right. He makes me feel that I can do it. I don't get put out of his class.

The crucial factor was that the teacher and the young people were very clear that it was the teacher who made the difference and that not all teachers were, in their opinion, effective or inclusive.

Teachers

As one might expect these young people had a lot to say about their teachers and the role they played in creating inclusive or exclusive classroom cultures. They understood how complex and stressful the teacher's job could be and they spoke highly of the many teachers who, in their opinion, do a first class job:

> The teacher's job can be really hard. They have to try and help everyone and everyone wants this or that at the same time. It's hard for the teacher to cope.
>
> Teachers have a difficult job to do. Most of them do their best to help us to learn but some pupils are prepared to work and some are not. Some people like me can be a bit rowdy and sometimes distract others and the teacher gets mad and stressed. So would I.

The young people tended to refer to what they perceived as effective teachers as 'good' teachers. The researchers tried to tease out what this meant and concluded from the evidence that the young people were expressing, in their own language, the view that the most effective teachers made an effort to include everyone:

> Mrs X is a good teacher. She listens to you and treats everyone fairly. She is strict but she is fun as well.
>
> Good teachers have a relaxed kind of class. They respect you and are like a sort of friend. They see you as a person and listen to you. A lot are like that but a lot aren't.

However, there was also a considerable amount of evidence to suggest that not all teachers were equally effective in promoting positive behaviour. As far as these young people are concerned, the teacher is the key. They accepted that some young people can be so disruptive that they are unwilling to respond positively to any teacher but they were also well aware that teachers varied considerably in their ability to relate to young people. One very articulate boy summed it up eloquently as follows:

> Good teachers help you and spend time with you. They understand how you feel, they respect you and give you a chance. Bad teachers don't listen, treat you like dirt, pick on you, think they are always right and boss you around all the time.

The young people were not prepared simply to accept the treatment they received from 'bad teachers' which they perceived to be unfair. They consistently expressed their determination to resist what they perceived as injustice. Even though they understood that ultimately they would be the losers in that they might be excluded, they were not prepared to be passive victims of unfair treatment. They often made a conscious decision to challenge these teachers who in their opinion abused their authority.

> I always challenge Mr X because he never treats me right. As far as he is concerned everything is always my fault. If he shouts at me I am going to shout at him.
> I'm not letting her (teacher) get away with treating me as if I'm dirt. She is not getting away with that so I stand up for myself because it is just not right to treat someone as if they are worthless.

Pupil support bases

In Scotland there is an increasing trend to open in mainstream schools Pupil Support Bases. All of the young people interviewed had spent time in these Bases and wanted to share their experiences with the researchers. There was unanimous agreement among them that the Pupil Support Base was helpful and sometimes prevented them from being excluded:

> I don't see eye to eye with some teachers so I come here (Pupil Support Base). I know if I stay in class I'll just get thrown out of the school.

The young people often made a clear distinction between some of their class teachers and the teachers who managed the Base provision:

> The teachers in the Base understand my problems. They know about my life outside school. I can talk to them.

These young people wanted their class teachers to be more like the teachers who supported them in the Base. They recognised qualities in the Base teachers that were not, in their opinion, evident across the school as a whole. The young people also expressed a strong feeling that the Pupil Support Base was often used inappropriately by those whom they perceived to be ineffective teachers:

> I didn't get a chance to misbehave in Mr X's class. I just walked in and he shouted at me to go to the Base.

> Mrs X said she was not here to teach people like me. I'd only stepped over the door and she said – 'Base!'

A quarter of the young people in the sample did admit that they sometimes misbehaved in order to be sent to the Base. They preferred the supportive ethos in the Base where they felt more secure:

> Sometimes I don't like the teacher or the subject is boring. I cause trouble so that I get sent to the Base.

All schools had in place whole-school policies in relation to indiscipline and the promotion of positive behaviour. The majority of the young people were well aware of these policies and how they should operate in practice. These policies emphasised the importance of praise and rewards and teachers were expected to create learning environments that were motivating and stimulating. The young people were, in general, supportive of these policies:

> We've got a behaviour policy in this school. You can get badges for good behaviour and you can get stickers in your card and get vouchers for McDonald's.

However, there was a widespread view expressed by all of the young people that all teachers were not consistent in applying school policy. Some teachers took a very rigid approach whereas others used the system more flexibly and interpreted policy in relation to individual need.

Conclusion

One of the most effective ways of securing young people's rights is through improving and extending educational opportunities available to them. Currently in Scotland one of the features of good practice which is highlighted within the context of education is the need to ensure all young people:

> have the right where appropriate to participate actively in decisions about their education and welfare. Their feelings and views should be valued and respected.

(SOEID 1999: 22)

In the wider arena of school effectiveness research, the absence of the student voice has been an issue for a decade or more. Nieto (1994) argues that:

> One way of beginning the process of changing school policies is to listen to students' views about them; however, research that focuses on student voices is relatively recent and scarce.
>
> (p. 396)

Rudduck *et al.* (1996) acknowledged that there are obvious problems in legitimising the contribution of the pupil voice in schools' own improvement practices. The University of Strathclyde study, by giving a voice to some of the most disaffected students within secondary schools, has confirmed Rudduck *et al.*'s conclusion that:

> ... young people are observant, are often capable of analytic and constructive comment and usually respond well to the responsibility ... of helping to identify aspects of schooling that get in the way of their learning.
>
> (p. 8)

Young people designated as having SEBD are often characterised as getting in the way of the learning of their peers. However, the incidence of learning difficulties among these young people with social, emotional and behavioural difficulties suggests that they too need to have a voice to express their experience of learning failure. Rudduck *et al.*'s view that we should take seriously young people's accounts and evaluations of their learning, teaching and schooling is borne out by the insights the young people displayed in this study.

The researchers tried to ensure that young people whose behaviour could be challenging and who were often excluded had an opportunity to exercise their right to share their feelings and views. The aim was to raise confidence and self-esteem and ensure the young people felt their opinions were valued.

The Strathclyde study allowed the young person's view to emerge and gave them a voice. It is clear that, when this happens, these young people are keen to have their voice heard. They want to have their say and it is important to remember that what they have to say may or may not correspond to the teacher's viewpoint and experiences. Nonetheless one must acknowledge these perceptions and accept them as valid because they are an expression of what the young person believes.

As professionals we must accept that all young people have the right to have their voice heard. This can be particularly difficult if the messages they convey cause us to reflect upon and critically analyse our own practice. In relation to the present research study the young people had much to say to us as professionals and hopefully we are listening to, valuing and responding to their views. We may be surprised just how knowledgeable and articulate young people can be and so we give the last word to one wise young man.

> An inclusive teacher never makes you feel like a second class citizen. They listen to you and don't just ignore what you think.

References

Allan, J. (1999) *Actively Seeking Inclusion*. London: Falmer Press.

Campion, J. (1992) *Working with Vulnerable Young Children*. London: Cassell.

Charles, C. M. (1996) *Building Classroom Discipline: from models to practice*. New York: Longmans.

Chazan, M., Laing, A. F., Davies, D. and Philips, R. (1998) *Helping Socially Withdrawn and Isolated Children and Adolescents*. London: Cassell.

Cole, T., Visser, J. and Upton, G. (1998) *Effective Schools for Pupils with Emotional and Behavioural Difficulties*. London: David Fulton.

Cooper, P. (1993) *Effective Schools for Disaffected Students: integration and segregation*. London: Routledge.

Cooper, P., Drummond, M., Hart, S., Lovey, J. and McLaughlin, C. (2000) *Positive Alternatives to Exclusion*. London: Routledge.

Cullingford, C. (1999) *The Causes of Exclusion*. London: Kogan Page.

Fogell, J. and Long, R. (1997) *Spotlight on Special Educational Needs – emotional and behavioural difficulties*. Tamworth: NASEN.

Garner, P. (1999) Schools by scoundrels: the views of disruptive pupils in mainstream schools in England and the United States. In M. Lloyd-Smith and J. D. Davies (eds) *On the Margins: the educational experience of problem pupils*. Stoke on Trent: Trentham Books.

Hamill, P. and Boyd, B. (2000) *Striving for Inclusion – the development of integrated support systems for pupils with social, emotional and behavioural difficulties in secondary schools*. Glasgow: University of Strathclyde.

Hewett, D. (ed.) (1998) *Challenging Behaviour – principles and practice*. London: David Fulton.

McIntyre, D. and Cooper, P. (1996) *Effective Teaching and Learning: teachers' and pupils' perspectives*. Buckingham: Open University Press.

Mittler, P. (2000) *Working Towards Inclusive Education – social contexts*. London: David Fulton.

Montgomery, D. (1998) *Reversing Lower Attainment – developmental curriculum strategies for overcoming disaffection and underachievement*. London: David Fulton.

Nieto, S. (1994) Lessons from students on creating a chance to dream. *Harvard Educational Review*, **64**(4), 392–426.

Olsen, J. and Cooper, P. (2001) *Dealing with Disruptive Students*. London: Kogan Page.

Pomeroy, E. (2000) *Experiencing Exclusion*. Stoke-on-Trent: Trentham.

Porter, L. (2000) *Behaviour in Schools – theory and practice for teachers*. Buckingham: Open University Press.

Rudduck, J., Chaplain, R. and Wallace, G. (eds) (1996) *School Improvement: what can pupils tell us?* London: David Fulton.

SCCC (Scottish Consultative Committee on the Curriculum) (1994) *Special Needs Within the 5–14 Curriculum – Support for Learning*. Dundee: SCCC.

Scottish Office (1995) *Children (Scotland) Act*. Edinburgh: HMSO.

Scottish Office (1998) *Report of the Consultative Steering Group on the Scottish Parliament*. http://www.scotland.gov.uk/library/documents-w5/rcsg-18.htm.

SEED (Scottish Executive Education Department) (1999) *New Community Schools – The Prospectus*. Edinburgh: HMSO.

SEED (Scottish Executive Education Department) (2000a) *Standards in Schools (Scotland) Act*. Edinburgh: HMSO.

SEED (Scottish Executive Education Department) (2000b) *Implementing Inclusiveness – Realising Potential*. The Beattie Committee Report. Edinburgh: HMSO.

SOEID (Scottish Office Education and Industry Department) (1994) *Effective Provision for Special Educational Needs*. Edinburgh: HMSO.

SOEID (Scottish Office Education and Industry Department) (1999) *A Manual of Good Practice in Special Educational Needs*. Edinburgh: HMSO.

Strauss, A. and Corbin, J. (1990) *Qualitative Analysis for Social Scientists*. Cambridge: Cambridge University Press.

Tattum, D. (1982) *Disruptive Pupils in Schools and Units*. Chichester: Wiley & Sons.

Thomas, G., Walker, D. and Webb, J. (1998) *The Making of the Inclusive School*. London: Routledge.

UN (United Nations) (1990) *Convention on the Rights of the Child*, Articles 12 and 23. New York: UN.

The need to listen if we are to learn from each other is a recurrent theme in this volume and Hamill and Boyd are powerful in illustrating this. This chapter leaves us in no doubt that all pupils have something worthwhile to contribute to the debate about how best to support learners.

Chapter 13

Disadvantage and discrimination compounded

The experience of Pakistani and Bangladeshi parents of disabled children in the UK

Qulsom Fazil, Paul Bywaters, Zoebia Ali, Louise Wallace and Gurnam Singh

This chapter discusses a study of the circumstances of 20 Pakistani and Bangladeshi families with one or more disabled children living in Birmingham. Parents and other adult carers were interviewed about their material circumstances, use of services and wellbeing. Importantly, the study found that these parents did not have as high levels of informal extended family support as can be assumed. Nor did they access formal support without difficulty. Thus, often disadvantage and discrimination compounded to make for difficult lives.

Introduction

[...] This article reports further evidence of the interaction of disability, ethnicity and disadvantage from a qualitative and quantitative action research study of families of Pakistani and Bangladeshi origin with a severely disabled child living in a Midlands city.

Families with disabled children in the UK experience many interlocking facets of disadvantage and discrimination (Ahmad 2000a). This has contributed to the development of the concept that it is the family as a whole that is disabled by the unjust society in which it finds itself. Parents and siblings, like disabled children, are also subject to stigma, marginalisation and discrimination. Within this experience, two key dimensions are central. First, disabled families in general face greater chances of (long-term) material deprivation than families without a disabled child. Second, against that problematic background, they commonly experience a variety of obstacles in accessing the range of information and services which it is known would have a positive impact on their lives (Beresford *et al.* 1996). In combination, as Ahmad (2000b) rightly argues, such disabling conditions constitute barriers to disabled people exercising their rights and responsibilities as citizens.

As Chamba *et al.* (1999) have demonstrated, families from minority ethnic groups with a disabled child face additional barriers to full citizenship, compared to majority families, as the consequences of the further impact of individual and institutional racism on their material circumstances and access to services. [...] They underlined the differences which lie between and within minority ethnic groups, as well as those between the minority and majority populations. Within the minority populations studied, those from Pakistan and Bangladesh are worst placed in both the key dimensions identified. [...]

Parents of all ethnic identities describe problems in the coordination of services as well as in availability, quality and timeliness (Beresford 1995). The difference in familiarity with English coupled with the failure of service providers to work equally effectively in languages other than English, are major mediating factors in the reduced levels of access to services of minority ethnic families with a disabled child. As Ahmad (2000b) points out, language counts for much more than just a means of communication, but is a significant primary barrier to families securing the information – about their child's impairment and information about services – which is a precursor to service access.

Parents from minority groups face the additional problems of the stereotype of extended family availability and willingness to provide care. Even though there is evidence of increased levels of extended family involvement by Pakistani and Bangladeshi families, only a quarter of such families reported receiving 'a lot of help' from family members (Chamba *et al.* 1999). It is not clear whether these somewhat raised rates of informal help are the *cause* or rather the *result* of the absence of formal services. Other assumptions, for example, that minority families do not like to send their children to respite care facilities, also seem, on the evidence, to be a reflection of the perceived lack of trust that the service provided will be appropriate to the needs of their children (and will not expose them to overt racism), rather than a cultural preference.

In summary, while all ethnic minority parents of disabled children face significant additional disadvantage compared with the white majority, which is itself discriminated against, there are deep differences between different ethnic minority groups. A parallel form of the inverse care law operates (Tudor Hart 1971) in which those families most likely to be facing material deprivation and disadvantage (Pakistani and Bangladeshi families) are least likely to be receiving services, least likely to be able to understand professionals' information or processes, and least able to express their own requirements effectively in a language service providers will understand. [...]

Methodology

Pakistani and Bangladeshi families were identified to take part in an action research project. A new advocacy service was established by East Birmingham Family Service Unit (EBFSU), a local project of a national voluntary sector organisation providing preventive and support services for children and families. For the research project, 20 families to whom the advocacy service was to be provided were identified from new cases referred to EBFSU between October 1999 and March 2000. All contained one or more severely impaired children aged between 5 and 19 years old. Families were interviewed initially to identify their existing needs prior to receiving the help of an advocate.

Interviews were conducted with adult family members in their own homes at a time convenient to them. Each interview involved a semi-structured questionnaire devised by the research team which explored the family's social situation and contact with service providers. [...]

Results

The families

Fifteen families were of Pakistani origin and five were of Bangladeshi origin. The families were referred via local schools, community nurses, health visitors and social workers. In each family, all those adults who were involved in the caring of the disabled child were interviewed. In total, 39 people were interviewed: 20 mothers, 16 fathers and three family members who played a role in caring. We had anticipated that carers might also include older siblings and other extended family members. However, of the 20 families interviewed, only three carers were not parents. These carers included one sister and two grandmothers. Mothers were the main carer in 19 families and a father was the main carer in one family.

Four families did not have a father living in the household; all these families were of Pakistani origin. This was more than a quarter of the Pakistani families. It is unclear whether this is unusual, as the incidence of single-parent Pakistani families is unknown and, in any case, the numbers involved in this study are very small.

The average age of mothers and fathers was 35 years and 41 years respectively. The majority of families had more than four children, two families had seven children and five families had six children. Families had an average of 4.5 children. The majority of parents were first-generation Pakistanis or Bangladeshis. Only four parents were second-generation Pakistanis. All four of these were married to first-generation Pakistanis.

Findings: evidence of material disadvantage

Housing

Eight families out of 20 (40 per cent) owned their own homes, six families (30 per cent) lived in local authority housing and six (30 per cent) lived in houses provided by private landlords.

Thirteen out of the 20 families (65 per cent) said that their house was unsuitable. Of these, seven families (35 per cent) felt that their house was not appropriate for adaptation and wished to move to a more suitable house. The other five (25 per cent) had a range of reasons for the unsuitability of their house, from small items such as a raised stand to reach the toilet to needing a suitable area for their child to play in. The seven families (35 per cent) who said that their current accommodation was not suitable for adaptations and wished to move lived in some very adverse conditions.

These families had severely disabled children, did not have lifting equipment and had to carry their children up and down the stairs. Four of these families (20 per cent) slept downstairs in fairly small back living rooms. In this room they had the child's bed, and one or two settees. In the daytime, they used it as a sitting room and in the evening they slept on the settees so that they could keep an eye on their disabled child. These parents had been sleeping like this for many years and all four of them have been trying to move to suitable local authority accommodation for a number of years.

One father reported that discriminatory attitudes of landlords led to difficulties in finding private rented accommodation. He lived in a three bedroom house with five children and wanted to move. He explained his difficulty in finding accommodation in the private sector:

> Private accommodation is difficult as people see T's disability and will not rent a house to us as they are afraid that he will damage their property.

Employment

Nine families had a father working outside the home. Of those working fathers, five worked in shops or factories and four were self-employed.

The self-employed consisted of three taxi drivers and one shop owner. None of the mothers worked at the time of the first interview. During the period of the advocacy project, one mother started work as a dinner lady at the local school. Two mothers who were students were both single parents.

Costs of living and barriers to claiming income

Five (25 per cent) out of the 20 families reported difficulty in managing with their income and eight families stated that there were items that they needed, but were unable to afford. These families reported a need for essential items, including beds, cooker, clothes, washing machine and fridge. A particularly striking finding was that 17 families (85 per cent) were unaware of the Family Fund scheme from which such essential items could have been claimed.

Mothers with partners were, in general, not sure about the benefits that the family was receiving. They told the researchers to ask their husbands about benefits and finances. Benefits were perceived as being stigmatising. For example, one mother believed that they were entitled to family credit. When the father was interviewed he said that he was managing and did not wish to claim benefits as this would not reflect well on him. The mother reported that the family struggled on wages of £150 a week. They had six children. Another mother explained that her husband had not wished to claim benefits for the disabled child as he did not want people to think that he could not look after his child and that they were living off her money. He had been persuaded to claim by a community nurse.

The complexity of the issues surrounding making a benefit claim is exemplified by a third mother, who had been advised to claim benefits in respect of a daughter aged nine months who needed a lot of care with feeding (she also had a nine-year-old disabled daughter). She was afraid to make the claim for her daughter as she felt that by claiming benefits she would be labelling her baby daughter as disabled and 'tempting fate', as she was afraid that she would also become disabled like her older child. At the time she believed that her baby only needed care with feeding, not that she was disabled.

Findings: accessing services and support

Evidence of problems in accessing services

We asked families about the service providers that each family had contact with in the six months prior to interview. Families reported relatively little contact with professional service providers; few families were closely linked with service providers other than the school and the general practitioner. However, in general, families had difficulty in understanding the role of the service providers, identifying who they were and where they came from. In some cases, families knew nothing more than the first name of a worker who came to the house. [...]

The families most likely to be in contact with service providers other than the general practitioner (GP) and the school were those families with children who needed frequent medical care. These families had contact with community nurses and one family had contact with a health visitor. The person who had the most contact with the service providers depended on which of the two parents spoke English. [...]

Service providers who were particularly difficult to identify were housing and social services. Only one family had a social worker whom they could name. Housing staff were difficult to identify as the Housing Department did not allocate a named individual worker to a family.

Since families found it difficult to recall who visited and which organisations these visitors came from, there may be more service providers involved than we were able to identify. However, from the families' perspective, if a user cannot describe who a service provider is, where they come from, what services they can provide or how to contact them, their value is substantially reduced.

Outstanding service need

Fourteen parents stated they wanted contact with service providers. They had either previously been in contact with these services but had lost contact or had never been in contact before. The number of service needs for families ranged from seven families who had at least three service needs they wanted help for, to seven families who had fewer than three service needs they wanted help for. A number of parents did not know which service to contact but stated they wanted to contact a service that would satisfy their stated need (Table 13.1).

Families' experience of and contact with professionals and services

Schools

Parents said that they visited their child's school when they needed to. In general, the majority reported being satisfied with the school and felt that

Table 13.1 Services families wanted contact with

Would like contact with	Number of families
Respite care	6
Practical help	5
Housing	5
Social worker	4
Somewhere to get a wheelchair	2
Someone to help with child's behaviour	2
Mobility allowance section	1
Somewhere to get household items, such as bed, fridge	1
Physiotherapist	1
To know more about the illness	1
Someone to sort out footpath	1

the schools were very good at looking after their children. One mother said that her child was doing things at school she did not do at home. She had learnt to use the toilet and was using Makaton language skills at school, even though she would not use it at home. She recalls finding out whilst visiting one day at school that her daughter was able to feed herself.

> I found out that she eats by herself at school one day, I saw her eating there and I was gob smacked, so now I cut her food and she eats it.

However, three families stated that they were afraid of visiting the school, as seeing the disabled children scared them. These families did not attend school reviews, as they stated that they found it distressing. We discovered from the schools concerned that very few of our parents visited the school for annual reviews.

Four parents had areas of dissatisfaction with the school. Three families were concerned that their children came home with bruises. One mother whose child came home with self-inflicted bruises felt that the school was not doing enough to keep him happy. She commented that:

> If H is happy he won't bang his head on the floor, I think that they should take extra care, the school is a special school, that's what special should mean, that they should give him special attention. Two weeks ago he came home with a big cut on his head, last week he had a black eye. I didn't have the time to go to the school because I am under so much exam pressure, trying to study, but I spoke to the school guide

[*a school guide accompanies the children on the bus to and from school*] and she said she didn't know what happened. Nobody had told her.

One family was concerned about the standard of their children's education (they had two children who went to a special school). The mother said:

> I feel that the school system is hopeless and that the children have got worse. They can't write, they were not this bad before they went to school, but since they went to this school they have got worse. They have picked up bad behaviour which they bring home and then carry out at home. S bites her hand and sucks her thumb, she never used to do this before she started at this school. I think she has picked up this habit from other children.

The extent to which a disabled child will be able to meet the parents' expectations for literacy and writing may be limited. In this case, after interviewing the teachers it was apparent that the parents had expectations for their child that exceeded the school's assessment. The family reported having little contact with the school. Such a gap in expectations and accompanying dissatisfaction with services is the kind of outcome that is likely if communication between service providers and families is weak.

Social services

Two families received help from social services in the form of extra care hours provided by a care worker. However, they reported problems in getting these hours sorted out. Both mothers said that social services often took weeks to deal with a request for care hours and then often allocated hours when they were no longer needed.

Four families stated that when they needed to contact social services they had to speak to the duty social worker. These families said that they got extremely frustrated with having to tell their story again and again every time they spoke to social services, and to a different social worker each time. The social services department had recently introduced a new system where families have to leave a message and then someone rings them back, which caused much frustration.

Respite care

Of the 20 main carers, only one mother said that she had recently had a break from caring. She had one disabled daughter, who she had left with her

husband and mother-in-law while she went to Pakistan. However, the belief
that Pakistani and Bangladeshi parents with a disabled child are not interested
in respite care was not confirmed. Nine of the families said they did not
want respite care, but three families (15 per cent) had taken up respite care in
the past year and wanted to do so again, and a further six families (30 per cent)
who had not had respite care wanted it. Two mothers (10 per cent) were
not sure about respite care, but said that they would consider it if they
needed to. [...]

Access to appropriate housing

Seven families were waiting to be moved to a new property. These families
have been waiting for many years with little recent contact. [...] Housing
services were reported by a number of families to be unsympathetic. One
family reported an attitude that can be seen as lacking in cultural awareness.
The parents had six children and wanted to be moved to a larger house with
more bedrooms. They had a daughter in her early twenties living with them.
The housing officer had advised them that their daughter should move out
and get a place of her own. This annoyed them as they said that if the officer
had been Pakistani then they would have understood that Pakistani families
do not let their daughters live on their own.

GPs

Families did not report any problems with the doctor and said that they were
happy with the service received from the family doctor. This service is the
one with which families had the most contact. However, contact with the
GP had clearly not provided a gateway to the range of health, social care and
other services which families would have valued.

Hospital specialists

In seven families, the disabled children were currently under the care of a
hospital specialist. Two fathers and one mother were able to name who they
saw at the hospital. Six out of seven mothers knew neither the name of the
specialist nor the hospital. Two families reported missing hospital
appointments for their child. One mother said that they found it difficult to
take their son by car and taxis cost a lot of money, so they missed many
appointments. Another family reported that they missed their last
appointment to see the specialist as they had forgotten.

Community nurses and health visitors

Four families reported contact with a community nurse and one with a health visitor. These families were very happy with the health visitor and community nurse involvement, and the support that they received from them. They said that the nurses, as well as helping them with the child's welfare, also helped them fill in forms for housing, social service care hours and occupational therapy services.

Physiotherapists

None of the parents had had contact with a physiotherapist in the past six months. The reason for this may be that the physiotherapists have all their contact with the child at the school. It is of concern that parents have little contact with physiotherapists and also that parents may not even be fully aware of the role of the physiotherapist. One family were not sure what the equipment they had been given was for – they sent it to school, but were not sure if the school were using it.

> He goes to hospital and he has these clothes to straighten his legs. Mom sends the clothes to the school and the school are supposed to put the clothes on him. They said that they would do it. They think that by having these clothes we might be able to straighten his legs but they're not sure. I'm not really sure what the clothes are supposed to do. [...]

An important barrier to access

Families were asked if they thought that the ethnicity of the service provider was important in service provision. Eight parents said that the ethnicity of the service provider was important. The majority of these were mothers and the main reason given for ethnicity being important was language barriers.

> If they had an Asian assistant at the school then we would have somebody who could speak my wife's language and she would be willing to go to school. It would help if somebody spoke Urdu but I managed to communicate with her (school nurse). My main problem is language. It would be better if someone spoke my language then I could ask the questions without an interpreter.

One parent's response suggested that more than just language was at issue:

> It would be a great peace for me if I could directly understand and speak to a Bengali doctor. It would really be peace of mind for me.

However, another mother talking about her experience with Asian staff within the Housing Department stated that 'ethnicity can make things worse, when there are Asians who do not listen'.

Findings: family support, mental health and social well-being

The belief that extended families are a rich source of help in Asian families was not evident in this sample. Only two mothers had help from a member of the extended family, the help mainly consisting of babysitting. [...] None of the parents in our study belonged to a support group and only two parents had contact with another parent of a disabled child. Three mothers expressed the view that they would like to meet other mothers with disabled children.

One in five mothers also reported no help from their partner. [...] Not receiving any help or break from caring inevitably leads to tiredness. Physical energy is an important coping resource and, as a result of increased workload, parents with a disabled child have an increased vulnerability to stress.

Not surprisingly, given the previous evidence, we found that not only were Pakistani and Bangladeshi families in the study socially and economically deprived, they also suffered from high levels of anxiety and depression. Mothers were found to report substantially more somatic symptoms, anxiety and insomnia, and symptoms of severe depression than fathers. Altogether, 11 out of 39 parents (28 per cent) were found to be above the severe depression threshold score of 10. This included eight mothers (40 per cent) and three fathers (19 per cent). [...]

In addition to being amongst the most social and economically deprived in the population, doing most of the caring and receiving little or no social support outside the family, some women also reported experiencing domestic violence and/or being blamed for bearing a disabled child. Four women reported incidents of continual domestic violence. Those women also reported that they did all the caring duties concerning the disabled child and that their husbands gave little or no help. [...]

Five of the women said that their partners blamed them for having a disabled child. One mother said her husband would not accept that his daughter was disabled, so she had left him after years of physical abuse. Six mothers reported that their marital relationship was directly affected as a result of having a disabled child. Two of these women's husbands had left them. They explained why.

> My husband blamed me for this [having a disabled child], he said that it is my fault ... he never comes to see him ... he says if I marry again he will take H.
>
> My husband couldn't take the responsibility for A, she needed a lot of care and attention so he left.

One mother had left her husband temporarily as he blamed her for producing a disabled child.

> Because of the disabled child we had lots of family problems, when I was expecting the second baby [her first child is disabled], I left my husband. Some people mediated and helped us get back together. He used to tell me that I was an unlucky person and that is why this has happened to me. Now that we have this house provided by the council for A he doesn't say such nasty things about the child as he can see the benefits.

Discussion and conclusion

The evidence of this small-scale study complements and supplements the data available from the national surveys about the experience of families with one or more disabled children. It reinforces the understanding of disability as a product of impairment coupled with socially created discrimination rather than individual tragedy. It demonstrates again that families of disabled children are caught up in the disadvantage which results. It extends knowledge of the ways in which different dimensions of structural and individual discrimination, based in disability, 'race' and gender, interact to create inequality and unjust suffering. A number of significant points emerge, of relevance to policy makers, practitioners and researchers, as well as to disabled people and the disability movement. [...]

All the disabled children in these families were attending school and most had been in contact with their GP in the last six months. However, contact with other services, desired by the families, had not followed. Neither the health nor education systems offered a clear gateway to information about and access to the range of services that may be available to disabled families.

It is not surprising, therefore, that, in this locality at least, there was also no single point of coordination of services for families, no first point of contact, no one to look at the families' circumstances holistically. Far from service provision being integrated across the different agencies and professionals so that families experienced a seamless, needs-led service, it was the absence of systematic services which came through most strikingly. Undoubtedly, limited skills in the use of English by the families was a major barrier – though not the only barrier – here. Over three decades after the main contemporary period of immigration from the South Asian sub-continent, service providers still had not got effective means of offering services to non-English speakers or to those who are not familiar with the basic structures of the British welfare system. [...]

The evidence of this study does not support either the view that 'Asian' families are necessarily part of a care-giving extended family or that Pakistani and Bangladeshi families do not welcome the offer of certain kinds of services, such as respite care. The interviews found a variety of circumstances being faced by families which were diverse in nature; some single parent, some two parent families; some with adults in employment, many without; some with grandmothers providing support, many without. Equally, the families had a variety of expressed needs and attitudes to service provision. [...] For all parents, the quality of the care being offered – its appropriateness to the needs of the child – is a key dimension of the decision to accept help. Two things are clear: service providers should not make assumptions about the services which a particular family might want or value, and the level of service provision is substantially below that which families currently desire. That applies to Bangladeshi and Pakistani families just as much as, if not more than, other groups.

Finally, the study gives evidence of families who are remarkably resilient. Under profoundly difficult material, practical and emotional circumstances, the parents, particularly the mothers, were continuing to provide care to their children. However, the costs to those families are substantial as evidenced in the high level of psychological ill-health which the parents demonstrated. Neither the disabled children nor their siblings were interviewed for this study, but they undoubtedly also bear the costs of the combination of disadvantaged circumstances and inadequate service provision that has been demonstrated.

This study set out to examine the circumstances of what were likely to be members of the most disadvantaged groups of families with disabled children in the UK, so it is not surprising that disadvantage and institutional discrimination were found. [...] The fact that the results are expected should not dull our response. The distance between the experiences of these families, and the model of a security net of welfare services providing care and protection to all the country's children, is immense. The widespread disadvantage and discrimination experienced routinely by families with a disabled child in the UK in the twenty-first century is compounded for the families who talked to us by everyday institutional and individual racism that is the backdrop to their lives.

References

Ahmad, W. I. U. (ed.) (2000a) *Ethnicity, Disability and Chronic Illness.* Buckingham: Open University Press.

Ahmad, W. I. U. (2000b) Introduction. In W. I. U. Ahmad (ed.) *Ethnicity, Disability and Chronic Illness*, pp. 1–11. Buckingham: Open University Press.

Beresford, B. (1995) *Expert Opinions: a national survey of parents caring for a severely disabled child.* Bristol: Policy Press.

Beresford, B., Sloper, P., Baldwin, S. and Newman, T. (1996) *What Works in Services for Families with a Disabled Child?* Ilford: Barnado's.

Chamba. R., Ahmad, W., Hirst, M., Lawton, D. and Beresford, B. (1999) *On the Edge: minority ethnic families caring for a severely disabled child.* Bristol: Policy Press.

Tudor Hart, T. (1971) The Inverse Care Law. *Lancet*, 27 February, 40–12.

The account of this research is a powerful reminder that there are very significant barriers to inclusion and social justice. The experiences of the families show clearly that access to support is made difficult on many levels. Their disadvantaged circumstances bring on more disadvantage. Although they show great resilience in caring for their children, their situations are compounded by issues beyond their control. The discrimination they face is a social creation and addressing this requires the whole community to be involved.

Chapter 14

Teachers and Gypsy Travellers

*Gwynedd Lloyd, Joan Stead, Elizabeth Jordan
and Claire Norris*

This chapter discusses some of the findings from a project looking at how teachers perceived, and respond to, the culture and behaviour of children from Traveller families. The authors discuss in particular the extent to which schools responded to cultural diversity when this challenges notions of 'normal' school attendance and behaviour. Important links are made between disciplinary exclusion from school and broader social exclusion which are fundamental to an understanding of equality and participation.

[...]

Gypsy Traveller children in Scotland

The Council of Europe identifies two main groups of Travellers, Gypsy Travellers and Occupational Travellers, the latter group including, for example, Show and barge people. (Others sometimes include a third group, 'new age' Travellers.) Our project focused on Gypsy Travellers and Show Travellers; however, the findings discussed below show a more complex situation for Gypsy Travellers, upon whom this paper concentrates. [...]

While there is some diversity of opinion over the correct descriptive terminology the term Gypsy Traveller seems to be the most often currently used by organisations representing the community itself such as the Scottish Gypsy Traveller Association. By Gypsy Traveller we mean those who consider themselves to be part of this community, whether still nomadic or housed, and who share the common knowledge, speech, customs and manners historically associated with that culture. Our definition is, therefore, principally one of self-ascription.

Research previously undertaken by the Scottish Traveller Education Project (STEP) and by Save the Children Fund (SCF) suggests a low level of school attendance by Gypsy Traveller children, especially at the secondary stage (Jordan 1996; SCF 1996). There is an official dispensation which allows for a reduction in the number of school attendances required from Traveller pupils, to allow for seasonal work travelling. Economic and legal changes in recent years do however make it increasingly difficult for Gypsy Travellers to maintain their nomadic lifestyle.

The research – methods

[...] The research questions sought to explore whether our initial under-standing, that Traveller pupils' behaviour was an issue in some schools, was substantiated by closer investigation. If some Traveller pupils' behaviour was an issue, how was it described and made sense of by teachers, pupils and parents? What responses were made to the behaviour and what strategies were used by schools? [...]

Interviewers used a semi-structured interview schedule as a topic guide but our aim was primarily to create an interview climate where teachers, parents, children and young people felt able to talk freely without too much control from the researcher. This approach is described by some researchers as a non-directive interview (Cohen and Manion 1994). This was particularly important for Traveller parents and young people, understandably suspicious, who needed to be reassured that we really were going to listen to what they had to say. Much of the content and direction of the interviews was determined principally by the respondent, the interviewer using the schedule to ask questions or raise issues if these had not come up. (The interview guides are given in the Appendix.) [...] Care was taken, however, to avoid making suggestions or leading respondents. [...]

Some deliberate validation was also built into the project through the process of interviewing of Traveller support staff. Their views were important – as a group they have a mixed 'outsider/insider' status working both on Traveller sites and with numbers of teachers and schools. They were thus able to offer a valuable comparative perspective. [...]

We interviewed both housed and mobile Show and Gypsy Travellers, identified and contacted for us by 'gatekeepers', individuals with an existing relationship of trust with traveller groups. The Travellers interviewed were not chosen as in any way representative of their communities; they had something to say and were willing to talk to us. We recognised that these groups are heterogeneous and so aimed to gather personal experiences from which we could form impressions and develop themes, rather than generalisations.

We make no claim for scientific neutrality, indeed we are explicit that our interest stems from a concern for social justice [...]

The research – findings

The research looked at the school experiences of both Occupational (Show) Travellers and Gypsy Travellers and the whole findings are described in a project report (Lloyd *et al.* 1999). A key finding of the study was the difference in the views of the school staff on the two groups of Travellers. Teachers in schools where Show Travellers had attended were almost all highly positive about having Show Traveller pupils in school and did not see their presence as disruptive, other than in relation to the disruption to the routines of the class because of irregular attendance. Although teachers saw irregular attendance and absence from school as perhaps the major issue for both groups, the pupils themselves, Show and Gypsy Travellers, identified name-calling by other pupils as the strongest negative feature of their school experience.

This chapter concentrates on Gypsy Traveller pupils, whose behaviour was perceived by staff to be problematic and who were sometimes formally excluded.

Was the behaviour of Gypsy Traveller children an issue for schools?

There were a wide variety of views and perceptions expressed by the staff interviewed. In some respects they reflect those likely to be argued about all children in school in that some children's behaviour is considered to be a problem by some teachers, in some schools and at some times. The notion of behavioural difficulties is inevitably subjective and contextually varied (Cullen *et al.* 1996; Munn *et al.* 1998).

> You get children with behavioural problems who are Travellers and you get children with behavioural problems who aren't.
>
> (B: Traveller support)

Most of the school and Traveller support staff did describe some incidents and circumstances where schools had defined the behaviour of some Gypsy Traveller children as problematic. A small number said that there had never been any particular issue with the behaviour of the Traveller children. Sometimes this was then contradicted by reference to circumstances where there had been problems. In some secondary schools not all staff were aware that the school had identified and responded to perceived problems. For example, the behaviour support teacher in a secondary school described the exclusion and referral to the Children's Hearing System of two Gypsy Traveller girls, but two of her colleagues appeared not to be aware of this. In secondary schools there were sometimes quite different views expressed by staff in the same school, for example the four teaching colleagues quoted below.

> We've never had any situation where the Travelling people have been different from anybody else.
>
> (A: deputy HT, secondary)

> There are conflicts, I hate to say there is a 'them and us', they have a way of life where they do certainly appear to care for each other but equally well, they see the rest of the community as being the great unwashed where the problems are.
>
> (B: PT guidance, secondary)

> They voice their opinion in not too pleasant a manner sometimes ... I could take it because I knew him, but certainly in front of a mainstream class it wasn't acceptable ... He didn't see a lot of point to the curriculum ... it was difficult for us too because if he was withdrawn from these classes it meant he was sitting down there and it was time that was special for others too. If he was there, he demanded attention. With the staffing level it was difficult to make sure the others were getting the attention as well. That was a problem.
>
> (C: special education teacher, secondary)

> He had real run ins with authority which was major, quite a major disruption, fighting and swearing and such things. On the other hand he was quite pleasant to adults. He did have a problem with integration ... there was little parental backup, the parents didn't see the value of school or higher education ... If we're talking difficulties, the biggest difficulty is attendance, they just don't attend ... no matter how nice they are, how well they integrate, the attendance thing is always the thing that hits most, even more so than just discipline.
>
> (D: guidance teacher, secondary)

There were no teachers who argued that the behaviour of all Gypsy Traveller pupils was a problem for the school. Several made a point of beginning with a positive statement, even when they subsequently mentioned difficulties with individual children.

> For the most part their behaviour is good, if not better than many of their peer group ... Within the school there is no doubt that we have come up against behavioural problems with the kids ... we have also had difficulties with those Travellers who have been settled, even though they have been settled for quite some time. One of the major issues is truancy.
>
> (F: PT learning support, secondary)

How did teachers make sense of Traveller behaviour?

Again, there was a considerable range of views and understandings of Gypsy Travellers' actions in school. The interviews often contained quite contradictory observations, for example several teachers stated they felt that the difficulties presented by a particular pupil were not related to cultural background but then went on to give examples that suggested that the teacher was indeed viewing the behaviour as significantly influenced by their background. Sometimes teachers were emphatic in their view that the cultural background of the pupil was not a factor in the teacher's perceptions, implying that perhaps to recognise difference was in itself inappropriate.

> I've never, never thought of him as any of the Travelling people, he was difficult because he could flare up very easily. My impression was that was part of his background and he had a sort of defence mechanism ... maybe the language is the one thing we've noticed more ... he's not scared to say what he wanted. I wouldn't say that was typical of Travelling people but he maybe, that might have been that they accepted it more on the site. We've never had any situation where the Travelling people have been different from anybody else.
>
> (A: deputy HT, secondary)

In some instances the teacher's own implicit prejudice or stereotyping was apparent. For example, a teacher in charge of a secondary special class, where several Gypsy Traveller young people had been placed, talked 'positively' about two pupils, contrasting this with looking like a 'tinker'.

> They were very acceptable, they were nicely dressed, they turned up nice, they didn't make themselves different in any way ... they were

actually very clean and tidy ... they didn't make themselves out to be Tinker girls – their hair was nice and whatnot ...

(C: special education teacher, secondary)

Perhaps paradoxically, the teachers who acknowledged that schools could face problems with the behaviour of Traveller pupils were those with the most knowledge of and empathy with cultural difference, as in the case of Traveller support teachers, They were the most likely to say there is an issue which they see in the schools they visit. They were clearer in their positive acknowledgement of difference and their perception of how this difference might become constructed as difficulty by schools.

Several support teachers and other staff made the point that all children can choose to be difficult in school and also that sometimes Traveller children face difficulties in their lives which are not peculiar to Traveller communities. Thus, though some Traveller children were seen to have required extra support in school because of family bereavement, alcohol or other drug use or physical or sexual abuse, in this respect they would be no different from children from the settled community.

Perceived lack of cooperation in class, e.g. not following instructions

Some difficulties may be the consequence of lack of knowledge. Schools' ability to operate is contingent on pupils knowing how to behave and knowing when they break the rules. Often the Traveller pupils might have missed the beginning of the first class in primary school, may not have been to nursery school and, therefore, have missed the everyday learning about how you act in class.

> The boys had no real knowledge of how to behave in a large group ... sorry, how we expected them to behave, which is maybe a different thing ... they would sit and talk, shout out, refuse to do any work, walk around the place – which in a class of 30 is something that is very difficult to accommodate ... I feel that in the case of the Traveller boys they were just behaving normally to them. They weren't setting out to disrupt.
>
> (G: PT guidance)

The structure of classroom norms may be implicit and difficult for the Traveller child to access. It may represent a difficult transition to insideness for children used to spending much of their time outside.

> I think the thing at the P[rimary] 1 level with the behaviour is that it is such a culture shock for the child, you know ...
>
> (E: Traveller support)

> Just a whole new ball game to be even within a building with corridors and so many rooms.
>
> (C: Traveller support)

> And rules – 'you sit down' [in teacher instruction voice].
>
> (F: Traveller support)

[...] It was suggested that Gypsy Traveller children may get into trouble for the same kinds of reasons as other children, for example, not having a pencil or not doing their homework, but that for some Traveller children these may happen more often because of the circumstances of travelling and life on site.

Difficulties related to late coming and to absence

Erratic patterns of attendance created difficulties. Problems of attendance were sometimes, but not always, associated with actually travelling. Several teachers mentioned problems of attendance by housed Travellers.

> One of the difficulties when they did come back was that if they had been off for a great deal of time, like other kids, they had fallen behind and therefore the disaffection if you like, started at that period when they came back and it was in all subjects.
>
> (F: PT learning support, secondary)

Unpredictable patterns of attendance were recognised by all the Traveller support teachers as disruptive to class and subject teachers. Sometimes it may be that this exacerbates a problem a teacher was already having with a class.

> It's a case where 14 Travellers arrived at a school within a week, most of them settled very well but there's five gone into the Pl class and one boy, by anybody's standards anywhere, has behavioural problems. You get children with behavioural problems that are Travellers and you get children with behavioural problems that aren't. But it has had a catalytic effect on the class who were difficult anyway. There is one child who has come in who the other children perceive as being beyond control.

And it's not just that he is a problem in that class, but he has awakened, or reawakened, the possibility for that type of behaviour, the other children had settled quite well. So in terms of that class, yes the child is being perceived as a huge problem. They're trying to deal with it positively but there is a huge problem.

(D: Traveller support)

Well you can appreciate you've got bad days and you've got a class like P's class which is disruptive and then you've got them settled to work and then the door opens and P comes in.

(J: learning support T, secondary).

Problems to do with missed curriculum and specific learning difficulties

Frustration was expressed by several teachers recognising the difficulties presented by irregular attendance and their wish to see children making identifiable progress.

If they move between areas, move between schools, they might find that in one school they have done a section of work, when they get to another school they are only starting it so they repeat it all but they've missed the bit that they did before.

(B: PT guidance, secondary)

Several teachers suggested that sometimes difficulties in schools might be related to a high level of dyslexia amongst Gypsy Traveller boys. This is a problematic assertion as it is difficult to separate the notion of a specific learning difficulty from the overall issues associated with a historically non-literate culture, inconsistent school attendance and missed learning.

Problems with friendships/peer group relationships

Varying patterns of attendance were also seen to lead to difficulties with friendship and peer group relationships.

The poor attendance means that they never establish real friendships because it happens so often. They're always on the outskirts in the class if they're not attending regularly. They're always on the fringe because they haven't built up relationships over the years and if they find they can't build relationships with children it's very difficult for them to mix in.

(H: Traveller support)

Some teachers felt that it was difficult for Gypsy Traveller pupils to establish friendships outside their own community. Sometimes children would spend break times checking on the wellbeing of siblings or of other Traveller children.

Difficulties related to name-calling/bullying of Traveller pupils and fighting

Some teachers felt that there would always be name-calling.

I would say that you are bound to get a bit of name-calling and that sort of thing, I think that's inevitable ... I'm sure there's a bit of name-calling but they never complain about it ... they tend to tough it out.

(D: guidance T, secondary)

Others thought that it was not an issue in their school although the evidence from the interviews with children, families and Traveller support teachers suggests that it is virtually universal and that many pupils do not feel supported by schools in facing it.

[Q. What about relationships with other children?] Poor. Two reasons: firstly they kept themselves to themselves, they don't naturally mix, this is girls and boys: secondly because of the background they come from, they do at times come up smelling or dirty, they get called 'tinkie' or 'blacko', in this part of the country it's 'tinkie' and 'blacko'. To this they would rarely react violently, they would come and complain and would use this as an excuse for not coming to school for the next three weeks.

(G: PT guidance, secondary)

I think he gets on well, but he is a wee bit smelly at times, a wee bit scruffy, he has an English accent, so he is different and he will be picked upon from time to time. Not because he's a Traveller but because he's different.

(A: deputy HT, secondary)

There's a lot of prejudice in the area about Traveller children. They use a horrible word, I can hardly bring myself to say the word, but they say 'scoot' as a derogatory word for a travelling pupil. They would use it for anyone they saw who was dirty or scruffy. That is one of the problems, I have to say, that many travelling children are not very clean which other children don't like at all ... it really is a form of racial prejudice and it has to be tackled as seriously as that.

(N: Traveller support)

[...]For most teachers in schools the bullying and name-calling was not seen as part of an overall racism, although one or two did see this broader view which also tended to be expressed more often by Traveller support teachers.

Certainly the anti-bullying policy and strategies [are] in place within the school. It's not seen as a racial problem just as a general bullying thing.

(N: Traveller support)

A number of teachers suggested that bullying and name-calling were sometimes used as an 'excuse' not to attend school. Most schools mentioned fighting in the playground as an issue, often as a response to name-calling but also sometimes between Gypsy Traveller children.

... it's playground and it usually focuses on the boys because there is a tendency for them to be fiercely competitive. They're fiercely competitive among themselves and it leads to rough play if they have a fall out, a quick aggressive battering is a very quick quite satisfactory solution to them.

(HT, primary)

It [i.e. exclusion] was for fighting. One boy was swearing at the teacher but mainly it's been fighting outside school.

(N: Traveller support)

[..] It may be that teachers in some schools have not reflected on their duties under the law to provide education free from discrimination and harassment or that they do not perceive this to be an issue with respect to Gypsy Traveller pupils. Traveller support staff were more likely to perceive the bullying and harassment as racist than teachers in schools.

Style of addressing adults and sense of justice

These were commonly identified as an issue for schools. Children often addressed school staff as if they were equal adults, sometimes making personal comments which the teachers found difficult. One Traveller support teacher argued that Gypsy Traveller children have not learned the 'social dishonesty' expected in the settled world.

> ... if you are talking to a Traveller child, he or she will speak to you as an adult. Now in school that can appear to be cheeky because children tend on the whole not to speak to teachers like that.
>
> (A: Traveller support)

> [...] I think one of the difficulties is the difference in Travellers' perceptions of fairness. It's difficult because by the time a Traveller boy is 12 he is thinking of himself as a man and speaking on equal terms with adults and this is not acceptable [to teachers]. It's just so difficult to match the registers.
>
> (L: Traveller support)

Several teachers like the one above commented on the sense of fairness expressed by Gypsy Traveller children and suggested that this sometimes got them into trouble at school.

> The boy that was with us lasted till about the end of third year then he just couldn't cope any more. It was very frustrating for us because he was quite a bright boy and what we could offer him in his support class did not give him the breadth and balance, it did not give him what he needed. Now for him to conform in a mainstream situation was very difficult for him, he was bright, he was cheeky, he had to be disciplined. He had a real sense of justice if he thought something was wrong. He had his own values if he thought somebody was being unfairly treated. His language, if he did get annoyed he found that very difficult to control and of course in certain situations it doesn't always work.
>
> (C: special education teacher)

Difficulties associated with transition to secondary school

Lack of knowledge of school and classroom routines is also mentioned in relation to the transition from primary to secondary school when

Gypsy Traveller pupils may arrive late and miss the introduction and induction phase. Attendance becomes much more sporadic and tails off completely for many Gypsy Traveller pupils (SCF 1996). Peer group relationships and bullying may also become more problematic.

> It's like going from P7 to secondary, October is too late to try and fit into S1.
>
> (F: Traveller support)

> Once the boys reached the age of 12, 13 they didn't want to come to school, they were disruptive, they couldn't be put in a class with other children, they just completely disrupted the place and we found that a tremendous problem.
>
> (G: PT guidance, secondary)

Another issue identified at the secondary school level was refusal to participate in particular subjects, for example PE. Several teachers argued that some secondary subjects were seen as irrelevant for Gypsy Traveller pupils. As for other pupils it may also be the case that sometimes a particular subject may be liked because of the teacher who teaches it:

> He liked science because he got on well with the science teacher and the science teacher really talked to him and they really got on well.
>
> (C: special education teacher)

Discipline at secondary level becomes more complex as subject teachers vary in their approach:

> Some secondary teachers are very free and easy about things like chewing gum and what the noise level is … and that's accepted that within a secondary school there are variations.
>
> (J: Traveller support)

Difficulties deriving from travelling life and being on a site

Traveller support staff felt that school colleagues had little understanding of the impact of life on a site, rather than in a house or of the culture and customs of travellers living in a trailer.

One of the things I feel about issues around behaviour is, for example, within a school, teachers don't understand the perspective of Traveller life and how the child's behaviour can change totally when they start getting ready to leave. There are other examples like a funeral or something major going on at the site, just like children in houses where they have something going on with their family but Travellers have more incidents like that and it comes through more in their behaviour.

(A: Traveller support)

Difficulties associated with local neighbourhood poverty, and delinquent subcultures

Several teachers mentioned that both housed and nomadic Gypsy Traveller families often live or stay temporarily in areas of multiple deprivation. Changing patterns of employment may make it difficult for Gypsy Travellers to obtain work and some were seen by schools to be living in circumstances of great economic disadvantage. A few teachers, especially where there were locally housed Gypsy Traveller families, talked about the problems for the school and for the families where Gypsy Traveller young people had become involved in the local delinquent subculture, for example, in one case with drug dealing. Some Gypsy Traveller parents also referred to this and, for some, their fears of their children getting into this kind of trouble were an argument against participation in secondary education.

Gender issues

Most of the teachers' views differentiated between boys and girls. As has been found elsewhere, boys were more likely to be in trouble in school, to be seen as aggressive and more confrontational (Crozier and Anstiss 1995; Lloyd 1992). Girls were more likely to be seen as accommodating to the school norms.

It's hard to say but our experience would be the girls integrated better. I can think of several girls, P's sister for example, who came into school and had friends and went through school and she was – you'd never know she was a Travelling person, you never associated her with P. She fitted in perfectly well, had friends, came to school.

(D: guidance T, secondary, male)

When girls were difficult they were regarded as particularly problematic, especially when they were involved in violence.

Exclusion

Although formal disciplinary exclusion did happen to Gypsy Traveller pupils, it seemed often more likely that conflict with teachers led to non-attendance. Where pupils were excluded there were issues around the formal procedures, for example, where the procedure was to write formally to parents inviting them to attend a meeting before their child would be readmitted, it was often the case that this meeting never happened. Some Gypsy Traveller parents may not be able to read such communications. Often, however, the pupil may be removed from the roll by their parents after a problem before reaching the stage of exclusion.

Some teachers suggested that Traveller pupils may have consciously or unconsciously behaved in a disruptive way leading to exclusion from school as a strategy to avoid attending school.

> ... he was finally excluded for urinating in a bowl up at home economics and making it very obvious that he done this and so on and so forth. Whether he was deliberately trying to get himself excluded, or he was making a statement, I'm not a hundred per cent certain, but he was not a pleasant lad to have within the building.
>
> (N: AHT, secondary)

One support teacher saw the continual exclusion of a boy from school in the context of what was being done by neighbours to his family.

> One of the wee boys I'm working with just now is in a situation where the family have been forced from the housing scheme they were in because of discrimination. His behaviour has always been a problem and he's been excluded.
>
> (P: Traveller support)

Another saw the exclusion having a negative impact on a pupil.

> In one particular case, I think this boy changed remarkably after he was excluded. I think he saw it as unjust. He's in secondary school and he became very withdrawn and quite hostile. He's been in a lot of confrontations with teachers since then although he hasn't actually been excluded ... He's now stopped attending and we feel it stemmed from the exclusion and his perception of a strong sense of injustice ...
> I think that he felt he was in the right to fight back.
>
> (N: Traveller support)

Although most of the excluded pupils mentioned were boys there was evidence of the exclusion of a few girls. Where there was exclusion it tended to be for reasons similar to those found in other research on exclusion, i.e. violence between pupils or general disruptiveness (Cullen *et al.* 1996; Lloyd 1999).

Lack of confidence by teachers

Several teachers and Traveller support teachers suggested that sometimes a lack of confidence on the part of colleagues may lead to difficulties in class.

> I think a lot of it just depends on how secure the teacher feels. And if they feel that they're in a class where they're on the borderline of being in control of that class, then anything like that is going to increase the level of insecurity and they're going to feel threatened, so they're going to see it as a behavioural issue. Whereas the teacher who feels perfectly confident in their relationship with the other children in the class, isn't going to feel threatened by that and it isn't an issue.
>
> (D: Traveller support)

Teachers and schools may be afraid of the impact on the class or the school of the presence of Gypsy Traveller pupils:

> ... there was a family who were known in the area, who had been made homeless and were living outside the area but because they had just lost their dad; there were nine children, it was two who were secondary age and the dad had been killed in a terrible road accident, just months before, and had been made homeless at the same time and they were living in temporary homeless accommodation and the mother thought for stability's sake the best thing to do was to get back to the school ... the school said no way are we letting these two in. It would undermine the entire school and the school formally believed this.
>
> (H: Traveller support)

The school eventually agreed a compromise arrangement of part-time attendance:

> ... they got a part-time learning support teacher just for them and they were not allowed to do anything without that teacher being with them, they weren't allowed to go the toilet, they were kept in and couldn't have lunch with the other kids.
>
> (H: Traveller support)

Even when teachers are positive and supportive they may sometimes feel insecure about how to approach Traveller children. One Traveller support teacher described her first meeting with a group of Gypsy Traveller pupils and feeling that her college teacher training had not prepared her for this.

> ... they were put in a little room on their own and told that a teacher was going to come and be working with them ... I tried saying to them 'What would you like to do?' and I was trying to be really positive about it and all I got was 'No way am I going to talk to you, we don't need another teacher, we've had enough of people like you coming in, we liked our last teacher, what are you doing here?' It was so negative from them ... in fact after a few months it was good but I did feel threatened. I felt like any minute one of them was going to throw a chair at me.
>
> (J: Traveller support)

Discussion

[...] Although the behaviour of Gypsy Traveller pupils may be perceived as a problem, often this is understood as the 'fallout' from repeated and sustained absences. The reasons for many such absences may be from self-exclusion or exclusion as the result of racist name-calling, or because of regular absences due to travelling. It was clear that some teachers did see some Gypsy Traveller children having behaviour difficulties but many also emphasised that other children from the Gypsy Traveller community showed good behaviour and furthermore that most of the school's behaviour problems were created by other kids from the settled community.

The findings did, therefore, confirm our initial understanding that the school behaviour of some Gypsy Traveller pupils was seen as problematic by school staff. Some of the teachers who were interviewed made sense of it by contextualising it within an understanding of the culture of Gypsy Travellers. Other teachers either did not have much knowledge of Gypsy Travellers' lives or, like the rest of the community, had partial, stereotyped or even prejudiced views. Equally a lack of knowledge, or indeed a rejection, by Gypsy Traveller pupils of the norms and values of schools was seen by staff as underpinning their actions. Staff in schools rarely reflected critically on the culture or organisation of their schools, tending, as we argued earlier, to see problems in individual terms. Traveller support staff were more aware of the interaction between the child and their culture and the norms and values of schooling.

There was a great deal of evidence from our interviews of individual teachers and schools taking action to facilitate the education of their Traveller pupils. There were several different strategies and responses discussed that accepted some of the practicalities of nomadism and worked with these, rather than against them, with variable success. Other responses may have exacerbated the social and peer group problems that may be associated with nomadism, for example when Gypsy Traveller pupils were segregated in school from other pupils.

In most schools there was a lack of awareness of the extent of name-calling or a reluctance to see it as an issue and, therefore, little attention was paid to addressing it as a school problem (Troyna and Hatcher 1992). From interviews with Gypsy Traveller parents and children it seems that much of what the school sees as indiscipline in the form of violence may be in response to name-calling – several pupils talked of the importance of fighting back when there was name-calling in the playground. Some schools are failing to make the connection between discrimination in the wider community and what happens in schools. When some teachers perceive an inappropriate or excessive concern with their rights by Gypsy Traveller pupils they may not understand that their lives may be characterised by a struggle to achieve what are seen as basic rights and that a strong response to injustice reflects a life where injustice is experienced as routine.

Kenny (1997) argues that 'Travellers do not claim to be completely different, they simply refuse to be measured by the norms of the sedentary' (p.25). Traveller support staff who were interviewed had made an effort to make sense of this to the teachers in the primary and secondary schools and attempted to mediate between the Gypsy Traveller families and the schools. For many teachers there appears to be some confusion/tension between their understandings of some behaviour as possibly culturally defined and their desire not to discriminate against their Traveller pupils. This often results in statements which deny difference and stress the particularity of the situation, which itself may lead to failure of the school to respond to the particular situation of some Traveller children, where an understanding of their cultural background and experiences could lead to a more empathetic response by the school. Sometimes an assertion that 'they are no different' or 'they are never treated differently from anyone else' may suggest a lack of recognition of the issue of difference. [...]

Although the number of Gypsy Traveller pupils in Scottish schools is not large, a discussion of teachers' views does raise some important issues about the ability of schools to respond to children who challenge the 'normality' of school attendance and behaviour. (Other children also do this, for example others with intermittent attendance such as children with chronic illness, and truants.) Gypsy Traveller pupils may challenge the fundamental and often unspoken bottom line of schooling which is that you come every day and do as you are told. There have always been groups of children who challenge these rules and schools vary considerably in their ability to include them. As Slee (1996) argues, the search for equity is itself a challenge to the structure and culture of schooling. By seeing these issues in individual terms, by not recognising difference, schools may continue merely to focus on behaviour, rather than explore the institutional response of the education system to a marginalised community.

References

Cohen, L. and Manion, L. (1994) *Research Methods in Education*. (4th edn) London: Routledge.

Crozier, J. and Anstiss, J. (1995) Out of the spotlight: girls' experience of disruption. In Lloyd-Smith, M. and Dwyfor Davies, J. (eds) *On the Margins. The Educational Experience of Problem Pupils*. Stoke-on-Trent: Trentham.

Cullen, M. A., Johnstone, M., Lloyd, G. and Munn, P. (1996) *Exclusion from School and Alternatives*. Three reports to the Scottish Office. Edinburgh: Moray House.

Jordan, E. (1996) *Education for Travellers: towards a pedagogy for the protection of diversity*. Paper presented at ATEE Annual Conference, Oslo.

Kenny, M. (1997) *The Routes of Resistance: Travellers and Second Level Schooling*. Aldershot: Ashgate.

Lloyd, G. (1992) Lassies of Leith talk about bother. In Booth, T., Swann, W., Masterton, M. and Potts, P. (eds) *Curricula for Diversity in Education*. London: Routledge.

Lloyd, G. (1999) Excluded girls. In Salisbury, J. and Riddell, S. (eds) *Gender and Policy and Educational Change: shifting agendas in the UK and Europe*. London: Routledge.

Lloyd, G., Stead, J. and Jordan, E., with Norris, C. and Miller, M. (1999) *Travellers at School: the experience of parents, pupils and teachers*. Edinburgh: Moray House.

Munn, P., Johnstone, M. and Sharp, S. (1998) Is indiscipline getting worse? Scottish teachers' perceptions of indiscipline in 1990 and 1996. *Scottish Educational Review*, **30**(2),157–172.

SCF (1996) *The Right to Roam: Travellers in Scotland*. Dunfermline: Save the Children Fund.

Slee, R. (1996) Disabilities, class and poverty: school structures and policing identities. In Christiansen, C. and Rizvi, F. (eds) *Disability and the Dilemmas of Education and Justice*. Milton Keynes: Open University Press.

Troyna, B. and Hatcher, R. (1992) *Racism in Children's Lives: a study of mainly white primary schools*. London: Routledge.

Appendix

Schedules used in interviews

These schedules were used flexibly as a topic guide.

School staff

Explain what the research is about. Confidential, no one outside the research team will have access to the data, and no schools or individuals will be named in the report.

- How many Travellers attend the school?
  Number in your class?
  Breakdown of number of girls/boys.
  How often do they attend?
  What time of year?

- How do you find having Travellers in your class?

- Are there any particular issues which arise when Travellers are in class?
  Are there any particular difficulties?
  Any difficulties experienced with classroom behaviour?
  Difficulties associated with learning difficulties?
  Could you tell us about peer group relationships?

- Are there any Traveller pupils whom you would describe as having behavioural difficulties?
  Could you tell us about that?
  What do you feel are the main difficulties?
  Are there any key differences between Traveller pupils who display difficult behaviour and those who do not?
  Differences between Traveller pupils and other pupils in this respect?

- Why do you think there are/were these problems?
  Intermittent nature of attendance?
  Because of differences in culture?
  Curriculum does not meet Traveller pupils' needs?
  Traveller pupils' difficult behaviour is different from that of their non-Traveller peers? Tell us about parent–school communication.

- Has anything been done to address difficult behaviour by these pupils?
  What are the strategies used in class to address such behaviour?
  Same as for other pupils?
  Other in-school support?
  Out of school support?
  Have any Traveller pupils been excluded? How many?
  If so, for what reasons?
  What was the outcome?
  Do you feel any strategies employed have been effective?

- Thinking about the curriculum, do you think it addresses the educational needs of this group of pupils?
  What are the particular difficulties for this group of children in accessing the curriculum?
  If they cannot read or write, what do you do about that?
  Do you feel the curriculum is relevant for this group?
  Do the learning styles of Traveller children match those of non-Traveller children?

- Thinking about the classroom behaviour of both male and female Traveller pupils, do you feel there are any differences in the behaviour of girls and boys?
  Do they reflect those in the non-Traveller population?
  If not, what are the differences?

- What about bullying/name-calling – is this an issue for Traveller pupils? How do you respond to it?

- Where do you get your support from?

Traveller children/young people

Introduction – the research we're doing is about how young Travellers feel about school and how they get on at school. None of what you say will go back to the school, it's entirely confidential.

- How many schools did you attend?

- Do your school friends/teachers know you are a Traveller?
  Do you like people to know?

- Did you go to school all the time or were you travelling during school time at some points?
  How was it going into school, when the other pupils had been there all the time?

- Did you like going to school?
  What did you like about it?
  What subjects did you like?

- Was there anything you didn't like about school?
  What kind of things?

- What were the teachers like?
  What did you like/dislike about them?

- Did you get on with the other pupils who were in your class?

- Was there ever any name-calling?
  If so, what happened?
  What did you do?
  What did the teachers do?

- Did you ever get into any trouble? If so, how did you feel about that?
  What did the teachers do?
  How did you react?

- What age did you leave school?
  Did you ever think about staying on?

- Looking ahead, what kind of school would you like for your children?

- Is there anything else about your experience of school that we haven't covered in the questions that you would like to tell us?

Thank you for answering our questions.

This chapter shows that a good test of a school's inclusivity is its ability to respond to diversity, even when this challenges established notions of appropriate school behaviour. Pupils from Traveller families will not necessarily conform to traditional ideas about participating in school, but they should no longer be characterised as on the margins of school life. A whole school approach is required, which is developed from greater understanding of Gypsy and Traveller life, together with a commitment to adapt expectations and teaching practices. As a starting point the issues need to move on from being considered on individual terms. Staff need to reflect on how the culture and organisation of schools create barriers to include young people from every aspect of the community.

Chapter 15

Peer support for young people with same-sex attraction

*Colm Crowley, Susan Hallam,
Rom Harre and Ingrid Lunt*

This chapter discusses the lack of support available to lesbian, gay and bisexual young people facing challenges and hostility at school and in their personal lives. We are offered insights from the participants of a peer support project in the north of England about the pressures they face and the impact this has on their learning. The young people express their views on their school experience and also reflect on what personal and educational support has been useful for them.

Introduction

In this chapter we set out the views and experiences of four 15- to 16–year-old teenagers (one female, three male) with same-sex sexuality on two related matters of critical importance to them: how they became sidelined and harassed at school to the extent that their studies were disrupted, and their experiences of attending a unique study club for young lesbian, gay and bisexual (LGB) people as a response. [...]

With the assistance of the Young Lesbian Gay and Bisexual Peer Support Project (PSP) in central Manchester, launched two years before (1996), we were able to begin our inquiry with a teenage LGB population concerned about their education, the trained teachers who volunteer to tutor them at the project, and the project's paid youth workers and professional advisers. Young people training and volunteering as peer supporters (some of whom had a role in initiating the project, giving it its peer-led hallmark) also took part in the investigation. [...]

Background

[...] Coyle (1998) concludes that, although many young lesbian and gay people succeed in resourcefully creating a workable and satisfying sexual identity, nevertheless the formation and negotiation of a lesbian or gay identity poses considerable difficulties for young people in the face of generally negative social attitudes. It seems to us then, that the numerous LGB youth groups in today's Britain provide useful opportunities for young people wanting to 'be themselves' among equals. They provide an experience that contrasts with their typical experience of lack of acknowledgement of their sexual orientation by the school system, combined with negative attitudes and even harassment from their heterosexual peers and society in general.

[...] One of the aims of the PSP Study Club is 'to provide a *safe space* [our emphasis] for young LGBs to work together, do their homework and get help with their coursework and other study' (Hierons 1998: 5) by way of response to any immediate special educational needs arising for students whose schoolwork is suffering from bullying. This curriculum-based part of the programme, the study support provision delivered by a pool of 20 qualified teachers who had undergone the usual reference and police check procedures for volunteers working with young people, was designed to be complemented by a peer-led workshop-based element dealing with personal and social education with a specific emphasis on LGB issues. This dual emphasis on support with academic achievement and personal development for those young LGBs who sought it, delivered in what Winnicott (1965) might well have agreed is 'a facilitating environment', combined to make the Study Club, the first project of the PSP to be launched, in our view a particularly interesting setting in which to begin our investigation.

Methods

[...] The approach chosen for this study was one that allowed us to access people's personal meanings. Personal accounts of individuals' experiences in narrative form are therefore the primary sources of data, rather than questionnaire or pre-structured interview formats.

The participants in this phase of the ongoing study were ten young people with same-sex sexuality and 16 professionals (youth workers and teachers) involved in the Peer Support Project. Four of these young people had used the study support provision, and it is their narratives that form the central focus of this paper. The six other young people were involved in peer support. Of the professionals, ten were teacher volunteers, four were paid project workers and two were advisers to the project. All participants were recruited on the basis of their availability at times when the researcher could visit.

They were approached in advance by the PSP organisers, and asked if they wished to take part voluntarily in the research interviews, which were held at the PSP premises. Anonymity (primarily by changing names) and confidentiality were assured; some of the participants nonetheless wished to be identified by their own names. [...]

Findings

[...] PSP's first provision was a twice-monthly Study Club for teenage students whose schoolwork was suffering because of homonegative harassment. Volunteers who were qualified teachers delivered the first academic hour, to be followed by a peer-led hour featuring issues of particular importance to young LGBs, which are almost invariably missing at school.

When as the main investigator I (CC) began my series of visits to the PSP (autumn 1998) the Study Club was nearing the end of its first year of active provision. But by then, with some 20 keen teacher volunteers available, no students were coming. As this continued throughout the six months of my visits, it was not possible to observe study support in action. Ten young LGEs had used the Study Club prior to this. It was possible to contact half of them again; all readily agreed to come along to talk to me, however one later cancelled due to taking up weekend work, so four were interviewed. In addition, ten of the teachers, six peer supporters, all four core staff members and some steering group members were interviewed. [...]

It is the stories of serious difficulties at school, how they led these particular four young people to attend this unique Study Club for LGBs and their reflections on the part it played in their lives that we set out here. We believe that, although the numbers involved are small, it is nevertheless important to present some examples of how the life world of these young respondents seems to them, particularly so, we feel, at the present time, when young LGBs have been the topic of so much public debate by older generations, a discourse in which their own voices have been significantly missing. Furthermore, while the numbers using this study support initiative have been less than was expected, it constitutes, in our view, a valuable instance of an attempt to respond to special educational needs that otherwise tend to be ignored. The Study Club's existence has provided an opportunity to consider the trajectory of young people aware of the implications of the disruption to their learning, moving from a position of isolation into a supportive setting with the aim of remedying the situation. Extracts from the interview narratives of Violet, Mark, Daniel (all 16) and Dave (15)[1] are therefore presented to illustrate two principal themes of concern to them: the pressure and hassles at school that disrupted their studies; and what the Study Club offered them as a response.

Pressure and hassles at school that disrupted studies

Mark outlines the particular challenges that young gay people have to contend with at school, certainly those who have not somehow remained 'invisible' to their peers:

> There's a lot of pressure and hassle for young gay students because, even if they're not out, teenagers tend to have this sixth sense to spot lesbians and gay men. They just home in on them and take the piss. So you tend to get a lot of hassle and a lot of disruption in lessons.

Violet tells how pivotal the issue of homosexuality is among groups of boys, and identifies the third year of secondary school (Year 9, at age 13–14) as being of particular note:

> The main insult is 'gay' – well two lads, if one touches another he goes 'oh you're gay, you're gay', and this lad'll get beaten up just for like putting his hand on his mate's arm, you know. It's so intense and it still is with some of the gangs at school. My friends have said to me 'when you're in the third year in school', which is when I got the most hassle, 'the biggest crime is to be gay'. Definitely never be a third year at high school. It's that age when they maybe first discover what homosexuality really is.

Dave is tall and played rugby at school. He says: 'I started getting camp since I was about 11.' He has had much hassle in the four years since then, and has felt quite isolated. This has been in spite of the relaxed attitude he feels most of his immediate year group (the girls in particular) have about him being gay. Although he was beaten up once, Dave attributes this not so much to being thought to be gay, but rather to being on his own 'in the wrong place at the wrong time'. However, he reflects that, were he not socially isolated from other boys at school because of his sexuality, he would have the backing of a group of them as friends, functioning as a protective deterrent. Not having this calls for continual vigilance, particularly outside of school. He refers to the 'constant fear' of attack when walking home on his own. As to overt negativity about his (perceived) sexuality, he explains about the sort of direct hassle he regularly receives:

> All the grief I get is sexually oriented so it's all about anal sex and stuff like that, it's like 'Oh, you've been bummed'. I'm like 'Why do you want to know?' They're all like that. Whenever I walk down the corridor they all pin themselves down the wall. [...] It's some sort of weird mind thing, boys haven't got open minds at all, the girls have.

Violet also takes the view that boys tend to be more prejudiced about sexual orientation. But she found she got more negative reaction from the girls at school.

> You generally find that the boys are a lot more homophobic than the girls, but I got my main hassle from girls. Because I'd have to go in the toilets, and when I'd go in the changing rooms I'd see everyone sort of go 'aargh' and cover themselves up. It's just pathetic the way they deal with it.

The situation for her appears to have been aggravated by her older sister having 'come out' as lesbian at school before leaving:

> I'd have gangs following me and there was a lot of name calling, all sort of 'lesbian', 'leb', stuff relating to being a gay girl, nothing else like 'bitch' or 'cow' or 'slut', it was all related to me being gay. There were lots of stories going round like, 'she was staring at me in the changing rooms the other day'. Because my sister's gay as well they made up this whole story about both my parents being gay, which they're not, and how we're like a big sort of cult, a gay household. People would say things to me like 'oh, so your sister's a lesbian, has she not been like, doing stuff to you, like, abusing you?' so it was a very, very difficult thing to work round. I wasn't actually out, I wasn't particularly out. It was because I had short hair, didn't wear high heels, didn't spend time doing what average 16-year-old girls do. I was going out with a girl, who I changed the name of to the nearest male name, saying 'I'm going out with this boy from ...' and because they never saw this boy or any photos, they sort of picked it up from that.

Daniel also points to his third year as being of particular significance for him, although he emphasises his growing discomfort in the prevailing majority culture rather than a sense of victimisation. Nevertheless, the impact on his education was dramatic:

> I knew I was gay when I was eight but I didn't really understand what was going on. It was when I was about 11 or 12 that I realised [...] what it all meant and everything. I was alright until I hit third year, that's when everything like was coming clear to me – from that day on I started missing school, going in late, missing lessons.

He tried a strategy of openness but also considered pulling out of school:

> I was thinking about coming out in school or leaving school. I wasn't happy because I couldn't be myself. I thought I was putting on an act. I told all my friends and they were OK about it but I'm sure people knew I was gay because I was becoming more camp and I was actually sticking up for gay people because they'd call them queers and everything and as soon as the word gay came up it was AIDS and HIV and it was just about anal sex and I'd correct them on it and they'd all look at me as if to say like, I was gay. If they were having a go at me I'd be bitchy and answer them back. All the people who were supposed to be really hard, they'd say something and I'd just answer back to them. And they were OK about it. I was expecting them to kind of, like beat the crap out of me every time I said something, but they didn't.

A continuing preoccupation with his position as an anomaly in relation to groups of other boys at school appears to have been Daniel's principal pressure. He was comfortable with his immediate circle of friends (girls), had come out to them and found acceptance. The process of unequivocally coming out to all was not, however, straightforward, and declaring his sexuality to his head of year does not appear to have elicited any significant assistance with his dilemma. The unresolved situation appears to have weighed heavily on Daniel, judging by the eventual outcome:

> A couple of times I did almost come out. One time I was close but somebody just put me off in the conversation, so I didn't come out. I told the head of year and I think he told the teachers I was having lessons with. It ended up where I actually left school. I wasn't doing good in my subjects because I, like, didn't go into school at all.

Mark tells of his trajectory from being popular and included to being progressively sidelined:

> I used to play football and I used to have a big group of friends [...] and then I started sort of being shunted – when the abuse started – like pushed to one side. [...] I didn't start acting, I don't think, any more effeminate.

A teacher's collusion in his marginalisation appears to have been the catalyst for a marked escalation in this process. Mark believes that her comment to the class about him, after sending him out for forgetting some books, sealed his fate as the target of a constant
barrage of abusive taunts:

> I've had about ten separate people on different occasions tell me [that] the teacher said to the rest of the class 'That boy needs a good kick up his butt to get himself in gear and I know that's not the only thing he gets up his butt' and it's at that point that the bullying really started.

Apart from one frightening situation where he narrowly escaped from a group threatening him with a hot iron, the sort of hassle Mark received did not involve physical violence. It does not appear to have been any less traumatic for him however:

> You have these images of someone walking across the playground and getting beaten to a pulp, but that wasn't the sort of abuse I got. It was emotional and mental abuse that I got and I don't know which is worse.

Mark's coping strategy was to try to shut it all out, but he found the constant effort of this draining:

> You tend to switch off as soon as you walk into school, because you know that if you didn't you'd end up an emotional wreck. Switching off for so long makes you very drained. I used to sleep in the car on the way home and then I used to sleep on the couch and my mum used to wake me up to have my tea and then I used to go upstairs and go to sleep and then wake up, get back in the car spend the day at school come back and sleep and that was it. I used to spend say 12 or 13 hours a day asleep. It was a lot of strain I think. [...] Yeh [I was] very depressed. I mean, I got panic attacks after, when I finally got out of the school environment.

It was not until he actually left school to transfer to a college that the seriousness of the situation fully sank in, Mark reflects.

Learning disrupted

All four Study Club users interviewed reported major disruption to their education as a result of the hassles they had at school. Mark explains the effect that having to switch off emotionally can have on learning:

> I sat in science once and the teacher left the room for a couple of minutes so it was 30 unsupervised children and I started getting a load of abuse from the sort of lads that sit on the back rows. I ignored them and totally switched off and went into my own little world and didn't come out of it again till 3.30 when the bell rang. So everything that anybody actually said to me that day went in one ear and came out the other, and no work got done and nothing sunk in. There were days that I know Violet has had like that, and my friend Daniel's had like that where you just switch off totally and you don't learn anything, at which point you flunk your exams.

When things got bad for Mark he started forging notes from his parents and was absent for 40 per cent of that half term. It was not until Mark had missed about three consecutive weeks that the school contacted his parents he says. When he explained to his mother what had been going on she praised him for attending as much as he had, and went with him to talk to his head of year. Mark recalls some reluctance on the school's part to involve the educational welfare officer (EWO), and when Mark suggested a strategy of directly coming out to his peers, his head of year stressed that there were pros and cons and that the decision must be his own. Mark did so at the beginning of the following term, but instead of taking the steam out of the situation, as he hoped, he explains:

> That [didn't] work because it just grew into a much bigger thing. [...] It got worse.

He missed 50 per cent of that half term, and finds it amazing how much absence it took before the school contacted his parents, given the events of the previous term. This time his mother took matters further and phoned Mark's head of year requesting a meeting with him and the EWO to resolve things. Mark recalls how much stress that both of his parents, too, had been under throughout this time:

> It was very emotional for both me and my Mum – my Mum was in tears and I was in tears at this meeting.

The EWO immediately agreed a transfer. Aged 15, with much valuable lesson time lost and with only six months to go before his GCSEs, Mark was now faced with moving to a college. Although he does not talk of missing school in the way Mark did, Dave too experienced disruption of his work in class by the constant name-calling and taunting, and could not make the progress he wanted:

> I was having a load of problems from people in the class just disrupting me all the time [...] just normal things like calling me names – queer and all this lot.

Violet talks of her preoccupation with the bullying preventing her from getting on with learning:

> I wasn't learning anything in school because I was too preoccupied with being bullied. I actually left school through the hassle and didn't do any kind of work. I stayed at home for two weeks.

And while Daniel experienced less dramatic hassle from his peers and had a teacher he could confide in, he was not happy at school because he could not, as he put it, be himself. He too missed a lot of school and finally stopped going altogether. Just as Mark's mother had done, Daniel's mother too asked for him to be transferred to a college before his GCSE exams. However, Daniel concludes that reluctance on his school's part to relinquish their funding for him (a consideration to which Mark also attributes his school's 'refusal' to involve the EWO until his mother later did so herself) accounted for procedural hold-ups. The delay resulted in it being 'too late to get transferred' until the following academic year. There ensued for Daniel 'just over a year of not doing any homework, or anything' until he could finally start at college. Daniel and Mark both described their parents as being supportive about their sexuality throughout their tangles with the world of education and indeed this was so with all four respondents. When Violet's situation worsened at school, her parents also attempted to intervene on her behalf. She remembers:

> I was staying at home and my parents were worried sick and kept ringing up the school saying 'Do something'.

However, Violet found the school's response ineffective:

> The deputy head rang up my Mum saying 'We've set up a support group … we've talked to the kids'. I went back to school and I was still getting all this hassle […] all that happened with this support group thing was just one lad said to me 'You alright?' and I was like 'Yeh, cheers'. Even if I'd said 'Oh no, I'm having loads of problems' […] he wouldn't have known what to do and so there was nothing. […] The teachers weren't really around. But it wasn't like me going out into the yard and getting beaten up, if it was something like that I would have reported it. Walking up the corridor and getting things shouted at you, or sitting in a classroom and getting things shouted at you, you can't really report that, you know. My Mum would say to me 'So what are the names of the kids who're doing it? ' and I'm like 'Well everyone's doing it' and she was like 'Well how can we stop it then? 'and I'm like 'The only way we can stop it is if you convince 700 school kids that being gay is OK'.

Violet's perception that it would take a whole school approach to make a difference seems to get to the heart of the matter. The respondents who had the most upheaval felt badly let down by their schools; for example, two commented that had the same hostility and harassment occurred for racial reasons their schools would have spared no effort in cracking down on the perpetrators. In only one case do they report that a teacher took the initiative in investigating what was going on and how they were coping. Typically, responses came only after a dramatic level of absence, or as a result of direct requests for help from the young people themselves or their parents. And rather than any of them receiving any information about or referral to the Study Club from their school or the education services, it appears to have been these young individuals' strong will to get on with their lives and not to let their academic futures be undermined that led each of them to make use of it.

What the Study Club offered

For Daniel, Mark and Violet, who had been regularly coming to the LGYM youth group for some time, coming to use the newly set up PSP Study Club in the same premises was an easy step. Daniel, for example, who had been brought by his mother to the youth group some years before, decided to attend after some talks with one of the youth workers there about the amount of school he'd been missing. Dave's experience was different. He made his own way to the Study Club after he saw an article about it in the first copy of *Gay Times* he bought in a newsagents when he was 14. But it was a friend of his, also gay, who actually first went along and checked it out after Dave told him about it, and he then gave Dave the confidence to go. Nevertheless, coming to the Study Club for the first time was a big step for Dave:

> I didn't know anybody. Even if there was just me, two teachers and Daniel, it might sound weird, but it was a bit scary because it was actually gay people there. [...] In my time I've not actually been ... the majority of people have been straight but [this was] solely for gay people. [...] I found out in *Gay Times* because if I need something I'll go and try and find it. It was a big step for me, it was something that made me feel good.

The Study Club had provided Dave with a good reason to move from the isolation he had been feeling into a larger world of other gay people. He did not need it once it had served as his stepping stone to the LGYM youth group that met later in the afternoon.

> It was even scarier because there was loads of gay people and [...] I'd never seen so many in my life. It was an added bonus to know I don't have to be scared any more of being proud that I'm gay, because there's all my friends here that, if I have any trouble, they'll support me. [...] I started going to the youth group every Tuesday and Saturday so it was giving me a lot more courage to rise above all the stuff that's been happening to me at school for the past four years. And then I've come out, and then I've not needed the study group since. Because basically people know that I'm gay. If it happens in the classroom, I'm normally sat round with my mates, and I'll just tell the person to shut up and like, 'I don't want to know about your sex life so you don't want to know about mine', and they'll actually stick up for me as well, they'll tell them to shut up and get on with the work. I can manage it now. I never used to be able to, because I was always the shy and intent person with no friends.

The Study Club providing a means of contact with gay peers, when young people might not be ready to go directly to the more social and boisterous setting of a youth group, was something that Paul, one of the volunteer teachers, remarked on too:

> The interesting point was he didn't come to do maths, he came along so he could make contact with the group. He did all the maths and I just sat there and said 'oh yes, that's right'. And I think there's an awful lot of that.

Having got to the point of wanting to come out at school, Dave was fortunate to have been offered practical support in responding to continuing hassles by one of his teachers who had noticed. He now feels that he can get the aid of the deputy head and this particular teacher should he need to, and he attributes this helpful response to their being relatively young. It was when she started to come to the LGYM youth group regularly that Violet began to get moral support regarding the trouble she was having at school. She decided to attend the Study Club as well, simply to keep up with her schoolwork while the hassles continued:

> I just came in to do my work, but I'm sure if I said 'can I talk about the problems I'm having at school?' they would have been perfectly happy to discuss it with me. I think it's very important to have a sympathetic teacher, or a gay one, if you prefer, but I didn't actually need that.

Nevertheless, Violet travelled to the PSP Study Club in preference to what was provided locally.

> There was a homework club in my school as well as an after school thing [but] I wouldn't have used it [...] because it's still in the area. It would have been the same teachers and things and I just wanted a whole different sort of atmosphere. That's what I needed and it worked.

Daniel too was not enthusiastic about going to study support elsewhere:

> I don't think I would. Because [with] the teachers who are gay, I could be myself, I could be camp or whatever. But if it was just a straight teacher I couldn't be myself. It's kind of comfortable being taught by somebody who is gay.

Daniel had been absent from school a lot and had not been doing well in his subjects. He came to the Study Club 'about two or three times and

then went into college [...] so I thought I don't need to go anymore'.
Although Daniel stopped attending, he continued to go to the youth
group where he kept up the new friendships he'd made at the Study Club.
Now 16, he had started work and was thinking of coming to the Study
Club again:

> Well, it has been a help. [...] I would like to give it a go because I don't
> want to just slack off on my education altogether, because I'm not going
> to stay in this job forever.

Violet enthuses about the curriculum-based support at the Study Club:

> You just turn up and there's lots of teachers and they say 'what do you
> want to do today?' and they'll just take you in a room and teach you.
> I did what I had the most difficulty with and that's maths and science.
> I learnt a lot'cos you tell them what you need to do, like what you're
> doing at school at the moment, or just anything you don't understand,
> I mean you can do anything. You can say 'I've got this massive piece of
> course work to do and I need help with it' and they'll help you, or you
> can say 'can you give me some revision tips?' and they'll do that. You
> could just even come to use the space, you know, and not even have a
> teacher help you. You can just come and revise or read, so it's a space to
> do your schoolwork and it's brilliant.

Although Mark and Violet were doing different subjects, they were both
coming up to their GCSE examinations at the time they attended the Study
Club. Mark recalls:

> [We] comforted each other because she was going through a lot of
> the hassles that I went through when I was in the same situation in
> high school. By this time I was in college, so I managed to get
> through them.

Mark transferred to college with just six months to go to his GCSE
exams and he wanted to make up for time lost at school by attending the
Study Club:

> It was all of them teachers here. They gave us a load of past exam papers
> to revise from and anything I was unsure of I had in a file – at high
> school I missed a lot [...] because of disruption in the lessons – and

I'd say 'look, this I'm unsure about' and he'd go through it with me.
[... It's a] bit of a success story because through the study group I got
four Bs and a C.

Yet, for the teachers who volunteered, it was typically their empathy with the
young LGBs' personal struggles that drew them to the project and made it all
worthwhile, as Ross explains:

> To a lad who was going through some chemistry work, towards the end
> of the session I said 'How do you cope with things at school?' and he
> was quite openly able to talk to me about his bullying experiences, how
> he found it very difficult and how he had to leave school for a while. And
> I hope that ... from someone who is a teacher ... although I didn't go
> through the bullying experience at school, I coped with it in a rather
> different way, yet I'm someone who is sympathetic and we can talk
> about it, and I think that's quite important.

Interestingly, the peer-led personal, social and health education (PSHE)
element that was intended to follow the first hour of academic work was not
talked about by any of the above respondents, by the teachers or by the peer
supporters interviewed. As three of the four respondents who had been
Study Club users were already attending the LGYM youth group (which
had a Saturday session in the same building beginning soon after the study
club) they were already well provided for in this respect, as PSHE work is
central to the ethos of this particular group. And Dave, the respondent who
came initially to the Study Club, appears to have moved, after only one
session, seamlessly into the LGYM group where he found the peer company
he needed. Staff believe that the remaining six Study Club users not
interviewed most likely followed a similar pattern in relation to the LGYM
youth group, although this could not be verified. In any case, the intended
work-shop approach to the peer support element would not have worked
well with typical attendance being in ones and twos, which might explain its
non-occurrence.

   The lack of a PSHE element does not appear to have been a deterrent to
the respondents; on the contrary, they seemed satisfied to focus on their
academic aims with the support of teachers who were sympathetic to their
sexuality and understanding of their predicament at school. Apart from
mutual support, when their attendance at the study club coincided, they
seemed content to pursue their social contact and explore their LGB
identities with their peers at the youth group.

Low uptake of the service and subsequent closure

In view of the consistently positive tone of the respondents' comments on what the Study Club offered, it was perplexing that there was no uptake of its services during the half-year period of my investigation. Prior to that, only ten teenagers had used it. Teachers' impressions overall were that they had been pleased with the service, but needed only short-term help. Once the Study Club's initial high profile in the national and local media had died down, publicity presented difficulties: budgets for advertising were minimal and it was doubted whether schools had ever displayed any of the material sent to them. What is particularly striking is the absence of any referrals from the most obvious sources, schools themselves and the education services in the area. Following an evaluation (Smith 1999), it was discontinued owing to the low attendance.

Key issues as revealed in respondents' narratives:

1   All respondents report persistent and intrusive verbal abuse, sufficiently daunting to affect decisively schoolwork in the classroom. Substantial disruption of attendance also resulted for three of the four.
2   All respondents also mentioned their failure to maintain the necessary homework schedules. They did not use homework to compensate for disrupted school hours. Our conclusion must be that the form of persecution they endured had a severe effect on morale.
3   The lack of support they have generally had in school from teachers also stands out. Even when support was forthcoming it appears that it was inadequate, particularly in the time it took for those charged with the task of providing support to react.
4   Little short of a whole school approach would appear to offer a thoroughgoing solution, and none of the schools involved appear to have had one.
5   Lacking an adequate institutional response, all respondents turned to their families. However, gaining their parents' support necessitated discussing their sexuality with them, in itself a major undertaking for most young teenagers. In the case of these respondents, they were fortunate to have particularly supportive families. Had they not felt able to risk telling them the root cause of their school-based problems they would have lacked this important support.
6   This study's findings prompt the speculation that there must be others in a similar school predicament who had perhaps received negative parental reactions, increasing the pressure they might be under. The self-selection of

these respondents as Study Club members, at least for a while, shows that they had retained some measure of academic ambition. A supplementary study of the lives of those who receive neither parental nor study support needs to be undertaken.

We are not taking a stance of being disinterested observers in relation to these issues. We take a human rights position in relation to sexual orientation. While harassment and discrimination abound, and cause psychosocial disadvantage, it should not be necessary to demonstrate that one is being disadvantaged in order to claim the basic human right to be allowed to get on with life unhindered as a human being (Ellis 1999). [...]

Warwick *et al.* (2000), referring to the UN Convention on the Rights of the Child, argue in addition that 'the right to express one's views and have them considered should apply to all young people regardless *inter alia* of poverty, class, race, gender or sexuality' (p. 132) – a sentiment that underpins the collaborative approach we have taken with our respondents in providing a platform in the academic literature for their voices. To this we would add that quite simply the right to be different is at the heart of the matter for these young people, and we strongly feel that this right should be recognised and supported by all professionals working with young people.

Note

1   The names of all Study Club users have been changed to maintain their anonymity, although they had all said they wanted their own names to be used.

References

Coyle, A. (1998) Developing lesbian and gay identity in adolescence. In J. Coleman and Roker, D. (eds) *Teenage sexuality: health, risk and education*. Amsterdam: Harwood Academic Press.

Ellis, S. J. (1999) Lesbian and gay issues are human rights issues: the need for a human rights approach to lesbian and gay psychology, *British Psychological Society Lesbian and Gay Psychology Section Newsletter*, 3, 9–14.

Hierons, D. (1998) *Young lesbian, gay and bisexual peer support project: project evaluation report*. Manchester: Young Lesbian, Gay and Bisexual Peer Support Project.

Smith, K. (1999) *Views and Opinions of Young Lesbians, Gays and Bisexuals on the Work of the Peer Support Project*. Manchester: Young Lesbian, Gay and Bisexual Peer Support Project.

Warwick, L., Oliver, C. and Aggleton, P. (2000) Sexuality and mental health promotion: lesbian and gay young people, in P. Aggleton, J. Hurry, and L. Warwick (eds) *Young People and Mental Health*, Chichester: Wiley.

Winnicott, D. W. (1965) *The maturational processes and the facilitating environment: studies in the theory of emotional development.* London: Hogarth.

The young people represented in this chapter did not feel included or valued within their schools, but they did gain positive experiences of being part of a community through peer and other support. Tackling homophobia is just as much a challenge for inclusive education as disability discrimination or racism. These young people's experiences at school highlight powerfully that this challenge can often be ignored until a crisis has occurred. An inclusive organisation needs to get to the 'heart of the matter' by developing a culture where the right to be different is recognised and supported.

Chapter 16

Exclusion

A silent protest

Janet Collins

This chapter challenges stereotypical views on truancy of young people. The author also considers how non-participation in the classroom whilst being physically present, contributes to pupils' social exclusion. Janet Collins' analysis provides a greater understanding of how maximising pupils' participation reduces their experiences of social exclusion in secondary schools.

Introduction

Elsewhere, issues of combating social exclusion are held to be synonymous with a reduction of truancy and exclusion from schools. In the UK, for example, New Labour have expressed a commitment to reducing the number of pupils truanting or excluded from our schools. The Social Exclusion Unit's (SEU) remit is to report to the Prime Minister on how to:

> make a step-change in the scale of truancy and exclusions from school, and to find better solutions for those who have been excluded.
>
> (SEU 1998: 1)

The aim was to reduce truancy by one-third by the year 2002 (SEU 1998: Annex A). As this chapter will illustrate however, the social exclusion of pupils goes way beyond simple measures of school attendance. Equally important are issues related to the motivation, engagement and active participation of pupils in school. Drawing on in-depth case studies (Collins 1994; 1996) this chapter demonstrates how attendance in school does not necessarily ensure social inclusion or a commitment to learning. In particular, it highlights the plight of children who may well be physically present in the classroom but who are unable or unwilling to participate in the learning opportunities provided there. Understanding the possible causes of this, often habitual, non-participation is an important first step towards increasing pupil participation and reducing social exclusion. Comparing the findings of research into truancy and my own work with non-participating pupils it would appear that both forms of behaviour might be influenced by similar 'individual', 'social' and 'in-school' factors. Consequently, insights gained in the study of one should help to shed light on the other. However, in-depth case studies of the kind presented in this chapter help to provide detailed analysis of the complex and interrelated factors which impact on individual pupils' behaviour. These challenge some of the sweeping and occasionally stereotypical views expressed in larger scale surveys of truancy and social exclusion.

The chapter begins with an account of the longitudinal research study on which it draws. It then identifies four non-participation or, to borrow a term from Young (1984), 'truanting in mind' behaviours. Following an exploration of the possible causes of habitual non-participation, i.e. 'individual', 'social' and 'in-school' factors, each section suggests strategies that may reduce incidence of non-participation in schools. Given that non-participation and truancy may have similar root causes, the implication is that these strategies may be effective in reducing social exclusion by combating both.

The original research began in an inner city primary school in which I had previously taught. The school had a large number of pupils who were identified as having serious emotional and behavioural difficulties. Invariably the attention of teachers and support staff was focused on those pupils who exhibited loud, aggressive behaviour and who posed a potential threat to the smooth running of the school. In this climate I felt there was a danger that the social, emotional and educational needs of the relatively quiet and undemanding pupils would go undetected and ignored. Ultimately, this research grew out of this concern and a growing frustration at my inability to communicate with, and therefore teach, a group of pupils who seemed unable or unwilling to participate in the learning activities in my classroom. These pupils were physically present in the classroom and their quiet, seemingly compliant behaviour did not present obvious problems in terms of discipline or classroom management. However, initial observations and one-to-one conversations revealed an acute lack of engagement in the learning process. These pupils appeared to be so intent on surviving in school without being noticed by teachers or peers that they paid little attention to what they should have been learning. In my opinion this coping strategy was every bit as detrimental to learning and social inclusion as physical absence or the more obvious signs of disaffection.

Beginning what was originally a three-year research project my aims were to understand the possible causes of the pupils' non-participatory behaviour and to design and implement teaching strategies that would empower the pupils to play a more active role in their education. The research focused on in-depth case studies of twelve pupils, ten girls and two boys, who were, at the beginning of the research, all in the same Year 6 class in primary school. Exhibiting quiet and non-participatory behaviour in class was the one criterion that united the group of selected pupils. In many other respects the pupils were extremely diverse. Ten of the twelve selected pupils were girls, which raised the issue of a possible link between non-participatory behaviour and gender. In terms of racial origins the group was mixed. Two pupils were of African-Caribbean origin, whilst one was of mixed race and another Asian. The case studies were constructed from observations while the pupils worked with their regular teacher during the last two years of primary school and the first year of secondary school. They also drew on a series of in-depth open-ended interviews with the pupils, their parents (or nominated significant others) and teachers. Each interview lasted between 30 minutes and an hour and was tape-recorded, transcribed and analysed following ethnographic principles.

During the first two years of the study I also worked directly with the pupils as part of an intervention programme. This chapter draws on the full range of data gathered during the study. All names have been changed.

During the three years of data collection, and despite the fact that the pupils transferred from one primary school to seven secondary schools, I was able to maintain contact with ten of the twelve pupils and their families. During that time 11 of the pupils had good attendance records and Charlene was the only pupil with a record of intermittent truancy. It is perhaps indicative of the relationship between Charlene's family and the school that I was unable to obtain an interview with members of her family. I finally lost contact with Charlene altogether during the second year of the research when Charlene and her family 'disappeared' from the area without leaving a forwarding address.

Truanting in mind

Absenteeism from school is a large and very visible problem. The official figures published by the SEU are likely to be alarming for parents and teachers alike. Moreover, there is growing evidence that the official figures are a gross underestimation of the real truancy levels. Surveys involving anonymous pupil questionnaires (for example, Gray and Jesson 1990; O'Keefe 1994) suggest that the incidence of both blanket truancy and post-registration truancy are much greater than was believed by the schools or than is reflected in official figures. Whilst there is some disagreement about the actual extent of the problem there does seem to be a general agreement that truancy levels are too high and that strategies which reduce truancy are to be welcomed. One can understand the attraction for governments in being seen: to measure truancy levels; to set targets for improvement; and to be able to measure improvement in a school's performance.

What remains significantly less visible is the plight of children and young people who, despite their attendance in school, remain as disaffected and uninterested in what school has to offer them as their absent and often more vocal peers. Indeed, the current emphasis on measuring and improving school attendance masks a serious underlying issue, namely pupils' disaffection with school and lack of engagement with the learning experiences which school offers. Getting pupils into school is only the first step towards solving the problem of truancy and social exclusion. There is also a need to ensure that all pupils are active participants in the social and academic life of the school. Whilst this remains an under-researched area there is some evidence that researchers and policy makers are increasingly aware of the problem. Speaking at the TES conference in 1997 David Blunkett talked about how youngsters who are dispirited about their chances of finding employment are likely to drift away from the education process.

> ... we all know that the 1 in 12 who get no qualifications at all, by the time they reach 16, are primarily, but not exclusively, those who have not been attending school. It is not merely a matter of actually being there, it is sometimes 'being there but not being there', if you know what I mean.
>
> (Blunkett 1997)

Blunkett and others recognise that school attendance does not necessarily equate with a commitment to learning. Pupils who are 'there but not there' do not actively participate in classroom activities and consequently run the risk of becoming socially excluded. They may be thought of as 'playing truant in mind whilst present in body, [seeing] neither the relevance nor the reason for all they are asked to do' (Young 1984: 12). Although they complete the minimum of work, they appear to have little interest or investment in the outcome. 'They conform, and even play the system, but many do not allow the knowledge presented to them to make any deep impact on their view of reality' (Barnes 1979: 17). Currently we have no evidence of the numbers of pupils who play truant in mind and without systematic research on a large scale the issue of 'truanting in mind' will effectively remain an invisible problem.

The fact that pupils who exhibit this behaviour may not present their teachers with acute attendance and discipline problems is likely to contribute to this invisibility.

In the context of this chapter 'playing truant in mind' describes situations in which a pupil is physically present in the classroom but who, for whatever reason, does not participate in the experience which has been planned and presented by the teacher. Identifying this kind of truancy can be difficult. Pupils can truant during any activity irrespective of whether it requires observable physical action or not. However, participation, or lack of it, is more easily observable in some situations than others. For example, pupils who are required to read silently could be actively engaged or they could simply be waiting for the lesson to be over. In a classroom of sighted children those who are looking in the right direction with their eyes open are more likely to be reading than those who are not. Admittedly the child who has his or her eyes closed might be thinking about the text but they might be thinking about completely unrelated matter. What is going on in the child's mind and the extent to which the pupil has indeed read and understood the texts can only be ascertained by talking to the child and/or by assessing their ability to complete a task that requires knowledge of the text.

Elsewhere (Collins 1996: 36–47) I identified four types of withdrawal or truanting in mind behaviour. I described these as 'being invisible', 'refusing to participate', 'hesitation' and 'an inappropriate focus'. Although all the children in the study exhibited these behaviours, here they are described in relation to observations of Justina. In many of the lessons I observed Justina would have no direct contact with the teacher. Often there was evidence to suggest that where she sat or how she behaved made her 'invisible' and minimised her contact with the teacher. Alternatively, she would be invited to participate but would 'refuse' to join in. Sometimes her refusal would be direct and possibly supported by a seemingly valid reason. On other occasions she would not acknowledge the request; she would remain still and quietly avoid making eye contact with the teacher. Whilst these behaviours were relatively easy to detect the remaining two presented more of a problem and required closer observation. In both of these situations Justina appeared to be busy, however, closer analysis revealed that she was not actively engaged in the task. When Justina 'hesitated' she appeared busy but she never really became engaged in the task and would remain on the periphery of an activity. Sometimes she actually seemed to be too afraid to join in.

In craft, for example, Justina spent significantly more time watching her partners working than she did actively engaged in the task. Similarly, during a practical lesson Justina walked round the science lab, touching some of the equipment with the tips of her fingers but rarely carrying out the intended experiment. On both occasions she seemed reluctant to 'get her hands dirty' by handling the equipment.

(Collins 1996: 43)

In both these cases it would appear that the teachers were expecting pupils to play a physical and active role in the lesson. They were expected to learn by doing. Having the experience of making a model or carrying out an experiment was deemed by the teacher to have educational value. In the case of the craft lesson Justina might have learned something from watching her peers. However, as Justina walked around the science lab on her own she never even observed someone else carry out an experiment. Consequently, it is difficult to know what science was being learned. The fact that the teacher did not comment on her behaviour might, however, have reinforced her non-participation.

The final, and to my mind the most disturbing, form of truanting in mind is where pupils have 'an inappropriate focus'. In these instances pupils are actively involved in an activity which has little or no bearing on the learning task presented by the teacher. During my observations of Justina this concerned me because in the majority of instances the teacher was either unaware of what she was doing or, worse, condoned the behaviour. The most dramatic example of an inappropriate focus occurred during a French oral lesson during which Justina did not speak a single word of French.

Her one interaction with the teacher was conducted in English and focused on a point of detail about the setting out of her work. He seemed oblivious to her lack of participation in the oral part of the lesson. When, out of sheer frustration, I asked Justina to read what she had just written she said, 'I don't speak French because it confuses me'.

(Collins 1996: 45)

Despite this refusal to speak the language Justina later described herself as being 'really pleased with myself in French. I've got really loads of ticks in my book and I am glad I know a lot about it now'. Her physical presence in the classroom and positive statements from the teacher reinforced her image of herself as a successful student. In one respect she was a model pupil. She did not cause the teacher any discipline problems. She handed her neatly completed work in on time. However, in other far more serious respects she was a failure, she had learned nothing of the spoken language. I believe this kind of behaviour may be more problematic than physical truancy. Justina's presence in the classroom did not ensure that she learned the language. However, her physical presence masked the fact that there was a serious problem.

Sadly, none of the teachers in the study appeared to notice or be alarmed by the pupils' lack of participation in curriculum activities. Moreover, even if individual teachers had noticed the truanting that went on in their lesson it would take time and energy to establish if this pattern was repeated in other lessons. I think it unlikely that teachers would easily be able to find the time or motivation to ask their colleagues about pupils like Justina who appear on the surface to be model pupils. Recognising that non-participation or truanting in mind is detrimental to learning is an important first step. Suggesting possible solutions requires an understanding of the possible causes of this behaviour.

Possible causes of truancy

As part of a two-year NFER funded project Kinder *et al.* (1995) identified a number of possible causes of disaffection and truancy. This and other truancy studies (for example, Gray and Jesson 1990; Graham and Bowling 1995; Balding 1996) raise issues very similar to those raised in my own work with quiet non-participatory pupils. Thus it would seem that the causes of disaffection are similar for pupils who fail to attend school and those who 'play truant in mind'.

Kinder *et al.* (1995) organise their analysis around the three main arenas constantly highlighted by research into truancy, i.e.: *individual pathological or personality traits*; *family circumstances* or values and/or social factors within the non-attender's communities; and *school factors*, often located in either the curriculum or the ethos and relationships encountered there by the pupils. This chapter takes each of these in turn and compares Kinder *et al.*'s findings with those of other researchers in the field of truancy and of my own research with pupils who truant in mind.

Individual pathological or personality traits

Kinder *et al.* (1995) report that where individual characteristics were cited, these were largely viewed in terms of some kind of deficit in emotional or social health, such as lack of self-esteem, lack of social skills, lack of confidence or poor peer relationships. I also identified these factors as potential causes of truanting in mind behaviour. However, I rejected the individual deficit model implied in Kinder *et al.*'s work. Following Oliver (1988)

I regarded these issues as being socially constructed and created. Thus, for example, whilst truanting in mind was associated with a lack of confidence, the extent to which a pupil feels confident varied considerably from situation to situation.

> Generally speaking quiet pupils are likely to be more talkative at home and with people that they know well …They tend to be shy when they are being watched by others and their shyness is particularly acute when they are asked to speak in front of the class or during assemblies.
>
> (Collins 1996: 20)

As pupils are more likely to feel confident and participate in situations in which they know people well this suggests that their confidence is socially created and constructed. Moreover, there is evidence to suggest that there is no simple causal relationship between lack of confidence and behaviour. Lacking confidence can inhibit pupils and prevent them participating. However, failure to participate can also reduce an individual's confidence.

> Anxiety about talking to relative strangers can contribute to poor self-esteem, especially when individuals compare themselves with more confident friends and relatives. Quiet individuals see an ability to converse easily as a skill to be envied and an inability to 'perform' in this way can make quiet pupils feel inadequate.
>
> (Collins 1996: 22)

The impact of non-participation is particularly acute in conversations with teachers. The discomfort of quiet pupils is often so visible that teachers become reluctant to ask them to participate in class discussions. This reinforces the pupil's truanting in mind behaviour. For example, Mandy was clearly anxious about being asked questions in class. In order to reduce her anxiety the teacher chose other more willing pupils. Thus rather than increasing Mandy's confidence and skill the teacher reduces her opportunities to practice skills which have an important educational value. Knowing that she is unlikely to be chosen to answer the teacher's questions might reduce Mandy's need to listen to the rest of the discussion. This could provide Mandy with even more opportunities to play truant in mind thus reinforcing her image of herself as an observer not a participant. I would suggest that a similar self-fulfilling prophecy is at work in the case of pupils who truant from school. Perhaps failure to attend school also reinforces pupils' negative image of themselves that makes it subsequently more difficult to attend school.

As with pupils who absent themselves from school, pupils who truant in mind also lack social skills and have difficulty in forming and sustaining relationships with their peers. Consequently, during the first year of the research I initiated a 12-week withdrawal programme of collaborative group work. The aim of the programme was to improve the pupils' social skills and confidence and to enable them to work collaboratively with their peers. I saw this as an important aspect of my work because:

> ... where pupils have difficulties in peer relationships which interfere with their learning, it is important not only to help them as individuals to develop their confidence and social skills, but also to work with the class as a whole in order to ensure that they do not become the subject of teasing, ridicule or rejection.
>
> (Beveridge 1993: 96)

The effects of the programme were encouraging and led to a development into whole class teaching the following year. Throughout these sessions all the pupils played an active role in all the activities. This subsequently led to a longer programme of work in a whole class context (for full details see Collins 1996; chapters 9 and 10).

Social factors

In terms of social factors, a profile of truants is developing. According to the research truants tend to be 'older pupils, and from poorer backgrounds' (SEU 1998, section 1.5). The parents of truants are more likely to be in low skilled than in professional or managerial jobs, and more likely to be in local authority housing than owner occupiers (Graham and Bowling 1995). In addition some studies (for example, Gray and Jesson 1990) suggest that truancy is more common in inner city areas. Given that all the children in the study lived in an area with a high level of unemployment and the majority lived in rented houses or maisonettes, this profile may be as applicable to pupils who play truant in mind as it is to those who physically absent themselves from school. However, as I found during my research, making assumptions about pupils based on where they live is over-simplistic. Angie's educated and articulate parents resented being perceived, and subsequently housed, as if they were working class by English housing authorities when they arrived in the country from the Caribbean.

Another common thread between the two forms of truanting is that, in both, significant domestic problems and inadequate parenting skills may be linked with disaffected behaviour in school. Drawing on post-Bowlby accounts of parenting (for example, Chodorow 1978; Benjamin 1990) I highlighted the possible connections between parent–child relationships and the truanting in mind behaviour witnessed in school. In essence, I argued that pupils who had experienced anxious attachments in their relationships with parents or caregivers might subsequently experience difficulties in forming relationships with teachers and pupils in school. I believe that difficult relationships in school are one of the underlying causes of truanting in mind behaviour. However, once again I believe the situation is far more complex than large-scale studies would suggest.

In a section on significant domestic problems Kinder *et al.* appear to perpetuate a view that one-parent families are, by definition, problematic. They quote, but do not challenge, the following assertion made by a respondent.

> A number of [disaffected] pupils bring huge social problems into school, they are mainly from one-parent families where carers have multiple social problems of their own, including debt, drug taking and unemployment.
>
> (Kinder *et al.* 1995: 10)

By comparison, in my research, I found no evidence to support the view that one-parent families were necessarily problematic. There were examples of good parent–child relationships within one-parent families and examples of anxious attachments within two-parent families. In addition, other researchers (for example, Collins 1991) have found no evidence to support a link between lone-parenting and delinquency. Based on this research I believe it is time to dispel rather than perpetuate the negative image of one-parent families. In particular teachers should examine the ways in which stereotypical views, which regard nuclear two-parent families as the 'norm', may exclude or marginalise fathers and lone-parents. A re-examination of the parenting role should also influence the ways in which parents are portrayed in school. It is important that textbooks and other teaching materials do not portray lone-parent families as a mutant form of the so-called 'normal' two-parent family. Similarly, teachers should be aware of how their own assumptions about parents and families could colour their expectations of the children they teach. A serious issue in the parenting debate around truancy is teachers' refusal to accept and respect the home backgrounds of the pupils they teach.

In Kinder *et al.*'s (1995) research parentally condoned absence was seen as a major problem. By comparison, during my own research I was only aware of three instances of parentally condoned absence. Twice Rasheeda took time off school to look after younger siblings, whilst Mandy's mother registered her disapproval for the school's multicultural curriculum by forbidding Mandy to attend Eid celebrations in school. As has been said before, with the exception of time off for illness, Charlene was the only pupil who was physically absent from either primary or secondary school.

With these exceptions the pupils in my research had good attendance records and parents clearly thought it was important for their children to go to school and 'get a good education'. Sadly, the parents did not seem to be particularly concerned that their children exhibited quiet and non-participatory behaviour in school. Some parents were themselves quiet pupils. Others saw it as a harmless phase that their children would grow out of. All the parents seemed convinced that regular attendance and good behaviour was all that was necessary for their children to get a good education and 'make something of their lives'. This is not surprising given the official emphasis on school attendance.

My research would seem to support the Social Exclusion Unit's assertion that family and peer pressures are important factors behind truancy.

> Parents bear the primary responsibility for ensuring that their children attend school regularly and home circumstances exert an important influence over pupils' attendance and punctuality. Poor parental supervision and lack of commitment to education are crucial factors behind truancy.
>
> (SEU 1998, section 1.8)

Poor parental supervision and lack of commitment to education may help to explain pupils' physical truancy from school. However, on the whole, pupils who truant in mind have good attendance records. Parents have clearly done their job in getting the pupils to school. In order to explain why they do not participate in school activities it is necessary to consider other, in-school factors.

School factors

The Social Exclusion Unit recognises that 'how schools operate can make a great difference in shaping whether children do in fact truant' (SEU 1998, section 1.7). In addition OFSTED (1995) found that in some schools poor attendance was centred among pupils who were weak readers and that non-attendance could also be a result of anxiety about GCSE coursework deadlines.

Balding (1996) found that anxiety about bullying was frequently cited as a reason for truanting. Kinder *et al.* (1995) cites a number of in-school factors directly associated with truancy and disaffection. These related to the school itself, relationships with peers and teachers, and the curriculum. In my own work I have also identified a number of in-school factors directly associated with truanting in mind behaviour.

Unlike Kinder *et al.* I did not focus on the 'most disaffected age group'. Instead I chose to work with younger pupils, i.e. from Year 6 to Year 8. Nevertheless, some of the pupils and parents I interviewed expressed strong feelings about the curriculum offered by the school. As has already been mentioned, Mandy's mother had strong negative feelings about a multicultural curriculum that she felt was inappropriate for her daughter. For different reasons the Black and Asian parents were equally disaffected by what was on offer.

> What's used to defuse the argument is multicultural education and 'let's do some bhaji, let's cook an Indian food, I'll wear a sari today, and that's multicultural education' – that is not multicultural education, multicultural education is the culture that's multifaceted and unfortunately education in England is very one-sided, it's really a culture to satisfy whites' perspectives of Black people.
>
> (Aberash's stepfather)

According to Aberash's stepfather at least, the mismatch between the school and the individual's lived experience was not restricted to racial issues.

> Crack exists and some of the biggest runners for crack and cocaine are eleven and twelve. They are not adults. Another issue is child abuse. There is a patronising way in which we talk to kids about child abuse, yet they go home and they get abused at home. It's like I've seen teachers talking about racism to black children in a way that makes them laugh. Teachers don't come out and talk about these issues as they really are.
>
> (Aberash's stepfather)

This is not a call for teachers to accept and condone drug abuse, child abuse and racist behaviour. However, it is a genuine plea for teachers to talk about such issues in a way that is real and meaningful to the pupils for whom it may be part of their daily-lived experiences. Without this, pupils may come to regard teachers and what they teach as irrelevant.

Despite their frequent truanting in mind, few of the pupils I interviewed saw the school curriculum as irrelevant. However, all the pupils were very clear about the lessons they liked or disliked. Basically, the pupils liked lessons that were taught by good teachers, i.e. those who seemed to respect the pupils as individuals and who were always willing to provide support and help when it was needed. This would appear to support previous findings that so far as young pupils are concerned 'how children are taught matters to them more than what they are taught' (Wade and Moore 1993: 29). In considering the qualities of an effective pupil–teacher relationship, it is generally accepted that pupils learn most effectively when they feel valued and secure, trust their teachers, and both understand and accept the full range of classroom demands.

Sadly, many pupils who exhibit truanting in mind behaviour have difficulty in forming relationships with their teachers. Rasheeda admitted that there was little communication between her and her teacher.

> 'Cause he has to work, some work to do and I have some work to do and if I say like speak to him a lot, he says 'just carry on with your work'.
>
> (Rasheeda, Y6 pupil)

She seemed unaware that both she and her teacher should be engaged in the same task, namely her education. The way in which pupils who truant in mind exclude themselves from learning relationships is also demonstrated by Diana's comment about what she sees as the teacher's role.

> . . . when I am stuck he has to help me ... work and everything but most of the time he's ... he's like talking hisself like doing things on the board and things so you can't really talk to him when he is trying to learn the children.
>
> (Diana, Y6 pupil)

In this account she effectively precludes herself from any participation in the whole class discussion for fear of disturbing the teacher. Moreover, she does not include herself in the group of pupils being taught. Little wonder that she feels free to play truant.

In terms of truanting in mind behaviour, issues of teacher expectation, feelings of security, teaching style and classroom organisation appeared to be more significant than teacher popularity or the subject being taught. Observations suggest that pupils are more likely to participate when the teacher clearly expects participation and they are explicit about the reasons for this participation. Conversely, teachers who ignore or condone truanting in mind behaviour actively discourage participation. Classroom observations, particularly during the intervention programme, suggest that, where collaborative working is supported by the teacher, pupils find it easier to talk in small group discussions rather than in whole class lessons. Consequently, there is greater participation in lessons in which the learning has been organised around small group activities. Similarly, structured but open-ended activities provide a secure environment that discourages truanting in mind. The current government policy of encouraging more whole class discussion bodes ill for pupils who truant in mind and who might well benefit from small group activities. The needs of all pupils should be considered in discussions of classroom organisation and management.

Reducing truancy and social exclusion

There is general acceptance that physical truancy is a problem for individuals and for society. In terms of truancy in mind the first issue for pupils, parents, schools and government agencies is to recognise and accept that this may be a serious problem. However, my research suggests that not everyone understands the need for active participation. Some of the pupils, teachers and parents who participated in this study seemed to assume that physical presence in the classroom was synonymous with learning. The research discussed above suggests that this is not the case. The need for active participation in education should be recognised and made explicit to all concerned. This should be supported by research into the causes and effects of truanting in mind behaviour. Given the potential similarities between the causes of both forms of truancy this might be done in conjunction with research into physical truancy. The next step would be to devise, implement and evaluate initiatives for reducing truanting in mind behaviour.

Once the need for active participation has been established, my work with pupils who truant in mind suggests that the three strategies for reducing physical truancy identified by Kinder *et al.* (1995) are likely to be effective for both groups of truants.

In terms of reducing truancy in mind the strategy of *maintaining and monitoring attendance* would have to be interpreted in terms of organising and managing the classroom in such a way as to maximise participation. This would require careful observations and monitoring of the four types of truanting in mind behaviour identified above. In secondary schools and large primary schools where pupils are taught by a number of different teachers there would have to be school-wide monitoring of nonparticipation and some means of sharing knowledge of pupil behaviour.

Experience of working with quiet pupils highlights the need to *provide direct support for the emotional and behavioural needs* of those who play truant in mind. Once again, this begins with the recognition that, despite their good attendance records, these pupils do in fact have emotional and behavioural needs that are not being met. In addition to improving relationships in school there is a need to provide time to listen to pupils. I feel strongly that all professionals who work with children and young people should be trained to identify the signs of abuse or other forms of acute distress and be able to contact appropriate specialist support.

Where, as was the case in the school where I began my research, there is parental disaffection about the curriculum offered by the school, *offering alternative curriculum experiences* would be a good way to reduce truanting in mind behaviour. However, such a curriculum would have to take account of and respect the reality of the pupils' daily-lived experiences.

In conclusion, it could be argued that this small-scale qualitative research contributes to an understanding of social exclusion in a number of ways. First, it suggests a refocusing of attention from simple measures of attendance to more subtle measures of participation in school. Second, it challenges some of the more general and stereotypical views expressed in large-scale research into absenteeism. Finally, based on the possible causes of truancy, it suggests possible strategies for increasing participation and reducing social exclusion for a potentially vulnerable and largely ignored group of pupils. What is required now is further research into the phenomenon of truanting in mind. [...] Sadly, given that these pupils do not demand attention I fear that their silent protest will remain unheard.

References

Balding, J. (1996) *Young People in 1995.* Exeter: University of Exeter: Schools Health Unit.

Barnes, D. (1979 first pub. 1976) *From Communication to Curriculum.* Middlesex: Penguin.

Benjamin, J. (1990 first pub. 1988) *The Bonds of Love.* London: Virago.

Beveridge, S. (1993) *Special Educational Needs in Schools.* London: Routledge.

Blunkett, D. (1997) TES Conference.

Chodorow, N. (1978) *The Reproduction of Mothering.* London: University of California Press.

Collins, J. (1994) *The Silent Minority: developing talk in the primary classroom.* Unpublished Ph.D. thesis: University of Sheffield.

Collins, J. (1996) *The Quiet Child.* London: Cassell.

Collins, S. (1991) Transition from lone-parent family to step-family. In Hardey, M. and Crow, G. (eds) *Lone Parenthood.* London: Harvester Wheatsheaf.

Graham, J. and Bowling, B. (1995) *Young People and Crime*. London: Home Office research studies, 145.

Gray, J. and Jesson, D. (1990) *Truancy in Secondary Schools Amongst Fifth Year Pupils*. University of Sheffield: QQSE Research Group.

Kinder, K., Harland, J., Wilkin, A. and Wakefield, A. (1995) *Three to Remember: strategies for disaffected pupils*. Slough: NFER.

Office for Standards in Education (OFSTED) (1995) *Access, Achievement and Attendance in Secondary Schools* (Report No. 16/95). London: OFSTED.

O'Keefe, D. G. (1994) *Truancy in English Secondary Schools*. London: HMSO.

Oliver, M. (1988) The social and political context of education policy. In Barton, 1. (ed.) *The Politics of Special Education*. London: The Falmer Press.

Social Exclusion Unit (SEU) (1998) *Truancy and Social Exclusion*. Report. London: Social Exclusion Unit.

Wade, B. and Moore, M. (1993) *Experiencing Special Needs*. Buckingham: Open University Press.

Young, D. (1984) *Knowing How and Knowing That*. London: Birkbeck College.

This chapter provides clear parallels between Collins' ideas and the development of an inclusive pedagogy. Through her analysis, Collins advocates the need for active participation in education to be recognised by teachers, parents and pupils. Collins' conclusions suggest a 'reducing truanting in mind' approach, improving pupil and teacher relationships and small group activities that can significantly support pupils' participation in learning in social contexts.

Chapter 17

Media portrayal of young people
Impact and influences

Catherine Clark, Amrita Ghosh, Emrys Green and Naushin Shariff

This chapter is an abridged version of a report undertaken by a group of young researchers aged 15–18 about how media portrays young people and what impact this has on them. The chapter provides insights into how the young people, supported by staff from the National Children's Bureau, employed a variety of research methods and developed their skills as young researchers. Their findings and recommendations raise our awareness about the negative and sensational reporting of young people in the media.

Introduction

The Young Researcher Network (YRN) is made up of several different partner organisations, including the National Youth Agency (NYA). The network values, supports and encourages research led by young people. It aims to empower young people to raise their voice and influence matters that affect their lives.

The National Children's Bureau (NCB) is a charity based in London, which works to advance the well-being of all children and young people across every aspect of their lives. NCB is one of the several member organisations that make up the YRN.

Background to the research

In early 2008, the YRN invited its members to apply for funding to support a group of young researchers who would carry out a piece of research on a topic of their choosing. Emrys Green and Naushin Shariff, who are both members of Young NCB, were the first of the four young researchers to be involved. Emrys and Naushin were both interested in the media, and how the media portrays young people. This was an issue that was important to them and something that clearly was affecting their, and other young people's, lives. Together they worked with Louca-Mal Brady from NCB's Research Department on the application, and were awarded the funding in May 2008. Amrita Ghosh and Catherine Clark, the other two young researchers, became involved in the project in June 2008, after responding to an email advertising the project. [...]

[This research was undertaken as part of a wider Young Researcher Network programme facilitated by the National Youth Agency.]

The broad aim of the research project was to explore how young people aged 13–18 are portrayed in the media, and find out what impact this has on them. Through gathering information from young people and journalists, we wanted to answer the following research questions:

- How are young people portrayed in national and London local papers and BBC/ITV news broadcasts?
- What do young people identify as positive, negative and neutral images? How do young people feel about these images?
- What do journalists think about young people's views?

Literature review

We asked Amanda, one of the researchers at NCB, to look in the NCB library at what research had been done already in this area and this is what she found.

Key points

- Existing research has found most media stories about young people are negative.
- Stories involving young people are most commonly about crime; gangs; education; and social exclusion.
- Young offenders are likely to receive negative coverage.
- The media often reports stories in a sensational way.
- The media does not always represent reality.
- Most young people feel the media represents them as antisocial and a group to be feared.

The majority of articles found were opinion pieces, or small scale studies, although it should be noted that the NCB library does not have all the publications on media studies. Several articles related to the Positive Images Awards, set up by the magazine *Young People Now* (YPN) in 2004. These awards aimed to improve the portrayal of young people by encouraging the media to look for the positive side when covering stories, and young people to contact the media.

As part of the awards' campaign, YPN commissioned research to monitor the newspapers' coverage of young people. The researchers monitored the media during a specific week each year, collecting all stories related to young people and classifying them as positive, neutral/balanced, or negative.

In terms of the findings in 2007 overall, 23 per cent of mentions were positive, 29 per cent neutral or balanced, and 48 per cent were negative, this was a slight improvement on previous years. During a week in August 2005, the results were 12 per cent positive, 30 per cent neutral and 57 per cent negative. In 2004, the results were 14 per cent positive, 15 per cent neutral and 71 per cent negative. When broken down by type of media, the results for 2007 showed that the most positive source was broadsheet papers, with 45 per cent positive, whereas only 10 per cent of broadcast news was positive, and 24 per cent of tabloid news positive. The three most popular topics covered were knife crime, education and gangs, then social exclusion and violent crime. This research claimed that news stories concerning young people should be more balanced. [...]

It seems that young offenders in particular are likely to be the subject of negative reporting. In 2002, a coalition of children's charities (Barnardos, The Children's Society, NCH, NSPCC, NCB), along with the National Association for the Care and Resettlement of Offenders (NACRO), set up the Shape project to challenge the way young offenders are represented. Part of this project was an analysis of the newspapers over a three-month period. In total 74 articles were published during this time. The tabloids had more articles (41) than broadsheets (33), *the Sun* had most with 13, *the Independent* had least with 5. Ghose (2004) pointed out the role newspapers, particularly local papers, can play in making life worse for young people who are in trouble with the law, by breaching their anonymity. Newspapers can apply to have the name of the young person revealed, and those applications are often successful.

An article by Hallsworth and Young (2005) looked at the representation of young people compared with the recorded levels of youth crime. This article is not based on an analysis of newspaper articles over time, but does claim that the term 'gang culture' was being used regularly. The authors criticise a story in *The Times*, in July 2005, that had the headline: 'Fear drives one teenage boy in ten to carry a knife'. This article tried to imply that there was a growing problem with knife and gun crime, without sufficient evidence.

Hallsworth and Young also focus on the media's use of the term 'gang' to describe a group of young people together. Cases in the media of knife and gun crime referred to as gang-related, are more likely to have been perpetrated by criminal groups, rather than peer groups of young people. Hallsworth and Young claim that society is frightened of young people who commit violent crimes, but these levels of fear are not supported by the recorded levels of crime. The British Crime Survey for 2003/04 showed that levels of violent crime had been falling slightly (Hallsworth and Young, 2005). Police statistics for violent crime during the same period contradicted this, showing a rise of 12 per cent but there had been changes in how they record crimes. Hallsworth and Young also refer to the Youth Justice Board (YJB) Marl survey of 2004, which showed that there had not been an increase in offending by young people since 2001. This article also mentions the use of meaningless statistics in newspaper articles intended to scare people, such as the following from *The Times* newspaper: 'Over half of young people claim to know how to obtain a knife'. This is no surprise, given that most people have access to kitchen knives.

There has been some research looking at how young people feel about the media, and about how they are represented. In 2006 the British Youth Council did a survey to find out young people's views on how they are portrayed by the media and by politicians. The survey had over 700 responses from 12–25 year olds. Amongst the key findings were that 98 per cent felt that the media always, often or sometimes represents them as antisocial. More than four out of five thought that the media represents them as a group to be feared. The respondents felt this may cause older people to be afraid of them, and may alienate young people causing more antisocial behaviour. The survey respondents wanted their achievements to be recognised, and to be given positive attention. They also thought that the media represented the majority of them on the behaviour of the minority.

According to Madge's research (2006) the strength of the influence the media has on children and young people increases as they get older. In terms of respondents, there were 2,000 primary and secondary age children and 500 adults. The focus of the project was to find out how children feel about their childhoods and the influence of the media. Adults felt the media had a strong influence on children. Children claimed that they were more influenced by their parents and families; adults claimed that children were more likely to believe the media and friends influenced them most. Adults also said they thought children were depicted 'very badly' in the media;

over 75 per cent thought children were depicted as 'troublemakers'. In addition, 47 per cent of adults said that children were portrayed in a negative way. Madge claims:

> Sensationalised images of youth predominate in the media and else-where, and display bias in the behaviour they report as well as the status of the children they depict. The well-behaved, well-adjusted 'ordinary' child may not be newsworthy but this does not explain the undue attention paid to negative messages about youth.
>
> (2006: 143)

This does raise the question of why the media represent children and young people in negative ways. Goddard (2005) reports on an event run as part of Young People Now's Positive Images campaign, where young people met with BBC television's head of news, Roger Mosey, to discuss the way young people are represented. Mosey felt that BBC news was not 'as good as it could be at talking to young people', although he thought the BBC was better than some other media, particularly newspapers. Mosey also said that the news has to reflect reality and one problem is that '25 people doing something good is not a story, while one person doing something bad is'. However, as his comments show, the media doesn't completely represent reality, as particular news stories are selected over others for coverage.

So it seems the public want negative stories. Hallsworth and Young (2005) claim that politicians use any mention of juvenile crime as an opportunity to demonstrate their toughness on crime. In addition, they argue that 24-hour news updates means that the public always want to hear the latest news, and also that the more sensational stories are repeated again and again, perhaps increasing their impact. However, it is possible for young people to challenge the way they are represented. Roger Mosey encouraged children and young people to start at a local level, possibly with local radio stations, because stories often start there, move onto local television then to national broad-casts. Van Ark (2004) advises that youth groups need to be proactive to combat negative images of young people, and suggests ways of putting stories across. There are groups that can train children and young people in dealing with the media, for example The Media Trust and Children's Express. Van Ark (2004) also mentions steps that can be taken if unfair publicity occurs: contact the editor of the newspaper or programme. The Press Complaints Commission has rules for coverage of children and young people. A negative story can be turned around; a story about gun crime is an opportunity for those who work with the young people who have been affected to talk about what is helping them. The Shape Project (2004) trained a group of ten young people from a variety of backgrounds to act as young media representatives, getting the campaign messages across to the press. They then had opportunities to speak to the media, and were briefed beforehand. As Van Ark (2004) says, young people who have contact with the media, whether to comment on stories, or to promote events and campaigns, need training, and there are also safety and confidentiality issues they need to be aware of. [...]

The research process

Media stories analysis and consultation

At the beginning of the research, stories were collected about young people aged 13–18 that appeared in the *Sun, Daily Mail* and *Guardian* national newspapers. Stories were also gathered from the *London Evening Standard*; the *East Anglian Daily Times* (regional newspaper); and from the BBC/ITV news. We collected these over a two-week period, from 30 June to 14 July 2008. Once all the stories had been collected, a consultation event was arranged and attended by the four young researchers and four other Young NCB members. At this event, we selected some of these stories and looked at what each one said about young people. The stories were classified into positive, negative and neutral categories based on how young people were presented in them. The Young NCB members that attended this event supported the research team with planning aspects of the project, and with three additional members, helped us with our dissemination strategy.

Focus groups

One of the aims of our project was to understand what young people feel about the way they are portrayed in the newspapers and on TV. To do this we used one of our qualitative methods – focus groups. A focus group is a method that is used by researchers to find out what people's opinions and views are. During a focus group the researcher(s) will ask questions to stimulate discussion within the group, while taking note of what people are saying about particular issues. Two focus groups were conducted: one in Suffolk, and the other in London. In total, 14 young people took part, all of whom were aged between 13–18 years. During the focus groups we used some of the stories that we had collected from the media as prompts, to encourage the young people taking part to talk about their views and feelings. We also asked them to draw a picture of a young person from the point of view of the media, and from the point of view of another young person.

Interviews

Interviews were carried out with journalists to find out what their views were on the way young people are portrayed, and how the media could respond to this. In total, seven were interviewed over the telephone. Four of these journalists wrote articles about children and young people in magazines; one wrote articles for both national newspapers and magazines; and two of them worked for a TV channel. The NCB's Media Department contacted the journalists on our behalf and asked them if they would mind being interviewed for our project.

Online survey

After the interviews with journalists and focus groups with young people had been completed, we designed and then ran an online survey to get the views of young people from across the country. Once the survey questions had been developed, a member of the NCB's research department input the survey into an online survey tool – Survey Monkey. The survey was advertised to young people through Young NCB's website, the Young Researcher Network, and several other networks that the NCB is part of. The survey remained 'live' for two weeks, and received 62 responses in total.

Ethics

To ensure that we gathered information for our project ethically we read and used both the NYA's and NCB's ethical guidelines to inform the design of our project. Before we began collecting our data, one member of the research team also attended a training session on ethics that was delivered by the NYA. [...]

Analysis and findings

To analyse the information that we had gathered, we worked together as a group and were supported by NCB's Research Department and the NYA. At the start of the analysis process, we developed codes and used these to extract themes from our data. These codes were taken from our main research questions, which helped us to stay focused on our original research alms.

The key themes that we identified are outlined below, with our main findings described under each theme.

Key points

- The media produces more negative stories than positive.
- The media focuses on minority groups.
- Bad news sells.
- Journalists are under pressure to cover negative stories.
- Negative media coverage can have a negative affect on young people's lives.

Media content

Many messages were found in our research. The most obvious message we found was that there was an imbalance in the amount of positive stories about young people and negative stories. Most of the stories published about young people portray them in a negative rather than a positive light. The young people who took part in the survey felt that there were more stories on them that are giving a negative image than positive, as can be seen in Figure 17.1:

Respondents to the survey were also asked to select what they felt were the three most common news stories involving young people. The majority who responded to the survey felt that knife crime was the most common story, with 76 per cent selecting this, followed by gun crime (22.4 per cent)

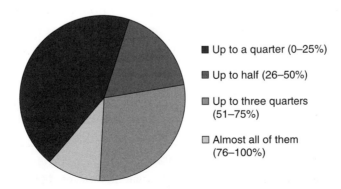

- Up to a quarter (0–25%)
- Up to half (26–50%)
- Up to three quarters (51–75%)
- Almost all of them (76–100%)

Figure 17.1 Out of all the stories on young people that the media covers, what percentage of these are negative?

and violent crime (15.5 per cent). Stories covering teenage pregnancy; school and education; and drugs were also felt to be common stories.

Another message from the research was the difference in the stories that are published within local and national papers. We found that national newspapers publish more stories that give a negative portrayal of young people. But on the other hand we found that the local/regional papers we collected tended to publish more stories that gave a positive image of young people. Although as stated above, the media as a whole tends to report more negative stories. This is reflected in the views of some of the young people that responded to the survey, particularly around how they feel they are represented by local and national media.

The reasons for this difference in local and national media reporting were not explored in depth during this research. However, it is possible that local/regional media are more likely to cover stories that will present the geographical area they cover in a more positive light whereas the national media are not constrained by geographical loyalties. The commercial media need to attract audiences to consume their stories. This is perhaps why many newspapers/editors choose to publish negative stories that will interest readers/viewers – we explore this in more detail under our next theme. We also found that media stories are not representative of the youth population as a whole, as they tend to focus on minority groups that are extreme examples of young people. For example, if the content of the story is negative it's usually very bad, focusing on young people who are criminals or badly behaved.

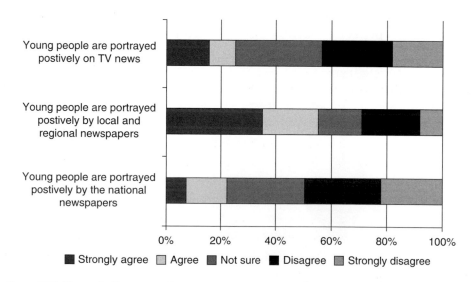

Figure 17.2 Please indicate to what extent you agree or disagree with the statements:

Positive stories are often linked with the self achievements of extraordinary individuals with rare talents, rather than average young people. Evidently not all young people are like these two extremes.

Barriers experienced by journalists

The journalists that participated in the research generally did not believe all of the bad press that young people so often receive. They recognised that young people are diverse: some of them behave badly, but the majority do not. Although they were also aware of the sensationalism that often characterises news stories, and felt that negative reporting by the media is likely to make young people feel negative about themselves, alienated and angry. All the journalists interviewed strongly agreed that not all young people are bad; one journalist commented that young people were a 'Fantastic bunch of people'.

However, our research found a common perception amongst the profession that negative stories sell. Several journalists that we interviewed mentioned the importance of targeting their readership and viewers. This is always the main focus, especially for editors, even if the values of the story aren't shared by the journalists who have covered it. The media needs to sell itself to the public, and it feels that negative, sensational news is what the public wants to hear about. As some of the journalists who were interviewed explained:

> If it's bad news it's news worthy.
> Bad news sells.

This arguably catalyzes the situation, as the public become more aware of particular issues and want more stories that cover those issues. The media will then publish more, further increasing awareness, and creating a 'thirst' amongst the public for negative press. Arguably then, young people are being commercialised, as they can be portrayed in particular ways that will attract readers or viewers who will consume the news. One journalist described young people as being like 'play toys', as they are an easy target for negative reporting and can be used by the media to sell its products.

Therefore, journalists must often conform to the requirements placed upon them by the institution they work for. Some of those that we interviewed explained that journalists often do not wish to disrupt the *status quo* and will conform to what their publication or TV channel sees as being the 'norm'.

When asked about changes in the portrayal of young people over time, some journalists believed the situation had worsened. Although we have established that this is very much a personal perception. The murder of James Bulger was mentioned as an example of negative news coverage from over ten years ago – suggesting that negative reporting of young people is not new. It was suggested by one journalist who participated that levels of violence may not be increasing; but due to excessive, sensational media coverage this can influence the public's awareness and perceptions of this. Moreover, a TV journalist pointed out that there is also an increase in young people becoming the victims of crime too.

The journalists who took part in the research agreed that it is more likely that positive stories will appear in the local/regional rather than national media, something that we have discussed above. One journalist explained the reasons for this being due to an: 'easier access to market due to a lower threshold of news need'. It was suggested that TV news channels are more likely to go for stories that involve powerful, visually impressive images, such as people who are angry and upset, rather than images of young people that have made a positive contribution.

We did find that some journalists were quite pessimistic about the situation, and felt it would be difficult to change the negative portrayal of young people and the public's demand for bad stories. Despite this pessimism they did discuss ways in which it might be possible to challenge this. On several occasions during our research participants commented on how young people can be empowered to change things through the use of online multimedia such as video sharing and social networking sites. One journalist we interviewed felt that instead of always interviewing adults about youth issues, the media should also be 'making more use of articulate young people'.

Young people's perceptions of 'self'

From the research that was conducted, a number of points were made by young people on the perception they had of themselves and how this could be influenced by media reporting.

Overall, it is clear that the media often present young people in a negative way, which the young people we spoke to said was often associated with 'hoodies', 'gangs', 'knives' and other generally negative images. Some of the young people who participated in the research felt that this can lead to stereotyping, and as a result, older people will feel that all young people are part of gangs or are badly behaved. Some of the young people we spoke to during the focus groups felt that these negative stereotypes were impacting on their daily lives: making them more conscious of how they dressed, how they presented themselves, and where they could go with their friends. For example, some young people wore hoodies because they're comfortable and fashionable. However, the negativity that the media often attaches to this item of clothing left some of the young people who participated feeling anxious about how other people may view them while wearing one. As this young person's comments during the survey demonstrate:

> Adults do not trust you if you wear fleeces with hoods on, or 'hoodies' – they presume you are in with a knife carrying gang and are on drugs.

Others reported feeling like older people were often intimidated by them:

> It makes me feel ashamed to fall into this stereotype ... some people may even cross the road if they see a group of us coming in their direction.

Our research found evidence that negative press can impact on young people's self-welfare, as a number reported feeling scared and intimidated by other young people after reading or seeing negative coverage. Evidence from the online survey found that some young people had experienced harassment at the hands of the police, for what they described as no apparent reason. They felt that negative media coverage had led the police to suspect them of wrong-doing.

During the two focus groups that were held in London and Suffolk we asked the young people taking part to draw what they thought a typical young person looked like from their perspective, and also what they believe the media thinks a typical young person is like (some examples of these drawings are in Figures 17.3 and 17.4).

We found clear similarities between the two groups with evident consensus around how the media portrays young people. In these illustrations young people were depicted in gangs, wearing hoods and carrying knives, guns, alcohol and drugs. They were described as living a 'gangster life' and 'rebelling against society', as 'troubled, violent and threatening', 'chav, ASBO yobs' who are 'rude', and concerned with 'fashion and appearances'.

The illustrations from their own perspectives differed in some ways. The Suffolk group described young people as being 'individuals', 'keen to learn', 'misunderstood' and capable of doing positive things. Whereas the London group emphasised some of the negative images that had characterised the illustration from the media's perspective. The London group also made

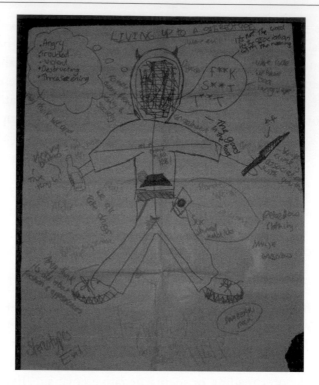

Figure 17.3 The media's view of young people drawn by young people participating in the Suffolk focus group.

Figure 17.4 An illustration of young people drawn from the perspectives of the young people who participated in the London focus group.

references in their drawing to young people's interests, such as music and spending time with friends. Clearly the focus groups showed the impact that the media is capable of having on young people, who felt that the media currently portrays them overwhelmingly in a negative light. When given the opportunity to express their own views of young people, it is evident from the London group that some of the negative images and stereotypes portrayed in the media had arguably begun to shape some of their own perceptions of young people.

Other participants were angry about the media's obsession with young people who misbehaved. They felt that behaving badly was often the only way to get any attention, something the minority of young people involved in criminal activity seem to get.

The young people who took part in the research recognised the important role the media has in informing people of what is going on, and that the public should be informed when bad things happen. However, they were critical of sensational reporting and felt that there should be some more positive news stories about young people to create a balance, as findings from our young people's survey in Figure 17.5 support (see below).

Conclusion and recommendations

Our research indicates that the media has the ability to influence people's perceptions and their views of particular issues, and as our evidence has demonstrated, it can affect the lives of young people. What concerns us about the findings of this research is the clearly negative impact that sensational, negative reporting is having on young people. Many who participated felt

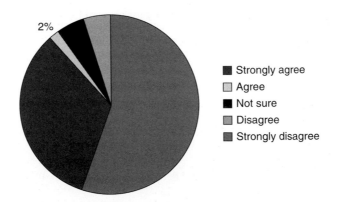

Figure 17.5 Please indicate to what extent you agree or disagree with the following statement – the media should cover more positive stories about young people.

angry and resentful that the widely publicised negative behaviours of minority groups within the youth population are dominating the headlines, and affecting wider society's perception of all young people. What is also concerning is the amount of negative coverage that young people receive, particularly in the national media, and the use of this bad coverage by the media for commercial gain. Clearly this situation places pressures upon journalists to cover instances where young people behave badly, rather than when they make a positive contribution.

At the beginning of this research we wanted to use the findings to raise awareness, and try to make a difference to the way young people are currently being portrayed. Our recommendations from doing this research have been included, and we hope that our audiences will take note of them. We would like policy makers and media professionals to seriously consider the damaging effects that constant negative and sensational reporting are having on young people.

Our recommendations

The data in Figure 17.5, demonstrates the overwhelming desire of the young people we surveyed to be represented in a more positive light. This is one of the clear recommendations from the research evidence we gathered:

• there should be a balance of negative and positive stories.

Our other recommendations include:

• young people should be given a voice to put across their views on this issue;
• negative, sensational reporting can have a negative effect on young people's lives;
• negative stories have the potential to be used for education.

References

British Youth Council and Youthnet (2006) The voice behind the hood: young people's views on anti-social behaviour, the media and older people. London: Youthnet, and British Youth Council.

Ghose, D. (2004) Newspapers give young people a bad reputation. *Young People Now*, no. 229, 7 April, p. 9.

Goddard, C. (2005) News has to reflect reality. *Young People Now*, no. 272, 2 March, p. 13.

Goddard, C. (2006) Media still has a long way to go. *Young People Now*, no. 327, 26 Apr, p. 8.

Hallsworth, S., and Young, T. (2005) On gangs and guns: a critique and a warming. *Childright*, no. 220, October, pp. 14–16.

Madge, N. (2006) *Children these days*. Bristol: Policy Press.

Van Ark, C. (2004) Paint a positive picture. *Young People Now*, 20 October, pp. 18–19.

[...]

The young people represented in this chapter felt there was an imbalance in the media portrayal of young people. Negative stories, a focus on minority groups, stereotyping of young people and the pressure by the media to sell bad news were all identified as factors which have a negative affect on young people's lives. Countering negative representations of young people is essential in asserting young people's rights to be treated with respect.

Chapter 18

The impossibility of minority ethnic educational 'success'?

An examination of the discourses of teachers and pupils in British secondary schools

Louise Archer

The focus of this chapter is the educational achievement of minority ethnic pupils of young people aged 14–16 from British secondary schools. Based on studies of Black, Chinese, British Muslim and ethnically diverse urban and suburban young people, the author explores the notion of success and then moves on to explore how differently racialised groups are constructed in relation to the notions of achievement and success and failure. The author specifically looks at ways in which minority ethnic pupils are othered and considers the model of 'trichotomy' and how it could be used to map how differently racialised positionings are played out in dominant educational discourses.

[...]

This article's approach [...]

In this article, I adopt a feminist post-structuralist approach to the concept of social difference (Archer, 2004), in which minority ethnic young people are understood as multiply positioned (and self-positioning) in relation to axes of 'race'/ethnicity, social class and gender, and so on.

My arguments are generated from analyses of data collected from four separate studies that I have been involved with to date. All the studies were conducted in British secondary schools and focused on the identities and experiences of minority ethnic young people: British Chinese (Archer & Francis, 2006), British Muslim (Archer, 2003) and ethnically diverse samples of urban (Archer 2005, 2007) and suburban young people (Archer *et al.*, 2004). These studies comprised interview and discussion group data from teachers, minority ethnic parents and minority ethnic pupils (aged 14–16 years). Thumbnail sketches of each study are presented below.

The *Dropping out and Drifting Away* study was conducted with 89 working-class, urban young people (52 boys, 37 girls) who had been identified by their school as 'at risk' of leaving education and/or not progressing into post-16 education. The young people were tracked over 1.5 years and were interviewed up to four times. Interviews focused on the young people's identities, experiences of education and the role of social and cultural factors in their engagement with schooling. Interviews were also conducted with 19 members of staff and 5 parents (see Archer *et al.*, 2005; Archer et al., 2007a, b).

The *Chinese Pupils* study was conducted with 80 British Chinese pupils (32 boys, 48 girls), 30 teachers and 30 Chinese parents (see Francis & Archer, 2005a, b; Archer & Francis, 2006, 2007). Interviews focused on the young people's identities (especially relating to gender. and ethnicity), experiences of education and aspirations for the future.

The *Under-performance* study was conducted with 90 suburban working-class pupils who had been identified from local education authority (LEA) data as 'underperforming' – defined for the purposes of this study as those achieving average to good results at Key Stage (KS) 2 but whose attainment dropped off considerably at KS3. Interviews focused on pupils' experiences of learning, views on achievement and the role of social and cultural factors. It also involved interviews with 22 teachers, head teachers and support staff, and 11 parents of underperforming pupils (see Archer *et al.*, 2004).

The *British Muslim Pupils* study was conducted with 64 British Muslim pupils (32 boys and 32 girls) aged 14–16 years (see Archer, 1998, 2001, 2002a, b. 2003). Single-sex discussion groups were used to probe pupils' ethnic and gender identity constructions, experiences of schooling, and aspirations for the future. [...]

Deconstructing/reconstructing 'success'

[...]The majority of UK educational policy and research literature is framed in relation to notions of underachievement. Yet a small body of work has begun to focus on notions of 'success'. For example, research has looked at educational success among 'dominant' groups, such as (white) middle-class families (e.g. Ball, 2003; Power *et al.*, 2003) and white, middle-class girls (e.g. Delamont, 1989; Walkerdine *et al.*, 2001). Research has also been conducted with 'successful' pupils from traditionally 'underachieving' groups, such as Black boys (e.g. Rollock, 2006), Muslim women (e.g. Ahmad, 2001) and working-class women (e.g. Mahony & Zmroczek, 1997). Importantly, these studies have not simply sought to identify factors that contribute to educational 'success', but have also sought to problematise the nature of this

Table 18.1 Summary of discourses of 'success' produced by pupils, parents and professionals

Type of success	Characterisation	Predominant pupil groups associated with
'Traditional' academic success	Highest levels of academic achievement in national examinations. The desired 'gold standard' of achievement	White, middle-class boys and girls Chinese boys and girls Some South Asian (non-Muslim) pupils
'Good enough' success	'Good' and middle levels of academic achievement seen as 'unspectacular' but unproblematic	Black girls Some South Asian (Muslim and non-Muslim) pupils Some Chinese boys Some White, working-class pupils (mostly girls)
'Value-added' success	A relational measure, reflecting average levels of achievement reached from considerably 'lower' starting point. Espoused in some education policy rhetoric in terms of individualistic 'realising potential', but not attracting much resources or attention in practice	Working-class pupils (especially girls) Some Muslim pupils English as an additional language/refugee pupils Some Black girls
'Desired-denied' and 'Potential ' success	A relationship to success in the absence of a recognised current/actual level of examination achievement. Positioned as problematic and requiring intervention within dominant discourse	Working-class pupils Black boys and girls Muslim boys (and some girls) English as an additional language/refugee pupils

'success', drawing attention to the continued hardships, tensions and inequalities experienced by 'successful' pupils.

In an attempt to help build upon and extend this area of enquiry, I would like to briefly discuss the notion of 'success' – with a view to specifying some racialised (as well as classed and/or gendered) differential forms of, and relationships to, success. Within the studies that I am drawing on here, there were various examples of pupils performing, trying to perform and/or desiring educational 'success' – and being differentially positioned by education professionals and parents in relation to notions of success. I suggest that these discourses might be organised into four different 'types' of relationships to educational success exhibited by minority ethnic young people. [...]

'Traditional' academic success (high achievement)

This form of success relates to pupils who are reported in the media each summer as gaining impressive, high results. It is particularly evoked by the notion of 'girls' overachievement', as articulated by proponents of the boys' underachievement debate. It is a form of success associated, predominantly, with white, middle-class pupils although there is a gender/ed element within this – as various feminist writers note, this high achievement is dominantly seen as 'natural' (and 'effortless') among boys but as achieved via 'plodding' hard work for girls (see Francis & Skelton, 2005). The only minority ethnic group consistently, popularly associated with this notion of achievement tends to be high-achieving British Chinese girls and boys (an observation borne out within the four data sets). However, it was also linked within some respondents' discourses to some south Asian (non-Muslim) pupils – notably high-achieving Indian pupils. However, as will be discussed in later sections of the article, this notion of success was always tempered and problematised in relation to minority ethnic pupils (only White. middle-class pupils – but particularly boys – could enjoy an unproblematised association with 'traditional' academic success).

'Good enough' success

This form of success is used to characterise pupils whose overall levels of academic achievement are good but not necessarily 'the highest' (e.g. Bs and Cs) – but whose achievement at this level is regarded as appropriate and respectable. This form of success tends to be seen as 'unspectacular' and attracts little attention or resources within the education system – even where pupils and/or their families feel that they are not maximising their potential. White, middle-class pupils tend *not* to be associated with this form of success because their achievements tend to be seen as residing more 'naturally' within 'traditional' forms of academic success (hence average/good achievements are treated as causes for concern/action). Across my data sets, this form of success was predominantly associated with working class and/or minority ethnic pupils, whose success at this level was interpreted by schools as being 'good enough' – although this view was not necessarily shared by pupils and parents (as discussed later in the article). Hence, within the data sets, 'good enough' success was characterised by pupils who expressed high aspirations but whose ambitions were regarded by their teachers as unrealistic. In the four studies, this form of success was most often experienced by Black girls, some Muslim pupils, some British Chinese boys and some White, working-class pupils (mostly girls). Within the talk of teachers, parents and professionals, it was also associated with some south Asian (both Muslim and non-Muslim) pupils.

'Value-added' success

This form of success represents a more personal or subjective experience of achievement. It does not indicate high grades *per se*, but rather is employed to indicate an identifiable level of achievement or improvement that has been generated in relation to a pupil's original starting position. For example, it refers to pupils who had previously been predicted to 'fail', or who came from severely disadvantaged backgrounds, but who at the time of the studies were performing better than previously expected or predicted. This form of success was associated with a notion of 'distance travelled' (or 'value added') and can be understood as a relational measure of success (as opposed to the supposedly 'objective' measure of traditional academic success). It tends to be espoused in some education policy rhetoric as an individualistic 'realising potential', but tends not to attract much resources or attention in practice as it is seen as a matter of individual responsibility, motivation and effort. Across the four studies, this form of success was particularly associated with working-class pupils (although it was notable that girls tended to adopt the responsibility for 'change' themselves, whereas parents or teachers were more likely to adopt the primary responsibility and action for helping boys). In particular, it was linked with working-class minority ethnic girls (especially, though not exclusively, Black girls) who subscribed to notions of personal effort and transformation. Within the talk of education professionals, it was also used to characterise the achievements of some Muslim pupils and English as an additional language/refugee pupils (e.g. to contextualise their levels of achievement in the face of significant personal and language barriers).

Desired-denied and 'potential' success

This discourse denotes a relationship to success in the absence of a recognised current/actual level of success or achievement. It also relates to those pupils who are positioned as 'underperforming' in terms of their abilities or potential for educational attainment. It reflects pupils' desire for success where they are positioned as having 'potential' (albeit unachieved). This discourse characterises much of the UK government's widening participation and 'standards' agenda. Despite indicating a (potentially) positive, desired relationship to success (albeit in the absence of 'actual' success), it tends to be positioned as a problematic position that requires urgent intervention within dominant educational discourse. Moreover, the source of the 'problem' tends to be associated with the identity and values of the pupil/group in question (irrespective of the young person's 'desire' for success).

Across the four data sets, pupils characterised in this way tended to come from working-class backgrounds, but this discourse was applied particularly to Black boys and girls and Muslim boys (and girls), whose attempts to generate value/self-worth within schools were being read within schools as running counter to the discourse of the ideal pupil. It was also associated with some English as an additional language/refugee pupils within the talk of some education professionals. [...]

Constructions of 'demonised' minority ethnic pupils (Black and Muslim pupils)

In line with previous research (e.g. Mirza, 1992; Sewell, 1997; Youdell, 2003), data from the four studies indicated that Black pupils (but particularly those of Caribbean origin) were frequently constructed as 'problem' pupils within schools. However, the increase in Islamophobia in the United Kingdom – and the cleavage between Asian 'achievers' and Muslim 'believers' within the popular imagination – also positioned Muslim boys within this category to an extent. Indeed, it has been argued that British Asian–Muslim boys are increasingly being positioned as the 'ultimate' demonised others within Western discourse (Archer, 2003) – a perception that appears to be filtering, to some extent, into their educational positioning.

Dominant constructions of 'demonised' minority ethnic pupils were organised around notions of rebellion/insubordination, loudness and inappropriate (hyper)heterosexuality. These combined with historical racist discourses to position these pupils as 'naturally' unambitious and unacademic due to their ethnic/cultural backgrounds. Each of these aspects will be discussed in turn.

'Loud' and 'challenging'

Interviews with teachers and with pupils evoked representations of Black pupils as overly challenging, confrontational, aggressive and influenced by their peers. [...] This notion of aggressive and confrontational behaviour has been particularly associated with Black boys (e.g. Sewell, 1997), yet it was also strongly linked with teachers' perceptions of Black girls too:

> I would say that a lot of the African–Caribbean girls and the African girls will challenge you, will have a lot to say about a lot of things.
>
> (Teacher, *Dropping Out* study)

The notion of being 'challenging' was frequently linked to the embodied practice of being 'too loud'. In particular, Black femininity was identified as problematically loud (visibly and audibly) and hence was seen as challenging within classrooms and schools. Furthermore, this 'loudness' was associated with a lack of educational motivation or application:

> Generally what I've experienced so far is that I haven't really come across that many Black girls who I've seen particularly motivated, they are generally socially want to be seen, they're very, they can be very loud and want to be noticed. But I mean they can be absolutely lovely girls, don't get me wrong, but I haven't seen that sort of input and that direct motivation at all yet.
>
> (Teacher, *Chinese Pupils* study)

In contrast, many Black young women explained their 'loudness' very differently – arguing that it is either a desirable and valued aspect of their racialised femininities (something to be proud of) or that it is a reaction to, and product of, the injustices that they experience at school. [...]

Hyper(hetero)sexual ('dangerous') masculinities and femininities

Black boys and girls were closely associated with notions of hyper(hetero) sexuality (see also Sewell, 1998). This 'excessive' sexuality was considered inappropriate and unconducive to being a 'good pupil'. Indeed, many of the working-class pupils across the studies were substantially invested in producing heterosexual, 'desirable' identities, which they achieved through the performance of 'style'. These performances of 'style' (coded, for example, through the wearing of branded clothes and 'bling') enabled the young people to generate a sense of value and self-worth (Archer *et al.*, 2007) – i.e. wearing 'cool' brands (such as Nike) provided young people with status and value within their peer groups. Yet these practices also brought pupils into conflict with schools in several ways. For instance, many of them got into trouble regularly for contravening school policies on uniform. Moreover, the young people's interest in, and attachment to, these performances of 'style' were interpreted negatively by teachers, as demonstrating an 'anti-school' attitude. In particular, some education professionals felt that these per-formances were antithetical to a 'good' pupil subject position and detracted from pupils' interest and investment in education. This was exacerbated by the coding of these racialised styles as 'black', 'male' and 'working-class' (see Archer *et al.*, 2007):

> A lot of the Black minority, I would say, is more focused on, because of media I would say, it's easy money, be a rapper, be an MC or just drug dealing because it's just easy, it's quick money, it's easy money.
>
> (Learning mentor, *Dropping Out* study)

Across the studies, Black, working-class masculinity was frequently positioned as the archetypal antipathy of the 'good pupil' subject position. For instance, it was evoked as a potential corrupting influence upon the achievement of 'other' minority ethnic boys, such as the British Chinese. Hence some teachers described 'laddish' British Chinese boys as having been 'infected' by Black, working-class masculine culture.

Hyper(hetero)sexuality was also evoked as an issue in relation to Black young women's achievement. In particular, some education professionals suggested that these girls' preoccupation with 'looking the part' was a major 'distraction' that mitigated against their engagement with education and schooling (see Archer *et al.*, 2007a):

> Well, what the girls do, obviously there's people like Beyonce [6], they do look up to them. Just looking good to them is good. 'Yeah, I want to look good' and, 'yeah, I'm going to have my man by my side' type of thing. But I would say the boys focus more on what's going on but the girls are just looking the part and having the materialistic stuff … They're too busy focusing on looking good and whatever. They spend their time in the toilets because every time, even if I go up there now, they're all doing their make up and their hair, trying to look the part because if they don't look the part … they will get teased. Because this culture is you have to look good, you have to wear the right stuff and they focus more on that than they focus on their education … Because of that pressure, if that was lifted they would have more time to do this and that, I feel. It's like the girls, 'why are you late?' 'Because I had to do my hair … for every guy to look at me and whatever'.
>
> (Learning mentor, *Dropping Out* study)

[…]

'Unacademic'/un-aspirational home cultures

As argued by Archer and Francis (2006), within UK education policy, minority ethnic underachievement is closely linked to the notion that these pupils (and their families) suffer from a lack of aspiration (e.g. see DfES, 2003,

2004, 2005). The issue of 'low aspirations' has largely been framed as the result of poverty ('We need to break the link between poverty and low aspiration once and for all' [DfES, 2005, p. 18]) but has also been linked with minority ethnic groups:

> There is a way to go before every child, regardless of their ethnicity, has an equal chance of reaching their potential.
>
> (DfES, 2005, para. 4.30)

Minority ethnic pupils have been targeted in particular for having low aspirations which, policy texts argue, require 'raising' or 'stretching'. For instance, the 2005 strategy paper explains:

> Our 'Aiming High' programme, focused on stretching the aspirations and achievement of black and minority ethnic groups, has begun to tackle deep seated underachievement.
>
> (DfES, 2005, para. 4.4)

As these extracts illustrate, policy discussions around aspiration and achievement are overwhelmingly framed in individualistic terms (i.e. aspirations are framed as personal choices) and are predominantly discussed in relation to pupils and parents. Scant consideration is given to the role that wider structural factors and/or teachers' attitudes and aspirations might play in shaping pupils' aspirations and achievement. Rather, the main thrust of policy discourse in relation to 'raising' aspirations and achievement remains grounded within a discourse of individualisation (called 'personalisation'; see DfES, 2005, para. 4.1). This approach places the primary responsibility for action (and hence 'blame' for low aspirations/achievement) with pupils and parents, detracting from any role that might be played by dominant structures or systems (e.g. schools, education policies themselves).

These constructions, I would argue, draw further strength from wider popular racist discourses and constructions of Black/minority ethnic families as 'culture poor' (Benson, 1996) and historical racist discourses which position Black people as being of lower intelligence ('IQ') (e.g. see Mama, 1995). Hence, Black pupils are positioned as 'naturally' unambitious and unacademic due to their location within 'unacademic' families and cultures.

Thus, dominant education policy discourse effectively silences other competing explanations and accounts of minority ethnic underachievement – such as the role that structural inequalities and racism might play in producing the tail-off in achievement that has been noted within many Black pupils' school careers. Indeed, many Black and Muslim boys across the different studies talked about the 'impossibility' of success (success as 'desired–denied') due to the prevalence of racism in society and its institutions (e.g. see Archer, 2003; Archer & Yamashita, 2003). However, they mostly felt denied a language and a space through which to express their concerns. Indeed, their counter accounts were often dismissed by education professionals as merely evidence of a 'chip on the shoulder', or were even cited as evidence of the boys' 'low aspirations'. For instance, one learning mentor (whilst, understandably, wanting to encourage and motivate his students to achieve) unwittingly dismissed and denied the boys' experiences of (perceived) racism:

> The other day I had four Black students and I said, 'guys you're not going to get far if you continue like this and you don't improve, I'm here to support you, whatever' and one of them said, 'who's going to give me a job anyway? The other day a woman looked at me on the bus and just turned away because I'm Black'. I said 'no it's not, if you go with that attitude: you are not getting a job or you're not going to achieve anything'.
>
> (Learning mentor, *Dropping Out* study)

It might also be argued that the dominant policy focus on 'unaspirational' minority ethnic pupils and families ignores the ways in which minority ethnic families routinely describe experiences of exclusion in relation to the education system (see Crozier & Reay, 2005). For instance, a number of Black parents and pupils across the studies recounted feeling uncomfortable and dissuaded from attending parents' evenings or engaging with home–school activities due to previous negative experiences. As one young Black woman explained – when describing how she felt her teachers treated her mother – these issues were compounded across 'race' and class:

> Some of the things they say ... it's making them look at my mum stupidly, and I'm like don't talk to my mum like that, she's right there, she understands what you're saying, she's not dumb.
>
> (Pupil, *Under performance* study)

The dominant policy emphasis upon the low aspirations of pupils and families can also be criticised for missing the significant role of teachers and schools in propagating low(er) aspirations for minority ethnic pupils. As numerous other studies have documented over the years, education professionals often tend to express lower aspirations for minority ethnic pupils than for their white counterparts (e.g. Mac an Ghaill, 1988; Basit, 1997; Connolly, 1997; Mirza, 1992; Parker-Jenkins *et al.*, 1997; Sewell, 1997; Blair & Bourne. 1998; Office for Standards in Education, 1999; Bhatti, 2000; Blair, 2001; Osborne, 2001; Shain, 2003; Tikly *et al.*, 2004). [...]

Construction of 'other'/pathologised minority ethnic pupils

So far issues have been discussed in relation to 'underachieving' minority ethnic pupils – but what about those who do achieve? In this section of the article, I would like to consider the ways in which even those minority pupils who ostensibly perform successfully within the education system can be pathologised and othered. To illustrate my arguments, I shall draw extensively upon data from the *British-Chinese pupils* study, conducted by Becky Francis and myself. The British Chinese have been identified as comprising the highest achieving ethnic group in the UK education system. In this research we found that even traditionally high achieving minority ethnic pupils, like the British Chinese, were constructed by teachers in problematic terms. However, the nature and form of these representations varied considerably from those of Black and Muslim pupils. [...]

In particular, we found that higher achieving minority ethnic pupils like the British Chinese were constructed as 'too quiet', ' too passive', as learning 'in the wrong way', and as 'repressed'. Each of these elements is now discussed in turn.

'Too quiet' and 'too passive'/the 'wrong sort of learning'

British Chinese pupils were overwhelmingly represented as a homogeneous passive, quiet and hardworking mass, whose capacity for 'focused' and 'dedicated' hard work was both eulogised and pathologised:

> It's very concentrated, determined sort of aggressive learning almost.
> (Teacher, *British-Chinese Pupils* study)

Chinese parents also described their awareness that their children were positioned as 'too passive' in class. Furthermore, some teachers complained of Chinese pupils: 'they're not noted for being kind of up for it, and argumentative, and wanting to argue a debate in class'. Another teacher expressed a similar concern that 'my worry would be that they're *unnecessarily quiet* sometimes'. Notions of quietness, diligence and passivity were associated with being the 'wrong' sort of learner. As feminist literature has identified, the 'ideal' pupil is constructed in dominant educational discourse as male, assertive and confident, constituting a yardstick against which other pupils are judged negatively (Walkerdine, 1988, 1990; Francis, 2000). The association of 'quietness' and 'passivity' positioned British Chinese pupils outside the discourse of the ideal learner and outside constructions of normative masculinity and femininity:

> They don't appear to be quite so loud and I'm thinking loud in all senses, both noise, you know, typical movement ... or physically, you can either, you can choose the amount of space you take up, just ... But I think their culture says that you shouldn't actually, you should be slightly more, *withheld*.
>
> (Teacher)

These qualities of quietness and passivity were also encapsulated by geographies of space and embodiment. For instance, a male teacher talked about Chinese boys tending to sit near the back of the class and a female teacher commented on how they don't 'stand out' in class. Pupils were concerned that popular representations of British Chinese as quiet and shy position them as weak, effeminate, powerless and 'victims'. A number of young people also explicitly discussed how this popular stereotype exposed them to increased racism and bullying, precisely because they were assumed to be 'soft targets'.

British Chinese femininity was particularly pathologised and infantilised, with an image being evoked of Chinese girls as educational automatons, who are too quiet, too passive and too repressed.

> Chinese girl students I've had, they just, *they would just work until you told them to stop*.
>
> (Teacher, *British-Chinese Pupils study*; emphasis added)

As noted elsewhere (Archer & Francis, 2005a), this notion of a work 'machine' denies Chinese girls agency and humanity, and places them outside discourses of the 'ideal pupil'. Hence, British Chinese girls were often described as being too passive and conformist, and concerns were expressed that they are 'too quiet', 'reserved' and 'shy'. The cause of this 'quiet and submissive' femininity was located within the 'tight', 'close' family structure and Chinese culture – i.e. in the very relations that were also regarded as producing the girls' high achievement. [...] this construction resonates with popular discourses around South Asian femininities, with South Asian girls similarly positioned as victims of oppressive home relations (e.g. see Rattansi, 1992; Brab, 1994).

[...]

Repressed masculinities and femininities

Minority ethnic pupils (such as Indian and British Chinese young people) who come from backgrounds that are constructed within dominant Western discourse as being 'culture rich' (Benson, 1996) are often assumed to suffer from 'restrictive' home cultures. This stereotype has been noted particularly in relation to non-Muslim south Asian families (e.g. Rattansi, 1992; Basit, 1997; Archer, 2003; Shain, 2003), but is also applied to Chinese communities. Indeed, I have argued elsewhere that constructions of 'rich', 'tight' yet 'oppressive' cultures can be understood as part of a discourse of Orientalism (see Archer & Francis, 2006). As noted by Rattansi (1992) and Alexander (2000), minority ethnic communities that are perceived as being culture-rich (like south Asian and Chinese families) tend to be ambivalently positioned as being both a (positive) source of strength and cohesion and a (negative) source of oppression and restriction of young people.

> On the one hand, the invocation of strong cultural values and traditions are [sic] seen as a positive contribution to society, overtly challenging wider social decay, whereas on the other, they are [sic] seen as constituting a source of internal oppression for the young.
>
> (Alexander, 2000, p. 5)

[...] Hyper(hetero)sexual masculinities and femininity tend to be equated with blackness, working-classness and educational underachievement, against which controlled and 'appropriate' sexuality (as opposed to 'hyper'sexuality) is integral to constructions of the 'good pupil' and middle-class identities. Many Chinese boys were judged to fall outside 'normal' masculinity (as conveyed via notions of agency and heterosexuality) whilst also being positioned outside working-class/Black forms of 'hyper' heterosexuality. Rather, British Chinese boys tended to be positioned as effeminate and subordinate – and hence not 'properly' masculine (by virtue of their association with ' passivity', 'quietness' and 'hard work').

[...] For girls, a 'good pupil' identity is predicated even more closely upon conformity to a controlled form of sexuality, as encapsulated by Diane Reay's (2001) 'nice girls' and Emma Renold's (2005) 'square girls'. As these studies have powerfully demonstrated, notions of innocence and chasteness are epitomised within the dominant discourse of the 'good' middle-class schoolgirl. However, despite their high academic achievement, British Chinese femininities were constructed outside of this idealised space. Rather, they were represented as asexual and repressed (as opposed to 'good'/ innocent). This distinction was seen as being produced through different family relations. In particular, whilst Chinese culture and family structures were acknowledged as producing a close 'fit' between British Chinese femininity and the education system, concerns were also expressed that this relationship could be oppressive/repressive and could result in 'abnormal' young femininities.

British Chinese pupils' perceived passivity and their subservient dedication to 'hard work' was further pathologised, with several teachers worrying that perhaps such pupils are too/overly focused on schoolwork, to the detriment of their overall development. For instance, questions were raised about whether these pupils' dedication to academic study was too 'one-sided' and whether this hard work and focused dedication might be psychologically and physically unhealthy for young people. British Chinese pupils themselves described being painfully aware of being positioned in this way (as problematically passive, quiet and repressed) by their teachers (see Archer & Francis, 2005a, b, 2006). For instance, as one pupil (Rebecca) put it:

> I think they [teachers] probably [think] – because I've been told lots of times that they see us really hardworking and we should relax more and play more and go out.

This association of British Chinese identity with passivity was also extended to parents – who were often described as not engaging with schools in the 'right' way. In particular, Chinese parents were characterised as being too passive and deferential. [...]

Conceptualising the impossibility of minority ethnic success: a trichotomy

I have argued, above, that minority ethnic pupils are complexly and variously positioned within educational discourse and that these positionings are shaped by interwoven racialised, classed and gendered discourses. However, I have also argued that the common theme within all of these constructions is the exclusion of minority ethnic pupils from the notion of 'success', *irrespective of their actual levels of achievement*. In order to bring these arguments together, I would like to draw upon the conceptual device of a trichotomy (see Table 18.2), which I developed in Archer & Francis (2006). Through this trichotomy I suggest that, within educational discourse, constructions of 'successful' pupil identity are predicated on a Cartesian dualism (a mind–body split) which is worked out along the lines of class, gender, race and sexuality. Attributes appear in normal text, inferences regarding pupil identity appear in italics.

[...]

Table 18.2 Model trichotomy mapping the discursive production of 'ideal', 'pathologised' and 'demonised' pupils in Western educational discourse

'Ideal' pupil	Other/pathologised pupil	Demonised pupil
Naturally talented	Diligent/plodding	Naturally unintelligent/lacking ability
innovative/initiative	Conformist	Peer-led
'Outside culture'	Culture-bound	Victim of 'bad' culture
Leaders	Followers	Anti-social/rebels
Enquiring/engaged	Deferent, unquestioning	Problematically challenging and disengaged
Assertive	Unassertive	Aggressive
Independent	Dependent	Ungovernable
Active	Passive	Anomic
'Normal' sexuality	Asexual/oppressed/repressed	Hyper-sexuality
Normal	*Other*	*Other/abnormal*
(White)	*(Asian/Oriental)*	*(Black/White working class)*
(Outside class/middle class)	*(Deserving poor)*	*(Undeserving poor/underclass)*
(Masculine/masculinised)	*(Feminine/feminised)*	*(Hyper-masculine/Hyper-feminine)*

Source: Archer & Francis (2006, p.66).

The trichotomy proposes a framework for understanding how the normalised 'ideal pupil' emerges as the dominant male, white, middle-class, Western subject (see also Francis & Archer, 2005a; Francis & Skelton, 2005). The privileged identity of the ideal pupil is effectively preserved via a splitting and projection of undesirable attributes onto other groups. In this way, minority ethnic success is always–already positioned as 'abnormal'/other and as potentially undesirable – it is always characterised as the 'wrong' approach to learning. Consequently, instances of minority ethnic educational achievement may be experienced as precarious, because the successful pupil subject position can never be authentically inhabited. The trichotomy also provides a way of understanding why (as so many studies have found) the abilities, achievement and behaviours of minority ethnic pupils continue to be misread/misinterpreted in different, albeit patterned, ways and why these evaluations tend to be 'singularly resistant to influence' (Walker & MacLure, 2005, p. 103).

Likewise, the trichotomy enables us to understand how the identity of the 'ideal pupil' can be preserved as 'male' and/or 'white' in the face of evidence of 'actual' high achievement by girls and/or particular minority ethnic pupils. This is because, despite their achievement, they are positioned as achieving it *in the wrong way* (e.g. via feminised 'plodding diligence' or through overly passive conformism within the classroom). Hence the trichotomy explains why the notion of 'over' achievement is only comprehensible as applied to female and/or minority ethnic others since 'achievement' is preserved as the rightful domain of the idealised, dominant subject position.

[...]

Conclusion

In this article I have argued that minority ethnic pupils in Britain are complexly and variously excluded from the identity of the 'ideal pupil' – and that these positionings are shaped by racialised, gendered and classed discourses. Indeed, I have argued that 'success' is very much an 'impossible' subject position for minority ethnic pupils – there appear to be very few routes available to minority ethnic pupils to access and perform a legitimated or authentic version of educational success.

I have attempted to unpack notions of 'success' and have traced the ways in which 'race', class, gender and sexuality interplay within the differential positioning (and self-positioning) of pupils in relation to notions and practices of 'success'. I have drawn attention to how minority ethnic pupils are afforded only the narrowest spaces within which to negotiate and experience forms of 'success' and to embody and perform their gendered, racialised and classed identities. Hence, I argue that for minority ethnic pupils, inhabiting success is (in many ways) impossible – and that the 'change' it demands from those who are always-already judged to have the 'wrong' bodies, behaviours and identities constitutes a form of injustice that must be urgently challenged.

The question remains, of course, as to how such trenchant and persistent inequalities might be usefully challenged. As the article has attempted to argue, the power of these discourses, and the complex ways in which they coalesce, are slippery and resistant to rational intervention. It is somewhat beyond the scope of this article to begin to explore the possibilities for how the current dominant representational regime might be interrupted. But one tentative starting point might be to offer the trichotomy model as a device for use within initial teacher education and ongoing professional development among both policy makers and practitioners in the field – in the hope that it might operate as a potentially useful point for reflection. Indeed, given the scale of the task, it might be hoped that the primary audience for change might be national policy makers – since policy has enormous power to shape the climate within with practitioners are able to work and pupils are able to learn. Moreover, as the article has argued, there is an urgent need to loosen and broaden the dominant discourses within which minority ethnic young people find themselves positioned as learners.

[...]

References

Ahmad, F. (2001) Modern Traditions? British Muslin Women and Academic Achievement, *Gender and Education,* 13(2), 137–152.

Alexander, C. (2000) *The Asian Gang.* Oxford: Berg.

Archer, L. (1998) The Social Construction of Identities by British Muslim Pupils Aged 14–15 Years. Ph.D. thesis, University of Greenwich.

Archer, L. (2001) 'Muslim Brothers, Black Lads, Traditional Asians': British Muslim young men's constructions of race, religion and masculinity, *Feminism & Psychology*, 11, 79–105.

Archer, L. (2002a) It's Easier that You're a Girl and that You're Asian: interactions of race and gender between researchers and participants, *Feminist Review*, 72, 108–132.

Archer, L. (2002b) Change, Culture and Tradition: British Muslim pupils talk about Muslim girls' post 16 'choices', *Race, Ethnicity and Education*, 5(4), 359–376. <http://dx.doi.org/10.1080/1361332022000030888>

Archer, L. (2003) *Race, Masculinity and Schooling: Muslim boys and education.* Maidenhead: Open University Press.

Archer, L. (2004) Re-Theorising 'Difference' in Feminist Research, *Women's Studies International Forum*, 27, 459–473. http://dx.doi.org/10.1016/j.wsif.2004.09.003 (accessed on 8 June 2010).

Archer, L. & Francis, B. (2005a) 'They Never Go off the Rails Like Other Ethnic Groups'; teachers' constructions of British Chinese pupils' gender identities and approaches to learning, *British Journal of Sociology of Education*, 26(2), 165–182.

Archer, L. & Francis, B. (2005b) Constructions of Racism by British Chinese Pupils and Parents. *Race, Ethnicity and Education*, 8(4), 387-407. <http://dx.doi.org/10.1080/13613320500323971>

Archer, L. & Francis, B. (2006) Challenging Classes? Exploring the Role of Social Class within the Identities and Achievement of British Chinese Pupils, *Sociology*, 40(1), 29–49. http://dx.doi.org/10.1177/0038038506058434 (accessed on 8 June 2010)

Archer, L. & Francis, B. (2007) *Understanding Minority Ethnic Achievement.* London: Routledge.

Archer, L., Halsall, A., Hollingworth, S. & Mendick, H. (2005) *Dropping out and Drifting Away: an investigation of factors affecting inner-city pupils' identities, aspirations and post-16 routes.* Final Report for the Esmee Fairbairn Foundation. London, IPSE.

Archer, L., Halsall, A & Hollingworth, S. (2007a) Class, Gender, (Hetero)Sexuality and Schooling: paradoxes within working-class girls' engagement with education and post-16 aspirations, *British Journal of Sociology of Education,* 28(2), 165–180.

Archer, L., Halsall, A. & Hollingworth, S. (2007b) Inner-City Femininities and Education: 'race', class, gender and schooling in young women's lives, *Gender and Education,* 19(5), 549–568.

Archer, L., Hollingworth, S. & Halsall, A. (2007) 'University's Not for Me – I'm a Nike Person': inner-city young people's negotiations of 'new' class identities and educational engagement, *Sociology,* 41(2), 219–237.

Archer, L., Maylor, U., Read, B. & Osgood, J. (2004) An Exploration of the Attitudinal, Social and Cultural Factors Impacting on Year 10 Student Progression. Coventry: Learning and Skills Council.

Archer, L. & Yamashita, H. (2003) Theorising Inner-City Masculinities: 'race', class, gender and education, *Gender & Education,* 15(2), 115–132.

Ball, S. J. (2003) *Class Strategies and the Education Market.* London: RoutledgeFalmer.

Basit, T. (1997) *Eastern Values, Western Milieu: identities and aspirations of adolescent British Muslim girls.* Aldershot: Ashgate.

Benson, S. (1996) Asians have Culture, West Indians have Problems: discourses on race inside and outside anthropology, in T. Ranger, Y. Samad & O. Stuart (eds) *Culture, Identity and Politics: ethnic minorities in Britain.* Aldershot: Avebury.

Bhatti, G. (2000) *Asian Children at Home and at School.* London: Routledge.

Blair, M. (2001) *Why Pick on Me? School Exclusion and Black Youth.* Stoke-on-Trent: Trentham Books.

Blair, M. & Bourne, J. (1998) *Making the Difference: teaching and learning strategies in successful multiethnic schools.* London: Department for Education and Employment.

Brah, A. (1994) Difference, Diversity and Differentiation, in D. James & A. Rattansi (eds) *'Race: Culture and Difference.* London: Sage.

Connolly, P. (1997) *Racism, Gender Identifies and Young Children.* London: Routledge.

Crozier, G. &. Reay, O. (eds) (2005) *Activating Participation.* Stoke-on-Trent: Trentham Books.

Delamont, S. (1989) *Knowledgeable Woman: structuralism and the reproduction of elites.* London: Routledge.

Department for Education and Skills (DfES) (2003) *Using the National Healthy School Stand to Raise Boys' Achievement.* Wetherby: Health Development Agency.

Department for Education and Skills (DfES) (2004) *Schools Race Equality Policies: from issues to outcomes.* London: HMSO.

Department for Education and Skills (DfES) (2005) http://www.standards.dfes.gov.uk/ethnicminorities/raising_achievement (accessed on 8 June 2010).

Francis, B. (2000) *Boys, Girls and Achievement.* London: RoutledgeFalmer.

Francis, B. (2006) Heroes or Zeros? The Discursive Positioning of 'Underachieving Boys' in English Neo-liberal Education Policy, *Journal of Education Policy,* 21(2), 187–200.

Francis, B. & Archer, L. (2005a) British-Chinese Pupils' and Parents' Constructions of the Value of Education, *British Educational Research Journal,* 31(1), 89–107.

Francis, B. & Archer, L. (2005b) Negotiating the Dichotomy of Boffin and Triad: British–Chinese pupils' constructions of 'laddism', *Sociological Review,* 53(3), 495–520.

Francis, B. & Skelton, C. (2005) *Reassessing Gender and Achievement.* London: Routledge.

Mac an Ghaill, M. (1988) *Young, Gifted and Black: student–teacher relations in the schooling of black youth.* Buckingham: Open University Press.

Mahony, P. & Zmroczck, C. (eds) (1997) *Class Matters.* London: Taylor & Francis.

Mama, A. (1995) *Beyond the Masks: race, gender and subjectivity.* London: Routledge

Mirza, H.S. (1992) *Young, Female and Black.* London: Routledge.

Office for Standards in Education (Ofstcd) (1999) *Raising the Attainment of Minority Ethnic Pupils: schools' and LEAs' response.* London: Ofsted.

Osborne, J. (2001) Academic Disidentification: unravelling underachievement among Black boys, in R. Majors (ed.) *Educating Our Black Children.* London: RoutledgeFalmer.

Parker-Jenkins, M., Hawe, K., Barrie, A. & Khan, S. (1997) Trying Twice as Hard to Succeed: perceptions of Muslim women in Britain. Paper presented at the British Educational Research Association Annual Conference, University of York, September.

Power, S., Edwards, T., Whitty, G. & Wigfall, V. (2003) *Education and the Middle Class.* Maidenhead: Open University Press.

Rattansi, A. (1992) Changing the Subject: racism, culture and education, in J. Donald & A. Rattansi (eds) *'Race': Culture and Difference.* Buckingham: Open University Press.

Reay, D. (2001) 'Spice Girls', 'Nice Girls', 'Girlies', and 'Tomboys'; gender discourses, girls' cultures and femininities in the primary classroom, *Gender and Education*, 13(2), 153–166.

Renold, E. (2005) *Girls, Boys and Junior Sexualities.* London: RoutledgeFalmer.

Rollock, N. (2006) Legitimate Players? An Ethnographic Study of Academically Successful Black Pupils in a London School. Unpublished Ph.D. thesis, Institute of Education, University of London.

Sewell, T. (1997) *Black Masculinities and Schooling: how black boys survive modern schooling.* Stoke-on-Trent: Trentham *Books.*

Sewell, T. (1998) Loose Canons: exploding the myth of the 'black macho' lad, in D. Epstein, J. Elwood, V. Hey & J. Maw (eds) *Failing Boys?* Buckingham: Open University Press.

Shain, F. (2003) *The Schooling and Identity of Asian Girls.* Stoke-on-Trent Trentham Books.

Tikly, L., Caballero, C. & Haynes, J. (2004) *Understanding the Educational Needs of Mixed Heritage Pupils.* London: Department for Education and Skills.

Walker, B. & MacLure, M. (2005) Home–School Partnerships in Practice, in G. Crozier & D. Reay (eds) *Activating Participation.* Stoke-on-Trent: Trentham Books.

Walkerdine, V. (1988) *The Mastery of Reason.* London: Routledge & Kegan Paul.

Walkerdine, V. (1990) *Schoolgirl Fictions.* London: Verso.

Walkerdine, V., Lucey, H. & Melody, J. (2001) *Growing up Girl: psychosocial explorations of gender and class.* Basingstoke: Palgrave.

Youdell, D. (2003) Identity Traps, or How Black Students Fail, *British Journal of Sociology of Education*, 24(1), 3–20.

Louise Archer's study of young people reminds us of the multiple ways in which many ethnic-minority young people are othered. Her model of 'trichotomy' moves our thinking beyond stereotyping and suggests ways in which this model can be applied to policy makers and practitioners in reflecting on the othering of minority-ethnic young people.

Part 4

Thinking differently

Chapter 19

Learning without limits

Susan Hart

This chapter shares some of what was learnt from a research project in which a team of researchers and teachers sought to understand the distinctive features of teaching that does not rely on the concept of fixed ability. The key ideas were developed collaboratively through exploring and comparing the similarities and differences across nine teachers' very different, individual ways of working. They are illustrated through the distinctive features of the thinking and practice of one member of the team, Julie, who works as a history teacher in a secondary school. The chapter offers an alternative model of practice that does not rely on the ability grouping and categorising that research has shown has damaged so many young people and their life chances.

Beginnings of a project

Over the years since comprehensive reorganisation, many teachers committed to the comprehensive ideal have rejected ideas of fixed ability and developed their practice to reflect their beliefs. They share the view, so powerfully expressed recently by Clyde Chitty (2002) that 'comprehensive reform has no meaning unless it challenges the fallacy of fixed ability or potential in education. It should aim to dismantle all the structures rooted in that fallacy that act as barriers to effective learning while, at the same time, it should facilitate practices that enable everyone to enjoy a full education'. However, while such teachers have, individually, developed their practices in line with their ideals, the distinctive features of teaching approaches based on a more optimistic view of human educability have never been articulated in such a way as to present a convincing and practicable alternative to ability-based teaching.

Meanwhile, long-discredited ideas about IQ and fixed ability continue to have currency in schools. Indeed, the thrust of government initiatives to raise standards over the past decade has been to place more, rather than less, emphasis on the need to differentiate by ability. These developments have reinforced the belief that it is essential to categorise – and group – pupils by ability in order to provide challenging teaching for all young people and to raise standards. Ofsted inspectors are briefed to check that teaching is differentiated for 'more able', 'average' and 'less able' pupils. Teachers are expected to make explicit in their schemes of work how this differentiation is achieved. The new emphasis upon target-setting and value-added measures of effectiveness means that from the earliest stages of education teachers are required to make explicit predictions about future levels of achievement.

In all of these developments, what exactly is meant by 'ability' goes largely unexamined. One view is that 'ability' is synonymous with 'attainment'; to say someone is 'less able' is simply to say something about how their current abilities to do certain things compare with others of the same age. Another view is that 'less able' implies something stable and relatively unalterable about underlying cognitive capacities, allowing predictions about future potential to be legitimately made. Current reform initiatives do not explicitly state that 'ability' means 'fixed ability'. Nevertheless, as Gillborn and Youdell (2000) point out, constantly requiring teachers to predict future performance can only be justified if it is underpinned by the assumption that current differences in children's learning reflect stable, measurable and relatively unalterable differences of potential.

This chapter describes the outcomes of a project intended to explore and elaborate models of teaching which do not rely on the notion of fixed or inherent ability. The project, which draws on the work of nine teachers, was initiated by researchers at the University of Cambridge School of Education, who felt that there was an urgent need to challenge the ideas about ability underlying the government improvement agenda. This follows decades of research testifying to the injustices and damaging effects of ability labelling (Hart 1998). The projects' name, *Learning Without Limits*, was inspired by a powerful passage in Stephen Jay Gould's *The Mismeasure of Man* which seemed to capture our central concerns:

> We pass through this world but once. Few tragedies can be more extensive than the stunting of life, few injustices deeper than the denial of an opportunity to strive or even to hope by a limit imposed from without but falsely identified as lying within.
>
> (Gould 1981: 29)

The team realised that it would not be sufficient simply to re-open well-rehearsed debates about the impact of ability labelling on young people's education and life chances. We would need to propose an alternative to ability-based pedagogy underpinned by a more optimistic view of human educability. We needed to show how teachers can cater for diversity within their classrooms without assuming that students can legitimately be grouped into the 'more able', 'average' and 'less able'. This would allow us, we hoped, to propose an alternative improvement agenda backed up by evidence.

About the research

The project began by advertising nation-wide for teachers who shared the aims and values of the project. The response reinforced our conviction that there were many educators 'out there' all over the country who shared our concerns. Fifty teachers sent for information about the project, and 22 applied, explaining why they wanted to participate. We were deeply moved by some of the personal experiences described in those application forms, including one from a teacher who, aged 16, had been devastated to be told by her head teacher that it would be 'a waste of everybody's time' for her to stay on in the sixth form. We held 17 interviews, and a team of four primary and five secondary teachers covering a range of very different teaching contexts was established.

Over the following year we spent many hours in these teachers' classrooms, observing and interviewing both teachers and pupils. We also met to share our thinking and develop the research collectively. In constant collaboration with the teachers, we gradually built up individual accounts of the key constructs at the heart of each teacher's thinking, and an understanding of how these constructs worked together to create a distinctive pedagogy. We then summarised these and looked for common themes and differences, to try to identify the key concepts and practices that are distinctive of teaching that does not rely on ideas of fixed or inherent ability. From this collective analysis, we have identified one core principle, which acts as the inspiration and driving force at the heart of these teachers' practice. In addition, we have identified three core ideas that describe the mechanisms through which the principle is translated into practice in the classroom to create a distinctive and practicable pedagogy. This principle and its associated ideas are illuminated in the distinctive features of one teacher's work.

The principle of transformability

Julie is the head of Humanities in a secondary school serving a predominantly white, rural community. Her antipathy to ability labelling goes back to her own school days when she noticed the damage that can be done. She determined to create, in her own classroom, an environment where young people's learning powers would not be limited or demeaned by such labels. When she applied to become a head of department, she chose a school where she would have freedom to organise groups and develop her teaching in accordance with her values. In her application she explained her feelings on labelling some young people as 'less able':

> Less able to succeed in a rigidly structured testing system maybe, but not less able to develop into thoughtful, talented human beings with a great deal to offer society. It would seem reasonable to assume that as the human intellect and potential is so diverse, the way children and teenagers express their intellectual and creative capacity will also be equally as diverse. [...] Stories of students who achieved little at school but went on to great success in all walks of life should not surprise us. Millionaires who cannot even sign their name are a rare and probably somewhat exaggerated example, but the concept is clear. Not everybody is able to demonstrate their unique talents in the current rigid education system. Once such people leave the establishments that labelled them 'failures', they can draw on their untapped skills. Others, however, robbed of self-esteem and confidence struggle to make a go of their lives.

Looking at this now, we can see how it links to the core principle we call 'transformability'. Julie rejects ability labels because she knows that existing ability hierarchies are predicated upon particular systems of education, curriculum and pedagogy which do not provide adequate opportunity or flexibility for all to succeed. There is nothing natural or inevitable about the existing education system, any more than there is anything natural and inevitable about the attainment or ability hierarchies that it produces. Ability labels lead us to expect a stable relationship between present and future – that future attainments will broadly reflect existing patterns. But this will be so only if everything continues unchanged – if nothing is done to unlock some of the 'rigidities' that constrain learning. The driving force underlying Julie's work is a passionate conviction that she does have significant power to change current practices in a direction that she believes will be more enabling for young people.

Julie sees considerable scope for enhancing learning by freeing it from the limits imposed by organisational practices such as streaming and setting. These not only damage self-esteem, but lock young people into boxes that determine and justify the provision subsequently made for them. Julie sympathises with those who give up because they feel that they have been written off. 'It's hard to keep trying, isn't it,' she says, 'when you are told you are being entered for an exam where you can only get a D?' Her resistance to streaming, setting and attainment-based grouping in the classroom is not just in the interests of those who find themselves in the lower groups and sets. Her experience has led her to conclusions similar to those recently reported by Boaler *et al.* (2000) who, when investigating mathematics teaching found that teachers working with top sets often did not recognise or address the students' difficulties, while students, feeling under pressure to perform, were afraid to admit when they didn't understand.

Julie strives to increase flexibility and create space for individuality and creativity to flourish through offering a wide variety of learning opportunities with open access for everybody, though this work is inevitably constrained by the rigidities of examinations. She sees herself as actively working to create better learning opportunities for young people. So, when she looks to the future, she expects to see significant changes – not continuity – in young people's attitudes, responses and attainments, as a consequence of the learning environment becoming more supportive and enabling. With ability-based teaching, children's futures as learners are already to some degree laid down. Teachers see their task as one of ensuring that each child reaches his or her presumed 'potential'. In contrast, for Julie the future is in the making in the present. What will happen next depends upon what is done now. There is scope for all young people to become better learners if conditions are enabling and learning can be freed from some prevailing constraints. The exact nature and extent of future improvement cannot be known in advance, so the future is necessarily open and unpredictable. Julie is inspired by the sense that the making of the future is at least in part in her hands, that through her practice she can help to make the everyday experience of education more enriching and life-enhancing. Through the choices she makes, Julie works to *transform* both current patterns of interaction and future possibilities for learning by opening up opportunities that might otherwise have remained closed, and by taking concerted action to release learning from limits that might otherwise constrain future development.

This core principle of transformability is at work in everything that Julie does: her questioning, expectations, the tasks she sets, the environment she constructs, her interactions, assessments and feedback to pupils. She understands that the choices she makes have profound and transforming effects upon the quality of young people's educational experiences.

Mechanisms of transformability

An example of the principle in action can be seen in Julie's early efforts to win round a particular group. Joining the school in the summer term, before she had been able to introduce any changes into the systems of grouping already in place, Julie took over a bottom-set history group. They greeted her, she recalls, 'with something like "We're the thickos, we don't do any work but we managed to give our last teacher a nervous breakdown"'. Despite what was probably exaggerated bravado, she felt their remarks were highly revealing of their perceptions of themselves: 'They thought all they were good for was being pains and tried as hard as possible to fulfil that image.' Nevertheless, Julie was convinced that, in time, it would be possible to change their image of themselves, and that there were specific things she could do to enable that change to happen.

As Julie talks about how she set about trying to change the dynamics with this challenging group, she relates her choices and actions to what she thinks might be going on in students' minds. She shows that she recognises the young people as active agents who make sense of their day-to-day experience in their own terms and who act accordingly. She also understands that students' states of mind are profoundly affected by their experiences in school. She understands the subtle messages that environments, resources and practices can convey to young people about their worth and capabilities. She exploits this to help rebuild their sense that they are taken seriously as learners, that their efforts at learning are valued, and that they can derive enjoyment and satisfaction from learning. She tries to turn things around with this group by offering them experiences which gradually, incrementally, enable them to change the way that they think about themselves and what school has to offer them.

As she describes the steps she took, practically, in her own teaching, Julie emphasises the *connections* between these steps and the positive effects that she expected and hoped for in the self-image, attitudes and feelings of the students. She began by 'changing the whole image' of the room where they were working, to create a more stimulating and relaxed environment. She changed the way that desks were grouped and provided them with attractive new folders 'so that they could see that their work was going to be valued'. She also used a lot of model making in the initial stages, which they enjoyed and during which she had the opportunity to begin building relationships. Slowly things began to change.

Julie's main strategy is not to try to influence students' behaviour through exercising forms of control. Rather she tries to turn things around by connecting with their consciousness as people, by trying to understand what makes a difference to their willingness and power to make use of the resources available to them to sustain and further their own learning in school.

Co-agency – connecting teachers' power and learners' power

We call the immense potential that is opened up by connecting teachers' power and learners' power *co-agency*. Julie understands that if teachers' power is to be effective it must connect with and harness young people's own power to make a difference to their own future lives. However committed and thoughtful teachers are, they cannot make a difference unless students themselves choose to take up the invitations to learn that are extended to them. And they will not do this unless what they encounter in school connects with their own sense of who they are, what they can do and what they want for their lives. So a major priority for Julie is to try to understand school experiences from the young people's perspective.

As Julie talks about her teaching, she continually makes reference to the subjective conditions that she believes will lay the foundations for young people to become more powerful and committed learners. Young people are more likely to choose to engage and invest in school learning if they are enabled to feel competent and in control, to find learning stimulating and enjoyable, to feel safe and supported and to feel themselves an equally valued member of the school community. Julie plans tasks and activities that should enable everyone to participate and succeed; she chooses *not* to set different tasks for different groups or tables of pupils by reference to their perceived levels of achievement, as is common in ability-focused classrooms. She prefers to offer common tasks presented in ways that make them open, accessible and engaging for everybody:

> I tend to set work that everybody can engage in at one level or another, which doesn't mean that I am not aware of their difficulties, if they have any. It just means that I don't want to go round the room saying 'well you're very clever, so you can do this but you're a bit thick so I'll give you that'. Because that's what you are doing, isn't it really? And it's surprising how well students do perform at certain tasks if they are given the chance.

Julie is convinced that, whatever the good intentions, the message that young people pick up from different tasks and/or ability-based groups is that some young people are 'not good enough' to do the tasks offered to others. While it is essential that everyone has work that they can do, these differentiated approaches are not an option for her because of the negative impact they can have on people's states of mind. Sometimes she provides double-sided sheets – with the same task presented in different ways on either side – and trusts the students to choose which side they want to do. What often happens, she finds, is that 'students who you would think will struggle do both sides'. Julie vets her choices, in relation to routine tasks of planning, teaching and assessment, not just in terms of immediate learning intentions but also in terms of the anticipated effects of her chosen approaches on the states of mind that she knows will determine the quality of future learning.

Julie is also highly alert to shifting emotional states that cause young people to switch off or give up when they encounter difficulties or challenges. She makes choices that she believes will increase their sense of safety and therefore willingness to take risks in their thinking and learning. She is very careful how she responds when offering help as she knows that this will affect students' willingness to admit to difficulties and ask for help in the future. She recognises that it is much more risky to ask for help than to cover up difficulties by copying from others or going through the motions of a task in a superficial way.

She tries to reassure students that they are not being judged when they admit to difficulties, and is always prepared to explain again and again, until students are confident that they understand. She stresses how important it is 'not to make them feel stupid (by saying) something like "What do you mean, you don't understand that? We went through it last lesson"'. She realises how easily comments and assessments of work can be read and interpreted by students as judgements on their worth and identity as people. She uses a set of stamps with different positive messages to lighten the atmosphere around the making of judgements, as well as helping (as one of her students expressed it) creating 'a friendlier feel with the teacher' than is created by grades or by comments alone.

Perhaps the most important state of mind that Julie seeks to nurture is 'feeling equal'. Often in schools what comes across to some students is that they are not valued equally. They feel second-class, and 'their work becomes second class. It's a self-fulfilling prophecy'. This sense of inequality is derived from unintentional messages that often go unnoticed by teachers. Julie tries to undo the effects of such negative messages by, for example, offering open tasks, constructed so that everyone can take part whatever their starting points. She encourages collaborative interaction, where everybody is recognised as a resource for the rest of the group. She structures tasks and activities so that everyone can become, and experience being seen as, an expert in particular areas of the curriculum that they, and not others, have chosen to research.

The ethic of 'everybody'

While Julie is very appreciative of the diversity and individuality of her students, it is noticeable that she frequently talks about them collectively

She constantly refers to what 'everybody' must have the opportunity to do, learn and experience. She expresses concern to ensure that 'nobody' is excluded or deterred from engaging in the learning activities offered to the group. She makes her choices based on what she believes will make for better learning for everybody and not just better for 'some people'.

Though students are individuals with diverse interests, backgrounds, experiences, knowledge, understandings and skills, Julie's formulation of what will enable them to become better learners – the positive states of mind and strengthened powers as active agents in their own learning – is the same for everybody. To be a powerful and effective learner, *everybody* needs to have a sense of competence and control, to feel safe enough to take risks, to experience curiosity and excitement in learning, to feel equally valued and to derive a sense of satisfaction and success. What helps to create, restore or enhance these states of mind will not necessarily always be the same for everybody, but the framework of choice-making *is* common to everybody.

We can see, then, that with ability-based teaching, teachers reference their teaching decisions to different ability groups. They set expectations, form groups, design tasks, ask questions, interact to support learning and evaluate progress, on the basis of what is considered appropriate for 'more able', 'average' and 'less able' students. Julie, in contrast, has a single, common point of reference: the potential for enhancing the exercise of student agency. Because she has a single reference point, many of these decisions can legitimately be taken collectively. Julie does not need to start out from an assumption that because students are all different she ought ideally to make her choices 30 times over, or (as a minimum) three times over to take account of the differing needs of young people of different ability.

In Julie's approach, diversity in learning experiences, opportunities and outcomes is achieved through co-agency, through what teachers and young people do *together*. Catering for diversity is not simply a task for the teacher, as in ability-based pedagogy. The technical task of *matching* tasks and learners gives way to a deeper, more complex, interactive process of *connection*, a meeting of minds, purposes and actions (co-agency) in which the teacher acts to try to enhance young people's ability and willingness to make full use of all the resources available to them to sustain and promote their own learning in school. Since young people are active agents in their own learning, when connection is successful it inevitably results in different experiences and outcomes, since everyone is unique, everyone brings and contributes something different, and makes their own meanings through active engagement in the learning opportunities provided. The teacher's task is to make the good choices, those that will enable and encourage everyone in the productive exercise of their agency, and then extend an open invitation to learn that can be accepted equally by everyone.

Trusting the learner

Such an approach rests on a basic position of trust. Julie trusts young people to find relevance and purpose in relevant and purposeful activity. She trusts them to make choices and construct their own learning within the supportive framework she provides. She trusts them to contribute to one another's learning, to take up her invitation to co-agency and to participate in the worthwhile activity of learning. This basic position of trust assumes that young people will choose to engage if the conditions are right. So when learners choose not to engage or appear to be inhibited in their learning, she tries to re-evaluate her choices and practices in order to understand what might be hindering their participation and learning.

> Sometimes you come out of the lesson and you think 'That didn't really work' or 'I must change that next time' or 'so and so is sitting in the corner there and was very quiet and didn't seem to get anything out of that'. So that is what I am always looking for. I try to think beforehand but sometimes things happen that you don't allow for, or an activity just wasn't suitable for a certain student. So you have to try to change it.

Julie realises that she cannot just rely on her own observations to make accurate judgements about how students are responding. She encourages dialogue with them in order to find out what is going on in their heads. As part of the research, Julie involved the students in some activities to explore their experiences and perceptions of themselves as learners. For the most part, she found that her trust in her students was reciprocated by a trust in her. She was deeply dismayed, however, to find that one or two students admitted to feeling uninterested or even unhappy in her history lessons. Julie comments:

> This was a complete revelation to me and my initial reaction was one of incredulous indignation – how could students possibly feel like that in my lesson? However, after this initial reaction, I began to understand that for some students the whole experience of school was uncomfortable; given a choice they would rather not be there. This made me more aware that as a teacher one should never become complacent. It is necessary to try to empathise with all students and strive to find new strategies to help them cope with the emotional nightmare of being compelled to come to school and participate in lessons.

For students whose previous experience has generated such significant barriers to learning, there is a long path to travel to undo the damage and begin to build more positive states of mind. In her response to these students' comments, Julie demonstrates her acceptance of and empathy for young people as they are, while at the same time recognising the possibility for change. Her trust sustains her effort to go on searching for ways to reach out and make connections that will free young people to learn more successfully.

Summarising key ideas

So what have we learnt from the research about the distinctive features of teaching free from the concept of ability? We have found a common belief in **transformability** that informs everything that teachers do. Transformability contrasts with the fatalism associated with ability labels. It means that things have the potential to change, and that people have the power to change things for the better by what they do in the present. Teachers understand that they must harness their own power to young people's power **(co-agency)** if they are to be successful in making a difference to future development. They do this by constantly making connections in their minds between classroom conditions and subjective states; by considering the positive and negative effects of their choices on the students' exercise of agency. Choices must be made in the interests of **everybody**, because everybody counts and everybody's learning is equally important. Moreover, what the teachers are working to achieve – at the level of subjective experience – is the same for everybody. So they do not have to start out each time from a perception of the class divided up in their minds into different groups of learners with significantly differing needs. All of this depends on a fundamental **trust** which the teachers have in their students, trust in their powers as thinkers and learners, to engage if conditions are made right and to find and create meaning. Moreover, they trust that no matter what has gone before, there is always potential for growth and change as a result of what happens in the present.

Ideas in action

To conclude, I show how these ideas come together in the construction of a single lesson. As part of a topic on medicine with her Year 10 group, Julie decided to use an extract from Chaucer as a key resource for students' enquiry into people's views of doctors and medicine in the Middle Ages. A Chaucer text may seem to be a bad choice for a class where a number of students experience considerable difficulties with literacy. But Julie felt, on balance, that a successful experience of engaging with such a difficult text might do more to reshape these young people's view of themselves as competent readers and learners than an activity that spared them the challenges of using their literacy skills. She believes that it is what teachers and learners do with a text, not inherent difficulties within the text, that determines its suitability and its potential for becoming accessible to everyone. None of the students in the class would be able to make much of this Chaucer text, if simply given it to read. Yet *everyone* can get something out of it if it is presented in such a way that they feel empowered to engage with it and are helped to construct their own meanings in relation to it.

In thinking how to achieve this, Julie projects herself into the minds of her students and tries to imagine how they will respond. She decides that the priority must be to nurture students' sense that they *will* be able to do the task, to create positive expectations of success, while at the same time helping them to recognise and use fully their resources. She decides to begin with some questions which invite students to contribute their present-day experiences of doctors. She then asks different groups to discuss briefly and report on what they already know about medical practices and how people viewed doctors and medicine in other periods of history already studied. This is intended to help build a context for reading the text, drawing attention to areas of existing knowledge that they could draw upon as points of reference in interpreting the passage. She begins to build up a narrative context for reading the text, through introducing them to the *Canterbury Tales*, via a brief, entertaining video extract to heighten interest and curiosity in the topic. By doing this, Julie hopes to relax and reassure them that this is something that they are going to enjoy and be able to do. By offering visual support as well as background information, she hopes to strengthen their ability to picture what they are reading and so assist them in making the text meaningful. She then explains the purpose of the Chaucer passage, and reads it aloud to them, to allow students to hear it and begin to make their own meanings. Students are encouraged to spot difficult words and passages in the text, and annotate their texts to explain word meanings. They then work in pairs to construct their own understandings, with the support of a series of questions. Working together means they can share ideas and explore meanings, and the mutual support gives students a chance to do things with a partner that they would not or could not do on their own. Julie monitors closely individuals' responses during the course of activities – and particularly their body language – for signs of frustration or confusion so that she can judge when best to intervene to assist their learning.

As Julie makes her choices about the lesson she is constantly thinking about their subjective experience. She anticipates barriers to learning at the level of task and text and takes steps to minimise them.

> There are students in there who have difficulty with written sources –
> written anything really; the language of that particular source without a
> lot of guidance would have just thrown them and they would have gone
> into panic mode and wouldn't have been able to do anything.

She does not define this reaction simply as a problem for the less confident
readers and learners, but as a natural reaction for any individual – adult or
child – confronted by a complex text or task.

> You know that they are going to glance at it and think 'what on earth is
> that about?' as you know sometimes *we* (adults) can, when you see a
> poem or something for the first time, it takes a few readings and you feel
> a little bit threatened by it.

As well as providing the video introduction to heighten interest and reassure
them that what they were going to do was accessible, she makes a point of
acknowledging the difficulty of the source. She takes active steps to make
students feel comfortable and safe by explicitly acknowledging how they might
be feeling – not just legitimising their feelings but reassuring them in advance
that adequate support was going to be provided. She also builds into the activity
the support of collaborative working, reinforcing an ethos of collectivity: that
everybody has something to contribute to and learn from one another.

Julie decides what to do on the basis of what she believes will make it
more likely that everyone, rather than just some people, will feel empowered
to engage in the activity. To an observer, the lesson generates a lively buzz of
activity, and there is no evidence of anyone opting out or finding the text
just too challenging. In her own review of the lesson, Julie comments: 'I
don't think there was anybody in the room who was struggling with the
work. Even if they were being prompted a little bit, they were still getting it
done … The source was difficult but they managed to cope with it after we
went through it and they felt quite good about that.'

Julie's account of the thinking underpinning this lesson demonstrates her
understanding that learning tasks and activities are *made* accessible to
everyone through judicious thought and action on the part of the teacher.
Accessibility is a quality produced through choices and actions, not an
objective quality inherent in the relationship between particular content and
learning objectives and the characteristics of particular students. While fully
cognisant of the diversity of her group, Julie makes the text, and the learning
that it is intended to promote, accessible to everyone through *one* set of
choices judiciously selected to support and empower everyone.

No doubt there are some teachers reading about this lesson who feel that it would be completely unsuitable for some of the young people they work with. However, what is important and distinctive about Julie's pedagogy is not tied to any particular set of choices or classroom practices but to the principles and mechanisms through which decisions are made. Julie would not choose this text as a way of developing students' skills in working with historical sources if she did not think she could make the experience of working with it empowering for everybody. With different groups of students, she might make different choices about how to include everyone, but the basic process and points of reference for decision-making would be the same.

If all young people could have the opportunity regularly and routinely to participate fully and on an equal basis in activities carefully devised in this way, such experiences could, in time, dramatically influence how they see themselves as learners, their power and desire to develop their learning in school contexts. And if teachers like Julie join forces with one another to share and expand their repertoires and to make the experience of learning without limits more widely available across the education system, they will be able to bring closer to reality their vision of making the experience of education more enriching and life-enhancing for everybody.

An alternative improvement agenda?

We believe that transformability-based teaching could play a central and critical role in the construction of an alternative improvement agenda, based around a critique of intelligence testing and ability labelling. While the project started out from a critique of current reform initiatives, there clearly is overlap between our values and some of those underpinning the standards agenda. There is common concern that the talents and capabilities of many young people remain untapped throughout their compulsory education. There is a common wish to challenge assumptions that not much can be expected of young people from disadvantaged backgrounds, and a common commitment to concerted action to reduce class-based discrepancies of achievement (*TES* 2002).

The current programme of reforms rightly recognises the power that schools and teachers have to influence young people's development. The ideas in this chapter offer a readily sustainable and self-generating approach rooted in teachers' own values, commitments and aspirations. Improvement does not have to be imposed on teachers, and superimposed on existing teaching by managers or inspectors, because the driving force comes from teachers' passions and sense of social justice; teachers' desire and ability to make a difference *are* what makes teaching worthwhile.

Acknowledgements

I would like to thank all the members of the Learning Without Limits research team for their contribution to the ideas in this chapter: Narinder Brach, Claire Conway, Annabelle Dixon, Mary Jane Drummond, Nicky Madigan, Julie Marshall, Donald McIntyre, Alison Peacock, Anne Reay, Yahi Tahibet, Non Worrall and Patrick Yarker. I would also like to thank Julie Marshall, Annabelle Dixon, Mary Jane Drummond and Donald McIntyre for reading and commenting on early drafts.

References

Boaler, J., Wiliam, D. and Brown, M. (2000) Students' experiences of ability grouping – disaffection, polarisation and the construction of failure. *British Educational Research Journal*, **26**(5), 631–48.

Chitty, C. (2002) Selection by specialisation. In Chitty, C. and Simon, B. (eds) *Promoting Comprehensive Education in the 21st Century*. Stoke-on-Trent: Trentham Books.

Gillborn, D. and Youdell, D. (2000) *Rationing Education: Policy, Practice, Reform and Equity*. Buckingham: Open University Press.

Gould, S. J. (1981) *The Mismeasure of Man*. New York: Norton.

Hart, S. (1998) A sorry tail: ability, pedagogy and educational reform. *British Journal of Educational Studies*, **46**(2), 153–68.

Times Educational Supplement (*TES*) 4 January 2002.

We were pleased to be able to commission this chapter and inspired when we read it. For us, it illustrates how inclusive education is less about differentiating educational experiences to meet different needs, and more about challenging traditional practices and discourses to make education meaningful for everyone. The chapter is challenging to our thinking, yet entirely practical for professionals wanting to draw on its wisdom.

Chapter 20

Gender, 'special educational needs' and inclusion

Shereen Benjamin

In this chapter Shereen Benjamin shows that it is nonsensical to isolate special education needs from other aspects of diversity. With particular reference to gender and SEN she shows how the two social constructs interact and limit the ways in which pupils see themselves and are seen by others. She goes on to show that, by giving careful consideration to their processes and cultures, schools can generate conditions of greater equality in the drive towards inclusion.

Introduction

Two distinct strands run through many of the current debates on inclusion in education, and these are reflected in policy, practice and provision. The first strand increasingly addresses 'inclusion' as though it refers almost exclusively to educational provision for children considered to have 'special educational needs' (SEN). This strand is underpinned by particular understandings of perceived academic ability. The second strand, often referred to as 'social inclusion', addresses aspects of educational provision in relation to structural and systemic 'differences': principally those of gender/sexuality, social class and ethnicity. The separation of these two strands, however, has led to incomplete analyses of the complexities of school life, and can contribute to an erroneous assumption that SEN can somehow be separated from other axes of difference. If we want to understand processes of inclusion and exclusion in schooling, we have to look at the intersection of multiple axes of difference – for example what it means to be a girl from a minority ethnic group who experiences difficulties with literacy. This chapter looks at how the understandings of perceived academic ability that underpin SEN interact with differences of gender/sexuality in the schooling experiences of children and young people. It also takes account of how this interaction is further nuanced by social class and by ethnicity.

Statistical evidence gives a clear indication of the fact that provision for children and young people considered to have SEN is a gendered phenomenon. A recent survey of SEN provision in wealthy Organisation for Economic Co-operation and Development (OECD) countries found that boys are consistently over-represented amongst those pupils considered to need specialist educational provision, both in special schools and in special classes in mainstream schools (OECD 2000). This chapter starts with a brief review of this, and other, statistical evidence. But to begin to unravel the stories behind those statistics, we need to look at the links between SEN, and masculinities and femininities – what it means to be a boy or a girl – in schools and classrooms. The bulk of the chapter is given over to an exploration of how masculinities and femininities interact with understandings of 'ability', as well as with understandings around ethnicity and social class, in the complex processes through which boys and girls come to be identified as having SEN. It goes on to consider how schools and teachers can act on such understandings as they strive towards inclusion. The chapter draws on research evidence in the form of interviews and observations with children, parents/carers and teachers in primary, secondary and special schools.

Gender and SEN: What do the statistics tell us?

To almost any SEN practitioner, the answer to this question – of what the statistics tell us – is a very obvious one. Certainly, those of us who have worked in specialist schools and other settings for any length of time have become very used to seeing girls outnumbered by boys in most of our classes. The figures confirm this. In 2000, the OECD conducted a major survey into SEN provision in its member countries (OECD 2000). The findings on gender were fairly consistent across all the countries surveyed. Girls accounted for between 30 per cent and 40 per cent of special school pupils, with boys being a significant majority: in the UK 32.2 per cent of special school pupils were girls as against 67.8 per cent boys. The gender ratios in special classes in mainstream schools were very similar. When it came to the gender ratios of pupils with SEN in mainstream classes, the UK figure was again 32.2 per cent girls to 67.8 per cent boys, though the proportion in some countries evened out slightly, and in France came close to an even balance at 48.4 per cent girls to 51.6 per cent boys.

When we examine the statistics further, other interesting variations come to light. In 1996, a team of researchers in England noted that the over-representation of boys in special schools and units 'is especially marked in schools for those with emotional and behavioural difficulties (6–8 times as many boys), language units (4 times) and autistic schools (2–4 times as many). Moreover, these gender disparities are strongly influenced by 'race': children of African-Caribbean origin are over-represented in special schools and those of South Asian origin under-represented' (Daniels *et al*. 1996: 1). In the case of schools for children considered to have emotional and behavioural difficulties (EBD), it is worth noting that there is considerable evidence that African-Caribbean boys of both primary and secondary school age are at greater risk of exclusion from mainstream schools (Parsons 1996; Hayden 1997; Wright *et al*. 2000; Blair 2001), and that many of these excluded children are considered to have SEN, which are subsequently met in EBD schools or units. Traditionally, pupils of Asian origin have been less at risk of exclusion: there is evidence that this remains largely true for girls of Asian origin, whilst the proportion of boys of Asian origin excluded from school is growing (Mehra 1998). Meanwhile, Scottish Office figures confirm that working-class boys are found in greater numbers in the 'less acceptable' categories of moderate learning difficulties (MLD) and EBD, whilst the non-stigmatised category of specific learning difficulties is dominated by middle-class boys (Riddell 1996).

These statistics raise a number of issues that are of interest here. First, they raise all sorts of questions about the implications of labelling, and about the particular consequences of particular labels. Whatever we may feel about the rights and wrongs of assigning children and young people to specific SEN categories, we need to look at how the consequences of assigning them are gendered. Second, they raise the question of why the gender differentials are so consistent in the participating countries, and why these differentials have endured over time. Third, and perhaps most important, they require us to consider gender, SEN, and what I call the 'multiple axes' of difference of ethnicity, social class and so on, as inter-related and interactive. If we accept that inclusion is a desirable goal in society in general and schooling in particular, the policies, practices and provision we design at all levels will have to take account of differential school effects across multiple axes of difference (Lingard *et al*. 1998).

In order to explain the over-representation of boys amongst children considered to have SEN, we need first to think about how we understand the phenomenon of educational needs. At one extreme, we could argue that SEN are entirely biologically- and physiologically-produced. We could then argue that boys are over-represented amongst those pupils considered to have SEN because they are 'naturally like that', due, perhaps, to some at present unknown aspect of male physiology. Or, at the other end of the continuum, we could argue that SEN are entirely socially-constructed, and that boys' over-representation is due, therefore, to social practices and societal inequalities. Somewhere between these two extremes is an understanding that SEN have a material, organic basis, which can sometimes be easy to discern, but are sometimes far from obvious. This material or physical origin produces a range of possibilities for an individual, which then interacts with social practices. Thus girls and boys schooled in a society with sexist assumptions are more likely to experience different responses to their behaviour and go down different educational pathways, but this is not inevitable.

This chapter will focus mainly on the 'high incidence' category of mild to moderate learning difficulties (MLD). This category is characterised by debates as to how far these perceived learning difficulties have a material, biological origin and as to what that biological origin might be. The category also presents something of a challenge to sociologists who might prefer explanations that are entirely social (Nash 2001). The understanding I am working with here is that material factors interact with social phenomena, and that, in the end, it is unproductive to try to tease out the 'real' from the socially-constructed, though it remains vital to interrogate the consequences of SEN designation.

In Norway, where 70 per cent of pupils considered to have SEN are boys, Skarbrevik (2002) argues that 'the higher incidence of boys in special education during the school years is caused by an interaction between genetic or biological factors and a pedagogy that does not match the educational needs of male students' (Skarbrevik 2002: 97). In other words, he argues that boys tend to be predisposed to have SEN, and that this combines with teachers' boy-unfriendly practice to produce an over-representation of boys amongst pupils considered to have SEN. But this is far from being a plausible explanation in a UK context. It does not give us any way of coming to understand the active participation of boys in the processes through which they come to be perceived as having SEN. Nor does it take account of gender as a lived social, and not just biological, practice. What is missing is an understanding of the interaction between discourses and discursive practices – the taken-for-granted meanings and actions – of SEN with those of masculinities. Connell (1995) notes that:

> Rather than attempting to define masculinity as an object (a natural character type, a behavioural average, a norm) we need to focus on the processes through which men and women conduct gendered lives. 'Masculinity', to the extent the term can be briefly defined at all, is simultaneously a place in gender relations, the practices through which

men and women engage that place in gender, and the effect of those practices in bodily experience, personality and culture.

(Connell 1995: 71)

Children with SEN conduct gendered lives, as do all children. The statistics tell us that there is a story to tell about the processes through which children considered to have SEN conduct particular versions of gendered lives. This story has two aspects. First, how does the gendering of school and pupil cultures produce a system through which boys are disproportionately considered to have SEN, and through which the extra resources associated with SEN are allocated disproportionately to them? Second, how does the designation as having SEN constrain or create a specific range of possibilities within which children can conduct gendered lives?

Masculinities and SEN

Ryan spent most of his primary years in a mainstream school, transferring to the special sector at the beginning of Year 5 (aged 9–10). He brought with him an unhappy history of failing to make discernible academic progress, and of failing to make friends with other children in mainstream schooling. By the end of his first half-term in a small all-age special school, he declared himself to be much happier, and began to make academic progress, albeit not at a typical rate. His mother described how she made sense of the improvements in Ryan's attitude towards schooling:

> We didn't want to put Ryan into a special school, but now that he's here, our family life, well, our family life has changed beyond recognition, he's like a changed boy ... In [mainstream] school, all he could think about was playtime, it was a complete nightmare for him, you know, he couldn't make the football team, let's face it, he couldn't begin to even kick the ball or even know which goalpost to aim for, and his playtimes were a complete nightmare, so he never wanted to go to school. It wasn't even that they bullied him, the teachers there were very good, they didn't allow bullying, it was just, I don't know, in the atmosphere somehow, between the children ... He obviously wasn't a clever boy, not in the usual sense of the word, and the boys were either clever or good at football, it had to be one or the other, and poor Ryan, well, he just didn't fit in. There was another child in his class, she was a sweet little thing, Ryan used to like her, they sat on the same table, and they both went to [the Learning Support Unit] together, and she used to play with

the little infants at playtime, but Ryan could hardly do that, could he, a boy his size? So it really dented his confidence, but now that he's here [in the special school] he's much better, he even tells me he joins in with football at dinner time sometimes.

(Interview, Greyhound School)

It is no coincidence that Ryan's mother attributes Ryan's more positive attitude largely to his inclusion in playground football. Sport in general, and football in particular, is one of the foremost sites for the production of masculinities in schools in the UK. It is on the football field (or, in most urban schools, the allotted corner of the tarmac playground) that boys struggle over their hold on dominant versions of masculinity (Renold 1997; Benjamin 1998; Gard 2001; Skelton 2001). The version of masculinity being struggled over is one of physical strength and skill, where that physical strength is associated with the considerable material rewards of top footballers, with the ability to win fights, and with heterosexual prowess and attractiveness to girls (Epstein and Johnson 1998; Benjamin 2001). As Thorne (1993) and others have noted, failure to excel in playground football is associated, for even very young boys, with 'gayness', and seen as the antithesis of successful masculinity. This failure is particularly marked for boys with SEN. Thorne observed that very successful boys – those who have many resources 'in the bank' on which to draw – can afford to be least invested in continual demonstrations of 'macho' masculinity, since their hold on success is secure. The opposite is true for many boys with SEN. Like Ryan, they cannot lay claim to many of the traditional markers of success. A group of boys in Year 6 at Ryan's special school described the importance of football:

The boys talked at length about the material rewards of 'winning'. Alex described the opulent lifestyle that he saw as the justifiable reward for success on the football pitch, contrasting this with the abject poverty of 'failure'. There was, for him, no intermediate position. For all three of the boys, the 'winner' indeed gained everything – money, acclaim and security – while the 'loser' was left with nothing … Inclusion was a priority mentioned by all the boys. Conflating football success, financial success and inclusion, Joe remarked that 'If you score the most goals, everyone will want you to be in their team, and you'll earn loads of money and have a big house and car'. Respect was also part of the overall picture. Ennis said that, 'When you're the best in the team no one will laugh at you and call you names and say you're rubbish… Because they'll want to be your friends'.

(Benjamin 1997: 58)

The point here is that a constellation of practices around gender and SEN have made success in football, linked to very absolute notions of 'winning and losing', particularly desirable to these boys. They are boys for whom other markers of success have proved inaccessible: they have failed to make the normative academic progress required of primary school pupils, and their experience has all too often been of formal and informal exclusion from classroom and playground activities. Football is one of the few activities that they can make theirs, and that can allow them to dream of current and future success. The flip side of their investment in football is that the 'cultural package' that goes with it is also associated with aggression, homophobia and heterosexism (Epstein 1997; Kenway and Fitzclarence 1997). This can lead to a cycle in which boys' investment in football leads to or reinforces their disconnection from schoolwork, and channels them towards disruptive behaviour. Such attitudes and behaviour in turn reinforce their designation within SEN discourses, which may in turn have the unintended effect of re-inscribing them as academic 'failures'.

Femininities and SEN

Femininities produce a very different set of possibilities for girls with SEN. At present, a critical literature that specifically addresses 'femininities' has not been as fully developed as has the range of critical literature on masculinities, and this is particularly true of work in the field of education and schooling. The work that does exist points to the way in which femininity has been theorised as 'that which is different from masculinity which assumes femininity as a given' (Skeggs 1997: 20). Nonetheless, it is possible to draw out from the literature models of femininities that might help us understand something of the gendered lives of girls with SEN.

Whilst it would be inappropriate to argue for the existence of dominant femininities, there are clearly some femininities that are more associated with power than others. Recent work on children as consumers (Kenway and Bullen 2001) indicates the existence of feisty, in-your-face femininities, associated with heterosexual attractiveness and the desire to consume the 'right' goods and wear the 'right' brands: in schools, this type of femininity can encompass academic achievement, since better-than-average academic performance is also associated with choices and material success in adult life (NACETT 2000). Alongside this version is a more traditional version of femininity – the decades-old stereotypical 'dumb blonde' of popular culture – where heterosexual attractiveness connotes not so much a positive life choice, but the perpetual vulnerability of needing care and protection

(Walkerdine 1997; Benjamin 2002). The 'dumb blonde' is an easily recognisable stereotype, and one that draws heavily on discourses of social class as well as 'race' to position some girls and women as inherently and essentially childlike, appealing (to men), and lacking in intellectual ability of all kinds.

'Cleverness', for girls, has tended to be seen as something struggled for: where the achievements of boys who do well tend to be attributed to 'natural' brilliance, the achievements of girls have been attributed to their capacity for hard work, born out of a desire to please (Walkerdine 1988; Rossiter 1994), and out of physical inability to access, or disinclination towards, heterosexual attractiveness. Girls at the margins of SEN can blend into the normative range of the class by positioning themselves as hardworking and diligent, and their difficulties may escape 'official' detection. But girls whose difficulties are more severe may find their room for manoeuvre severely constrained by the expectation that they will remain rather endearingly vulnerable.

> I sit with the science group. Anna is struggling … She asks if I will help her, and to refuse seems inhumane. She doesn't seem to like writing. She wants me to point to each word as she copies it. I get the impression that she doesn't actually need this amount of help, but it's a way of securing and retaining my attention. Every time I turn to Joe and Kofi, who are sitting next to her, she stops work. They, also, are doing very little. I try to help Joe to write a draft of his conclusion. All he then has to do is copy it out, but he doesn't do this. Instead, he starts to tease Anna. He makes fun of her, talking in a voice that is clearly supposed to be an imitation of the younger-than-eight-sounding way in which she speaks. Kofi tells him to leave Anna alone … I try to reconnect him with his work, but he is not having this. He calls Anna 'Sabrina the teenage witch' and she retaliates by saying that she really *will* be a witch when she grows up, and will turn him into a frog. She turns to me and asks if this is indeed a possibility – can one realistically hope to become a witch? Her question is transparently coquettish.
>
> (Fieldnotes, Year 3, Bankside Primary)

Both Anna and Joe have been identified as having MLD. In the above extract, Anna is positioning herself squarely within a discourse of rather charming, ultra-childlike vulnerability, securing the adult help that will enable her to complete her work but also re-inscribing herself as needy of help. There is a tendency for SEN discourses in school to draw upon what has been called the 'charity/tragedy model of disability' (Barton and Oliver 1997; Allan 1999;

Thomas and Loxley 2001). The charity/tragedy model, which originated in the nineteenth century but continues to influence perceptions and practices today, positions people with disabilities as the helpless objects of pity, concern and charity, and is used to legitimate their control by non-disabled people. Likewise, SEN discourses can position particular children as the passive recipients of care and control (Tomlinson 1982), though this may not be the explicit intention of the educational professionals who work with them. As Riddell notes, 'there are clear connections between the child-centred approach in special educational needs and the individual tragedy discourse identified by disability theorists' (Riddell 1996: 4).

It is interesting to think about how class and 'race', as well as gender and SEN, are played out in the vignette. Anna had turned on me such a look of pathetic helplessness when I sat at her table that I could not do anything other than pay attention to what she was saying and doing. She was able to keep my attention focused on her through strategies that made her seem younger and less able to manage than was really the case: a conundrum of independence made to look like dependence, and activity made to look like passivity. The classed and raced stereotype of the 'dumb blonde' was a position made readily available to Anna who happens to be blonde, working class, and small for her age. Joe and Kofi aided and abetted her in this strategy. Kofi took up a 'gentlemanly' role in relation to Joe's teasing, positioning himself as Anna's protector. Joe's teasing worked to distance him from the model of needy, vulnerable child, enabling him to resist the position of 'helpee', and also drew attention to Anna's production of herself as needy and ultra-childlike. In parodying Anna's 'babyish' voice, he made the strategy look ridiculous, and also made me want to protect Anna from him, further inscribing Anna and myself within a helper/helped relationship. When my strategy for putting an end to the teasing was unsuccessful, Anna made use of a very different kind of feminine archetype – that of the witch – that Joe had introduced into the encounter. In momentarily abandoning the dumb blonde in favour of the mysterious and powerful figure of the witch, Anna threatened to strip Joe of his masculine power by turning him into a frog. But this re-positioning was short-lived, and she threw herself straight back into neediness and vulnerability, by asking me, with what seemed like deliberate childlike 'charm', whether she could really be a witch.

Something paradoxical is going on. If girls can be much more readily recognised as vulnerable and needy, and SEN discourses draw on vulnerability and neediness, why is it that girls are less likely to be identified as having SEN? Perhaps the answer to this lies partly in the fact that SEN discourses draw partly on the (feminised) notions of care and concern for the helpless, but also on the masculine notions of imposing control through a technical, managerial apparatus. Girls' expertise seems to lie in securing informal help: which can mean they access the help they need without recourse to the official channels of SEN identification and assessment, but could also mean that their difficulties 'may remain undiagnosed and invisible' (Riddell 1996), and that their access to SEN resources is unduly limited. Once identified as having SEN, however, girls find themselves all-too easily inscribed within traditional discourses of vapid and vulnerable femininities.

Addressing disparities in gender and SEN

In their study of differential SEN provision in mainstream primary schools, Daniels *et al.* note that:

> Boys' learning seems to be more teacher-dependent than girls', and boys have various anti-learning behaviours. Girls, on the other hand, have a capacity collectively to 'keep out' of SEN provision by generally supporting each other's learning, not demanding too much of the teacher's time, and giving each other appropriate help.
>
> (Daniels *et al.* 1996: 3)

Daniels and colleagues go on to recommend that mainstream schools should address the disparity in SEN provision through objective assessment criteria, resulting in equal provision for equal levels of educational need. This is fine, as far as it goes. But it does raise questions about how to prioritise educational needs that cannot be measured in the same currencies. How, for example, would we quantify the needs of a child with global learning difficulties, whose proficiency at reading is roughly that expected of a child four years younger, in comparison with a child who has, say, an autistic spectrum disorder, who is able to decipher print but has not yet developed the skills of making sense of what s/he reads? Perhaps it is more useful to keep in mind the necessity of equal provision across both genders, and to develop assessment and allocation systems accordingly, but in the context of attention to the gendered nature of school, classroom and playground cultures.

This is a long-term agenda, and, whilst the development of appropriate tools and strategies for the management of SEN is important, so, too, is an understanding of the implications of masculinities and femininities in the construction of SEN. Raphael Reed (1998: 72) critiques the tendency of school effectiveness and school improvement literature to demonise the 'under-achieving boy', and argues that, instead, what is needed is a reformulation of social justice ideals that will include 'a critical focus on gendered actions and school cultures alongside a continuing debate on the nature of the curriculum'. This critical focus has to take into account the reality that SEN are produced in relation to a school system in which testing, and the achievement of externally-determined 'expected levels' (DfEE 1999), have already, to some extent, positioned children with SEN as academic failures.

This kind of critical focus can be hard to operationalise in the current climate of accountability through test results and league tables, but it is not impossible. Hilltop Junior School in the Midlands, and George Holt Primary in London (not their real names) are high-achieving schools that prioritise inclusion in their development plans. George Holt is specifically resourced by its LEA to provide places for up to 12 children who have been identified as having EBD and who have been excluded from other primary schools.[1] The head teachers of both schools are passionate about a range of social justice issues, and maintain a belief in the possibility of addressing social inequalities through schooling. Both head teachers are committed to the inclusion of children for whom schooling has been a struggle, and they both share the view that this can be done without compromising 'standards'. Indeed, both schools are characterised by an orientation towards 'high standards', broadly conceived beyond the requirements of test results and performance management.

> Jack and Daisy are sitting on the same table, not next to each other, but near. Meg [the teacher] tells the class they can start. I'm not at all surprised when Jack's first response is to walk over to the waste-paper bin and spend ages sharpening his pencil. Daisy is alternately staring into space and swinging on her chair. The other children on the table – two girls and a boy – don't appear to be bothered by this, but get started on their own work. I begin to wonder whether Meg will have to intervene. One of the girls on the table nudges the boy, and indicates towards Jack. The boy gets up, goes over to where Jack is sharpening and re-sharpening his pencil, and offers to lend him one of his. Jack accepts, and returns to the table, where the boy shows him what to do. The two girls, who have been working together, lean over to help Daisy.
>
> (Fieldnotes, Year 5, Hilltop)

This incident, which I witnessed during my first classroom observation, turned out to be typical. Daisy and Jack are children who might, until recently, have found themselves in schools for children with MLD. They stand out fairly sharply in this mainstream classroom, as children for whom the ordinary work of the class is a struggle, and they are not always able to make sense of what is going on in the classroom. The class's literacy and numeracy targets, which are written on the board at the front of the classroom, are not accessible to Daisy and Jack, immediately positioning them as vulnerable. In many ways this is a constant conundrum in schools, since the curriculum necessarily contains activities and concepts that cannot be made meaningful to everyone. At Hilltop, this is a problem that is addressed head-on through flexible grouping policies that sometimes set children according to academic proficiency for discrete activities, and sometimes require them to work in mixed-proficiency groups. In the incident described above, and in many others I saw at Hilltop, both girls *and* boys appeared to be acting in the ways noted by Daniels *et al.*: the giving and receiving of help seemed to be taken for granted.

Hilltop emphasises education as a collective project, and a team enterprise, as does George Holt. Whilst neither school can completely resist 'the allure of competitive success in education which derives from [a] masculine world-view' (Potts 1997:185), they are able to mediate this through a very active construction of themselves as learning communities. George Holt has three 'golden rules': high standards, teamwork and celebrating success. Because these three rules operate very much as an integrated whole, they go some way towards re-configuring what counts as success: they carry with them the notion that individual success counts for much more when it is shared by the community, and that if an individual within the community 'team' is prevented from being successful, then the community is the poorer. I videotaped some Year 6 lessons at George Holt, and was struck, watching the videos, by the amount of 'helping' – the pursuit of shared, collaborative success – that went on, almost unseen, and again taken for granted.

> Ken tells the children to get into groups of four. There is instant noise and movement, as children negotiate their groupings. I zoom in on Stephen, who remains sitting, cross-legged, looking up and around him with a look of utter bewilderment on his face. I am somewhat surprised when Jermaine goes over to him, invites him to stand up, then puts an arm around Stephen's shoulder and negotiates for them both to join two girls. I wouldn't have been surprised if one of the high-status boys, or a girl, had looked after Stephen in this way. But I would have thought that Jermaine, who always seems to have an insecure grip on both academic

and micro-cultural success, and who often acts 'macho', would have been resistant to grouping himself with a boy with SEN and two girls.

(Fieldnotes, Year 6, George Holt)

George Holt Primary and Hilltop Junior both have robust SEN policies and procedures, with assessment criteria that are rigorously applied. This goes some way to ensuring gender parity in the allocation of SEN provision. Crucially, though, both schools address, on an ongoing basis, what Corbett (1999) has called 'deep culture', and this is what seems to make the difference in both schools. What they are doing is freeing up room for manoeuvre by both girls and boys: when 'help' is recast as shared pursuit of success, boys can take up helping and helped roles without consequent loss of masculine status, and girls who are struggling can access help without needing to position themselves as overly vulnerable or ultra-childlike. This is not to claim that either school has found the perfect solution. But both schools show us that, by paying attention to the gendering of SEN provision and to the gendered lives of children considered to have SEN, it is possible to address disparities in provision and generate conditions of greater equality in the drive towards inclusion.

Conclusion

Issues of gender are at the core of policy, practice and provision in relation to SEN, though they may not always be seen as such. Though the gendering of SEN provision is a crucial component in our (often unspoken) understanding of inclusion, it has been all too common for discussion of the intersection between SEN and gender to be limited to the popular notion of boys' 'underachievement'. This chapter has focused on the classroom experiences of girls and boys: it has explored both the ways in which assessment and common-sense understandings contribute to boys' over-representation amongst children considered to have SEN, and the differential implications and consequences of this over-representation. In drawing attention to masculinities and femininities as organising categories of analysis, I have shown how common-sense understandings and their gendered implications for SEN policy, practice and provision are played out in classrooms.

Studies of gender and SEN in the schools detailed in this chapter indicate that the reasons for, and implications of, gendered inequality are not amenable to easy resolution through simple, single solution 'quick fixes'. In two of the case-study schools, the inequalities and disparities generated for and by SEN provision were tackled head-on, through strategies that permeated the cultures of the two schools. Both schools were committed to high standards and inclusion, within an environment that encompassed – but was not determined by – standard measures of academic achievement. Neither school reduced the complexities of creating an inclusive learning community to the managerial level of targets set and met: rather, they both paid attention to the ways in which girls and boys lead gendered lives, and to the ways in which those gendered lives are nuanced by issues of perceived academic ability as well as by other indices of 'difference'. The experiences of the two schools suggest that change can be made at local (school and classroom) level when staff develop an understanding of how gender and SEN shape children's classroom lives, and when they are committed to opening up room for manoeuvre for girls and boys across the perceived 'ability' spectrum.

Note

1 The data from George Holt Primary School were gathered as part of the Inclusion in Schools Project, funded by the Open University. I am grateful to project co-directors Janet Collins, Kathy Hall, Melanie Nind and Kieron Sheehy for permission to use these data here.

References

Allan, J. (1999) *Actively Seeking Inclusion: Pupils with special needs in mainstream schools*. London: Falmer Press.

Barton, L. and Oliver, M. (eds) (1997) *Disability Studies: Past, present and future*. Leeds: Disability Press.

Benjamin, S. (1997) *Fantasy Football League: Boys in a special (SEN) school constructing and reconstructing masculinities*. London: Institute of Education.

Benjamin, S. (1998) Fantasy Football League: boys learning to 'do boy' in a special (SEN) school classroom. In Walford, G. and Massey, A. (eds) *Children Learning in Context*. Stamford, Conn.: JAI Press Inc.

Benjamin, S. (2001) Challenging Masculinities: disability and achievement in testing times. *Gender and Education*, **13**(1), 39–55.

Benjamin, S. (2002) *The Micropolitics of Inclusive Education: An ethnography*. Buckingham: Open University Press.

Blair, M. (2001) *Why Pick on Me? School exclusion and black youth*. Stoke-on-Trent: Trentham.

Connell, R. W. (1995) *Masculinities*. Cambridge: Polity Press.

Corbett, J. (1999) Inclusivity and School Culture: the case of special education. In Prosser, J. (ed.) *School Culture*. London: Paul Chapman.

Daniels, H. *et al.* (1996) *Gender and Special Needs Provision in Mainstream Schooling*. Swindon: Economic and Social Research Council.

DfEE (1999) *National Learning Targets for England for 2002*. London: Department for Education and Employment.

Epstein, D. (1997) Boyz' Own Stories: masculinities and sexualities in schools. *Gender and Education*, **9**(1), 105–115.

Epstein, D. and Johnson, R. (1998) *Schooling Sexualities*. Buckingham: Open University Press.

Gard, M. (2001) I like smashing people and I like getting smashed myself: addressing issues of masculinity in physical education and sport. In Martino, W. and Meyenn, B. (eds) *What About the Boys? Issues of masculinity in schools*. Buckingham: Open University Press.

Hayden, C. (1997) *Children Excluded from Primary School*. Buckingham: Open University Press.

Kenway, J. and Bullen, E. (2001) *Consuming Children: Education, entertainment, advertising*. Milton Keynes: Open University Press.

Kenway, J. and Fitzclarence, L. (1997) Masculinity, Violence and Schooling: challenging 'poisonous pedagogies'. *Gender and Education*, **9**(1), 117–33.

Lingard, B., Ladwig, J. and Luke, A. (1998) School Effects in Postmodern Conditions. In Slee, R., Weiner, G. and Tomlinson, S. (eds) *School Effectiveness for Whom? Challenges to the school effectiveness and school improvement movements*. London: Falmer Press.

Mehra, H. (1998) The permanent exclusion of Asian pupils in secondary schools in central Birmingham. *Multi-Cultural Teaching*, **17**(1), 42–8.

NACETT (2000) Aiming Higher: NACETT's report on the National Learning Targets for England and advice on targets beyond 2002. Sudbury: National Advisory Council for Education and Training Targets.

Nash, R. (2001) Class, 'Ability' and Attainment: A problem for the sociology of education. *British Journal of Sociology of Education*, **22**(2), 189–203.

OECD (2000) *Special Needs Education: Statistics and indicators*. Paris: Organisation for Economic Co-operation and Development: Centre for Educational Research and Innovation.

Parsons, C. (1996) Permanent Exclusions from Schools in the 1990s: trends, causes and responses. *Children and Society*, **10**(3), 255–68.

Potts, P. (1997) Gender and membership of the mainstream. *International Journal of Inclusive Education*, **91**(2), 175–187.

Raphael Reed, L. (1998) 'Zero Tolerance': gender performance and school failure. In Epstein, D., Elwood, J., Hey, V. and Maw, J. (eds) *Failing Boys? Issues in gender and achievement*. Buckingham: Open University Press.

Renold, E. (1997) 'All they've got on their brains is football': sport, masculinity and the gendered practices of playground relations. *Sport, Education and Society*, **2**(1), 5–23.

Riddell, S. (1996) Gender and Special Educational Needs. In Lloyd, G. (ed.) *'Knitting Progress Unsatisfactory': Gender and special issues in education*. Edinburgh: Moray House Institute of Education.

Rossiter, A. B. (1994) Chips, Coke and Rock-'n'-Roll: children's mediation of an invitation to a first dance party. *Feminist Review*, **46**, 1–20.

Skarbrevik, K. J. (2002) Gender Differences Among Students Found Eligible for Special Education. *European Journal of Special Needs Education*, **17**(2), 97–107.

Skeggs, B. (1997) *Formations of Class and Gender*. London: Sage.

Skelton, C. (2001) *Schooling the Boys: Masculinities and primary education*. Buckingham: Open University Press.

Thomas, G. and Loxley, A. (2001) *Deconstructing Special Education and Constructing Inclusion*. Buckingham: Open University Press.

Thorne, B. (1993) *Gender Play: Girls and boys in school*. New Brunswick, N.J.: Rutgers University Press.

Tomlinson, S. (1982) *A Sociology of Special Education*. London: Routledge and Kegan Paul.

Walkerdine, V. (1988) *The Mastery of Reason*. London: Routledge and Kegan Paul.

Walkerdine, V. (1997) *Daddy's girl: young girls and popular culture*. Basingstoke and London: Macmillan.

Wright, C. *et al.* (2000) *'Race', Class and Gender in Exclusion from School*. London: Falmer Press.

Like many of the chapters, this one addresses the minutiae of what goes on in schools and classrooms. It is unusual, however, in that Shereen Benjamin applies a sociological lens to the practices and processes she sees and describes. Such sociological approaches have been, and continue to be, crucial in the process of understanding the power dimensions at work in schools and to offering a critique of everyday practice.

Chapter 21

'Part of who we are as a school should include responsibility for well-being'

Links between the school environment, mental health and behaviour

Jennifer Spratt, Janet Shucksmith, Kate Philip and Cate Watson

This article examines how the school environment can affect the well-being of pupils. The authors draw on interviews and case studies within a Scottish study to explore the tensions between school structures and cultures and the promotion of young people's positive mental well-being. They ask us to reflect on how the approaches used by inter-agency workers can build new working cultures which may benefit all children and young people.

[...]

Introduction: mental well-being in the school setting

[...]

Our understanding of mental health and well-being has undergone a paradigm shift over recent years, with the emphasis moving away from the medical model whereby mental health was seen simply as the absence of mental illness (World Health Organization, 2001). Positive mental health, or mental well-being, has been reconceptualized as a condition to be valued in its own right. This can be seen as a shift from a 'deficit to a strength perspective' (Weare, 2004, p. 66). While mental health is thought to be too complex to define simply (Weare, 2000), the Mental Health Foundation (1999) has compiled a list of attributes that can be associated with mentally healthy children. These include the capacity to:

- develop psychologically, emotionally, creatively, intellectually and spiritually;

- initiate, develop and sustain mutually satisfying personal relationships;
- use and enjoy solitude;
- become aware of others and empathize with them;
- play and learn;
- develop a sense of right and wrong; and
- resolve (face) problems and setbacks and learn from them.

Most teachers will be aware that the reasons why children fail to develop in the ways described above may not necessarily be located in the children themselves. The environments in which children grow up have been shown to be highly influential in promoting or damaging mental well-being. Potentially vulnerable groups of young people include looked after children, refugees and asylum seekers, gay and lesbian young people, those whose parents have mental health problems or problems of drug and alcohol abuse, those who have experienced trauma or abuse and other disadvantaged groups (Alexander, 2001). It follows that the school environment too has the potential to either enhance or damage the mental well-being of both staff and pupils, and that school managers thus carry a significant responsibility to create an environment that promotes good mental health, acts to prevent development of problems in vulnerable groups and supports those experiencing difficulties. The international context for school-based mental health promotion is provided by the World Health Organization (2001), which supports the development of 'child-friendly schools', defined as follows:

> A child-friendly school encourages tolerance and equality between boys and girls and different ethnic, religious and social groups. It promotes active involvement and co-operation, avoids the use of physical punishment and does not tolerate bullying. It is also a supportive and nurturing environment; providing education which responds to the reality of the children's lives. Finally it helps to establish connections between school and family life, encourages creativity as well as academic abilities, and promotes the self-esteem and self-confidence of children.
> (World Health Organization, 2001, p. 1)

For schools to take on this role of promotion of mental health requires a change in the way schools understand and respond to issues surrounding mental health. Indeed, Weare (2004) argues that concepts of mental health are not well understood in school, having belonged until recently within a medical discourse. Moreover, she suggests that schools often find it hard to see the relevance of mental health to their central concern with learning.

This may in part be related to teachers' unfamiliarity with the language (Cole, Sellman, Daniels and Visser, 2002) and the tendency for the term mental health to be identified with mental illness (Tuffin, Tuffin and Watson, 2001) as schools are familiar with the language of social and personal development and the importance of self-esteem in learning – both important components of mental health and well-being.

[...]

Links between the school environment and mental well-being

[The evidence for this chapter was drawn from a Scottish study. Interviews were conducted with 66 policy makers working in health, education and the voluntary sector across the country. Six schools were the focus of intensive case study, where the views of a range of stakeholders were sought including parents, children and young people, teachers, health workers and voluntary sector workers.]

The importance of the school ethos and environment in promoting positive behaviour has been highlighted by many authors, for example Rogers (2000), but the implications of these approaches for the mental well-being of pupils are less well documented. Within our data, calls for schools to fundamentally re-examine how their structures and culture affected the well-being of pupils, especially those experiencing mental health difficulties, were made by a number of local authority representatives, most notably, although not exclusively, educational psychologists. The rationale for such an approach is outlined in the interview excerpt below:

> Youngsters do have emotional difficulties but I think by attaching that label to them you see them as the ones that have to change rather than seeing the actual environmental factors as being equally important and having to be modified as well.
>
> (Educational psychologist)

However, at a strategic level, issues associated with mental well-being were spread diffusely through a complex policy landscape. Local authorities had developed few specific policies for promoting good mental health, *per se*, but could point to policies on a range of related initiatives (e.g. anti-bullying, health promotion, inclusion and behaviour support), the management of which was dispersed through various departments and between a variety of personnel. Consequently, schools' responses to mental health issues rarely involved a significant overhaul of school policies and procedures, but were more likely to be fragmented initiatives such as anti-bullying weeks, or peer support schemes, which were bolted onto the existing systems. Funding for any posts relating to mental well-being, such as counsellors or health workers, tended to be short term, leading to fragile and patchy provision. Consequently, such work was unlikely to be embedded within the school and conflicts between the promotion of mental well-being and existing school culture were evident. Tensions were particularly apparent in the arenas of curriculum, pastoral care, discipline and teacher/pupil relationships, and each of these is considered below.

Pupils and parents repeatedly alluded to the importance of the curriculum for well-being. Difficulties with school work were reported to elicit feelings of inadequacy, to be generally detrimental to the pupils' feelings about themselves and to their perceptions about how others saw them. Yet, there was little evidence of schools considering their pedagogical methods in terms of pupil welfare. Commentators whose professional background lay outside education, such as voluntary sector and health workers, expressed concerns that the over-riding priority of many schools still lay with subject-orientated curriculum, linked to positive academic outcomes for pupils. In spite of recent policy shifts away from overemphasis on attainment in its narrowest sense (Scottish Executive, 2004), school managers, it was reported, continued to feel under pressure to concentrate on the measurable attainments of pupils. Pupils who were experiencing emotional difficulties and whose behaviour, whether withdrawn or disruptive, inhibited their engagement with the curriculum, or impinged on other pupils' opportunities to learn, did not easily fit into such a system, as illustrated by the following comment:

> I think for a lot of the teachers the focus is academic achievement and if the young person is not interested then you know ... the young person becomes rubbished rather than looking at it from a different place and again I know that it's not the teachers' problem, that's the culture we live in.
> (Voluntary sector worker)

Teachers and local authority representatives made frequent reference, during interviews, to the tensions they faced, in reconciling an individualized approach to the difficulties of particular pupils, with the structures and expectations of a typical school, particularly in the secondary sector. This was linked to the notion that the main business of the school (delivering academic goods to the majority) was somehow in opposition to prioritizing welfare. However, some respondents, such as this local authority representative, also challenged the notion that there was conflict:

> There are some schools – secondaries – who go along the attainment line, focus very much on attainment and don't recognize that there is more than one way of achieving that. If young people feel good about themselves, particularly at times when they are feeling vulnerable, they are more likely to come through unscathed and take advantage of what the curriculum has to offer.
>
> (Education authority, development officer)

Case study data demonstrated a range of approaches to offering targeted pastoral interventions to vulnerable pupils either through the existing guidance system, or with the support of other specialists such as counsellors, social workers or pupil support workers. However the driver of such systems was often improved educational outcomes for the pupil, and for the wider school, so the focus of the support was on teaching the child to conform, in order to 'fit' better into the system rather than examining the system to see how it could better meet the needs of the child. Such approaches to pastoral care served to locate the difficulty, in the eyes of teachers, firmly in the child, and thereby to relieve teachers from any responsibility to examine their own responses to those children. Tensions inevitably existed in situations where pastoral support was seen as a separate function of the school, rather than an integral part of all teachers' roles.

At the heart of this issue was how schools responded to those pupils whose difficulties manifested in disruptive behaviour, which breached the disciplinary codes of the school. Whether or not disruption was treated as a disciplinary matter or a pastoral care issue in the first instance rested largely with the classroom teacher in whose charge the behaviour manifested. Interviewees holding strategic positions in local authorities frequently referred to the consequences of misinterpretation of these behaviours resulting in harsh disciplinary measures that inflamed the situation, and led to escalation with the ultimate consequence of exclusion, as described below:

> It's still very difficult for the [teachers] to actually say ... once a kid manifests on a difficult morning ... difficult behaviour, for the teacher to stand back and say, 'Ah that's that difficult behaviour.' They often end up in a situation where you know it's ... discipline.
>
> (Behaviour support manager)

They called for schools to examine their responses and to support teachers to develop strategies for dealing with difficult behaviour, in ways that were less confrontational. Staff were urged to develop reflective responses that explored the causes of behaviour before taking recourse in purely punitive reactions.

Yet, school staff expressed ambivalence about altering a universal system of rules to accommodate the needs of an individual pupil, as exemplified here in a teacher's concerns about school uniform:

> There is one child who is here, and it's like you have got him here but he doesn't wear school uniform. He doesn't just not wear the uniform, he makes a public issue of not wearing the uniform … a very public non school uniform wearer … and you wonder, do other youngsters see that and think 'Well he gets away with it, why shouldn't I get away with it?' But then, I don't know, do you just have to say: 'Well uniform is not that important. The boy is here; he's not walking the streets. He's not heading to some kind of oblivion.' I don't know.
>
> (Secondary teacher)

However, responding to pupils' needs was not necessarily seen as 'letting them off the hook'. Alternative approaches could be taken, which both discourage the behaviour and value, rather than undermine, the pupil. Such responses included solution-focused approaches adopted by the classroom teacher that supported pupils to avoid recurrence of the same behaviour. Restorative justice approaches (Wachtel, 1999) also offered a possible way forward, by involving pupils actively in redressing the wrongs that their behaviour has caused (as opposed to passive punishments such as detention).

These approaches viewed pastoral care as an integral feature of discipline. However, commonly in Scottish secondary schools the two systems were managed as separate functions of the school, giving rise to the likelihood that children and young people whose neediness was wrongly attributed to wilful disobedience would be denied the support they needed, and indeed punished for their poor mental health. In such situations the school creates or exacerbates the very problems that the pastoral care system seeks to address, as described by Watson (2005). Where such dual systems operate, it is vital that they are closely inter-linked both strategically and operationally, to offer a fair and supportive system of discipline that does not seek to undermine the mental well-being of vulnerable miscreants.

[…]

It was evident from our data that pupils valued relationships with school staff that extended beyond the classroom, where both parties could play a slightly more informal role. For example, pupils reported a very high level of trust in staff who ran extracurricular clubs, and suggested that these would be the adults they would be most likely to approach with sensitive information.

Pupils and teachers alike recognized such activities as instrumental in developing firmer ties, as described by this secondary teacher:

> I guess I came into teaching because I like people. I like youngsters, you know ... I like to meet kids socially. I like to play badminton with them, and to cycle and to hear their chat. And yes, I do see my role as being more than a subject [teacher], though the subject is very, very important to me, but I like to think of it as more than that.

Non-teaching staff such as playground assistants, pupil support workers, school nurses and health workers also reported being approached by children in difficulties, as their roles allowed more time for one-to-one discussions, they were able to observe behaviour outside the classroom and they were viewed as less authoritarian than teachers. These workers often detected difficulties that had escaped the notice of classroom teachers, although less frequently were they granted the autonomy to respond to the child's difficulty.

[...] Teachers' own well-being impacts upon their ability to respond sensitively to pupils with difficulties (Kyriacou, 2001) and, as pointed out by Hornby and Atkinson (2003), 'Working with emotionally disturbed children can be particularly stressful and challenging as it can involve high levels of emotion' (p. 7). This was clearly in evidence among teachers interviewed in this study, who in some cases reported feeling completely isolated when faced with challenging behaviour, and reluctant to seek support due to their fears of loss of credibility with other staff [.] [...]

Our study identified instances where strategies that addressed teachers' capacity to work effectively with disturbed pupils, for example, confidential teacher-to–teacher support systems similar to those outlined by Daniels and Williams (2000), improved their confidence and their own sense of well-being, as well as improving their relationships with pupils. It appears that by addressing teachers' competence to respond to challenging behaviour, a positive feedback is created, whereby improved pupil well-being leads to improved teacher well-being and vice versa, and the implications for this in terms of improved relationships could be far-reaching.

Interdisciplinary working and the school environment

With the advent of integrated service delivery, a wider range of professionals are now located on or close to school premises, increasing their own contact with vulnerable children and young people, but also providing possibilities for co-operative working with schools and teachers. Here, we consider the role of the non-teaching professionals within a school, in relation to mental well-being. Should they operate as trouble-shooters, to sort out problems for which no one else has the time or the skills to cope? Should they serve to contain the 'difficult' pupils, allowing everyone else to progress unimpeded? Or should their role be to support teachers to understand how to work more effectively with vulnerable pupils? Which of these ways of working would have the greatest impact on the school environment?

From the various systems we observed in operation across a range of settings, a loose typology emerged. Interventions fell into three main categories: export (remove the pupils from the school), import (introduce other types of worker to the school to take responsibility for mental health) or ownership (take steps to address mental health as a whole school issue), although on closer inspection, as outlined below, these distinctions are not always clear cut.

An export model would involve removing pupils from the school site and delivering specialized interventions or curricula elsewhere. In practice, we found a marked reluctance on the part of our case study schools to engage with this model, and a similar disinclination on the part of strategic planners to encourage such practices. However, education authority representatives commented on a degree of tension at the interface between some schools and external agencies, and reported having to create organizational barriers to prevent pupils from being 'fired into external agencies', with one referring to the tendency of some schools and head teachers to seek 'amputation' of problems. This chimes with Pettitt's (2003) observation that closer working between the Child and Adolescent Mental Health Service and education authorities initially gave rise to a large number of inappropriate referrals. Clearly, such an approach to meeting the needs of vulnerable pupils would do little to improve the whole school environment.

The emphasis among education authority representatives and other organizations involved in our study was to keep pupils in school wherever possible, an emphasis driven by the inclusion agenda and by national shortages of education psychology staff and CAMHS workers, but also by a genuine belief that this represented the best course of action for the pupils. While there are some circumstances under which a child or young person requires specialist interventions that are beyond the expertise available in school, and in these cases such supports would be made available, the emphasis was on rapid re-integration for the child wherever possible.

The alternative model saw specialists such as counsellors, therapists, social workers or health workers being located within the school, theoretically making themselves more accessible to staff, pupils and parents. This is the embodiment of Scotland's Integrated Community Schools initiative whereby children's services work together, with the individual child at the centre of service delivery.

However, in practice, our findings showed that in most cases these workers from other professional backgrounds were not well integrated in the school, having little communication with the wider staff, being bound by protocols of confidentiality from sharing problems, and not being fully included as members of staff, confirming observations made by Tett *et al.* (2001). Physical and temporal barriers between these workers and the teaching staff could be compounded by misunderstanding and professional mistrust giving rise to the rivalries discussed by McCulloch, Tett and Crowther (2004). Consequently, their role in the school was often seen as separate from the main business of the school, and in the eyes of some staff they were assigned the role of 'mending' those children who did not fit with the expectations of the school, as described by a counsellor:

> That was almost the test, you know, fix these kids, because there is in some ways, at some time an expectation that we will fix them. And that is an interesting thing that we are looking at, in terms of evaluation, is people's perception of significant change. What the person may deem as being significant to them may not in fact affect their classroom behaviour, so therefore the teacher sees a different change, or no change at all. So therefore, has the counselling in fact failed?

This type of arrangement thus also had little opportunity to impact on the school environment, and often gave rise to a situation where the work of the team was to support pupils to develop strategies to cope in the wider school, rather than encouraging the staff to develop a better understanding of the pupils. Ironically, of course, the success of interagency workers in maintaining pupils in schools meant that larger numbers of pupils with mental health difficulties were being kept in schools, and there was a greater need for teachers to develop new skills and understandings.

Paradoxically, a system of this type could make teachers feel less responsible towards pupils experiencing difficulties as they could assume that these were being dealt with 'elsewhere'. Consequently, despite their physical location, examples of this model could actually operate more as an 'export' than an import system, whereby pupils were removed from the mainstream school and supported away from other pupils, albeit on the school premises.

In the most proactive approach, which we refer to as 'ownership', the school puts the mental well-being of children and young people at the very heart of its value system as described in the quotation used in the title of this article:

> Part of who we are as a school should include responsibility for well-being.
>
> (Educational psychologist)

Schools that took ownership of mental health issues would undertake to review all aspects of their functioning to minimize the negative impact that school can have on some children and to improve the positive and supporting things that can be done. For example, one school in the study had revamped its support systems to bring learning support, behaviour support and guidance into one extended team, together with a team of pupil and family support workers who worked with vulnerable pupils and their families. This restructuring, it was felt, had improved pastoral care provision, providing much more effective detection of difficulties and rapid responses.

The term 'ownership' does not imply that school and teaching staff should work in isolation from other services, heroically dealing with all eventualities un-aided, rather that schools are prepared to learn from other agencies and develop new insights into the range of difficulties pupils face. In the first instance, rather than referring pupils to the 'experts', schools look to other agencies for advice and support, using them in the spirit alluded to by this learning support manager:

> The main aim of our service is to support the schools to support the children in whatever form that might take. We offer consultancy basis support to the schools. We would offer direct support to the schools, direct support to individuals, support to families, acting as a bridge between school and family.

By collaborating meaningfully with other children's services in the health and voluntary sector, schools can work to develop a much better understanding of issues associated with the mental well-being of pupils. Rather than seeing interagency support as an addition to their system, or a means to remove the responsibilities from teachers, schools should capitalize on the wealth of knowledge and skills they can bring to the school environment, and to develop ways of using these to develop the capacity of class teachers, and to address the fundamental environmental issues of the whole school.

Conclusion

Schools and local authorities are becoming much more aware of the issues of well-being, and in many cases are well versed in the rhetoric of pupil-centred practice, able to point to examples of efforts to improve the school environment through small-scale initiatives. Our findings suggest that these issues cannot be addressed simply by tinkering at the edges. Rather, they require a thorough review of established school structures and cultures to identify the points of tension between accepted policy and practice and pupil well-being. This raises fundamental questions about how schools see themselves, and what they view as their main purpose.

Gott (2003) expresses concerns about our expectations of teachers in relation to mental health, where their responsibilities begin and end, and whether we are expecting teachers to take on the roles of therapists for which they are not trained. The approach described here is not advocating that teachers deliver specialist interventions, but that the school and the staff develop teaching and learning strategies in their classrooms that can meaningfully engage vulnerable pupils (as suggested by Le Cornu and Collins, 2004) and that they reconsider disciplinary and pastoral care practices.

Ideally, teachers would foster the types of relationships with pupils that would enable them to be aware of young people whose behaviour indicated underlying difficulties, and to respond appropriately, referring children and young people to appropriate services only where necessary. By viewing other professional groups not simply as trouble-shooters, but as a source of advice, consultation and professional development, schools could learn to take ownership of the mental well-being of the school population, working in partnership with, rather than parallel to, other agencies. Such an approach should be seen as complementary rather than oppositional to curriculum delivery, attainment and achievement, as highlighted by Weare (2000):

> It is vital that those who seek to promote high academic standards and those who seek to promote mental, emotional and social health realise that they are on the same side, and that social and affective education can support academic learning, not simply take time away from it.
>
> (p. 5)

Unless schools address pupils' experience of the whole school environment, there is little hope that the targeted endeavours of specialists will have much impact. Cole *et al.* (2002) remind us of the 'other twenty three hours', in other words, the majority of the time that children and young people spend outside of their supported environment. There is little point in providing specialist interventions for those experiencing difficulties if the progress made in the targeted sessions is not supported (or is even undermined) by the wider school environment. By addressing mental well-being as a whole school priority, all pupils benefit, not only those experiencing difficulties. [...]

References

Alexander, T. (2001) *A Bright Future for All: Promoting Mental Health in Education*. London: London: Mental Health Foundation.

Cole, T., Sellman, E., Daniels, H. and Visser, J. (2002) *The Mental Health Needs of Young, People with Emotional and Behavioural Difficulties*. London: Mental Health Foundation.

Daniels, M. and Williams, H. (2000) 'Reducing the Need for Exclusions and Statements for Behaviour: Framework for Intervention. Part I', *Educational Psychology in Practice*, **15**(4), pp. 220–27.

Gott, J. (2003) 'The School: The Front Line or Mental Health Development?'. *Pastoral Care in Education*. **21**(4), 5–15.

Hornby, G. and Atkinson, A. (2003) 'A Framework for Promoting Mental Health in School'. *Pastoral Care in Education*. **21**(2), 3–9.

Kyriacou, C. (2001) 'Teacher Stress: Directions for Future Research', Educational Review. **53**(1),
    pp. 27–35.

Le Cornu, R. and Collins, J. (2004) 'Re-emphasising the Role or Affect in Learning and Teaching', *Pastoral Care in Education*. **4**, 27–35.

McCulloch, K., Tett, L. and Crowther, J. (2004) 'New Community' Schools in Scotland: Issues for Inter-professional Collaboration', *Scottish Educational Review*, **36**(2), pp. 129–44.

Mental Health Foundation (1999) *Bright Futures. Promoting Children and Young People's Mental Health*. London: Mental Health Foundation.

Pettitt, B. (2003) Effective joint working between Child and Adolescent Mental Health Services (CAMHS) and schools. RR 412, London: DfES.

Rogers, C. (2000) *Behaviour Management. A Whole School Approach*. London: Paul Chapman.

Scottish Executive Education Department (2004) *Ambitious Excellent Schools. Our Agenda for Action*. Edinburgh: Scottish Executive.

Tett, L., Munn, P., Kay, H., Martin, I., Martin, J. and Ranson, S. (2001) 'Schools, Community Education and Collaborative Practice in Scotland', in S. Riddell and L. Tett (eds) *Education, Social Justice and Inter-Agency Working: Joined Up or Fractured Policy?*, pp. 105–23. London: Routledge.

Tuffin, A., Tuffin, K. and Watson, S. (2001) 'Frontline Talk: Teachers' Linguistic Resources When Talking About Mental Health and Illness', *Qualitative Health Research*, **11**(4), pp. 477–90.

Wachtel, T. (1999) Safer Saner Schools. Restoring Community in a Disconnected World. Online at http://fp.enter.net/restorativepractices/SSSRestoringCommunity.pdf (accessed on 8 June 2010).

Watson, C. (2005) 'Discourses of Indiscipline; A Foucauldian Response', *Emotional and Behavioural Difficulties*, **10**(1), pp. 56–65.

Weare, K. (2000) *Promoting Mental, Emotional and Social Health: A Whole School Approach.* London: Routledge.

Weare, K. (2004) 'The international Alliance for Child and Adolescent Mental Health and Schools (INTERCAMHS)', *Health Education*, **104**(2), pp. 65–7.

World Health Organization (2001) Mental health: strengthening mental health promotion. Fact sheet 220. Online at www.who.int/mediacentre/factsheets/fs220/en/print.html (accessed on 10 June 2010 – fact sheet is frequently updated).

[...]

This article has focused on suggesting a number of interventions which would promote young people's mental well-being during their time at school. Significantly, the authors advocate adopting a more holistic approach to promote young people's mental well-being. It has considered the importance of partnership work, a theme echoed in many of the other chapters.

Chapter 22

Children and young people in hospitals

Doing youth work in medical settings

Scott Yates, Malcolm Payne and Simon Dyson

The issues facing young people in hospital is an area that has received little attention. The authors in this chapter provide us with an appreciation of how social isolation, separation from local peer groups and from trusted carers impact on young people's experience in hospitals. They also offer insights into how youth work can be an effective intervention tool leading to a wide-range of benefits for young people and staff working in hospitals.

[...]

[I]n the UK, the Kennedy Inquiry (DH 2000) into health-care provision for young people reported that facilities in hospitals were not designed with any acknowledgement of young people's needs, staff were not properly trained to deal with issues young people often face, and insufficient effort was made to communicate important information about illnesses and treatments in ways that young people could understand. Similarly, Atkin and Ahmad (2000) argue that health professionals are often not trained in understanding the perspectives of young people, leading to misjudged or inappropriate responses by staff and withdrawal or lowered adherence to treatment regimens by young people. In Australia, research has suggested that hospitals fail to design interventions that account for the needs and perspectives of indigenous youth despite their high incidence of presentation (Hulse *et al.* 2001) and that arrangements for transition to adult care for young people are often inadequate and have adverse health consequences (Kennedy *et al.* 2007). In France, Alvin *et al.* (2002) argue that emergency care for adolescents can be disorganised and problematic, and Latarjet and Choinere (1995) suggest that pain in young burned children is often poorly estimated and treated. In North America, lack of continuity of care has been blamed for exacerbating the problem of young male adolescents dropping out of the health–care system (Marcell *et al.* 2002).

In England, one response to these issues has been a small number of locally run projects employing youth workers in hospitals. Although some positive outcomes have been claimed for this work (e.g. Burke 2002, Hilton *et al.* 2004), it remains small in scale and limited to a small number of hospitals (Redfearn 2003).

[...]

The experiences of young people in hospital

Young people with chronic conditions – stigmatisation, stress and family conflict

There are a number of challenges connected to the experience of being in hospital itself, and hospital use for chronic health conditions in particular. We focus on three key areas: social isolation, stigma and self-esteem; depression and anxiety; and familial conflict.

The societal reaction to many chronic health conditions marks out young people as different from their peers, through lifestyle changes and treatment regimens, recurrent hospital visits, and physiological differences – such as the delay of puberty caused by b-thalassaemia (Tsiantis 1990) or motor restrictions associated with muscular dystrophy (Eiser 1993).

Such issues can be challenging as young people reach an age at which they 'become aware of their personal and social difference and [the] disabling responses of others' (Atkin and Ahmad 2001, p. 618). They often experience discriminatory behaviour, such as teasing or bullying, embarrassment, lowered self-esteem and feelings of stigma (Tsiantis 1990, Burke 2002). Recurrent periods of hospitalisation mean that they are often absent from school and other social activities for conspicuously long periods of time (Atkin and Ahmad 2001, Redfearn 2003). They may also become withdrawn, isolated and school-avoidant (Lewis-Jones 2006; see also Tsiantis 1990, Bell 2007).

Furthermore, the symptoms of conditions can be uncomfortable or painful, as can treatments required to manage them. Sickle cell disorders, for instance, can cause severe intermittent pain crises, and may require regular blood transfusions (e.g. Todd *et al.* 2006).

These unpleasant, painful symptoms and treatments can cause feelings of depression and anger (e.g. Tsiantis 1990, Bell 2007). Anxiety also tends to be increased for young people with life-threatening chronic conditions. Although the life expectancies of those with conditions such as sickle cell disorders, cystic fibrosis or kidney disease are increasing, these remain conditions associated with a relatively shortened lifespan. Young people often experience anxiety and difficulty in coming to terms with some aspects of their conditions and the uncertainty of their future (e.g. Atkin and Ahmad 2001, Bell 2007).

The aggregation of these issues is also challenging for families. Parents often find it 'difficult to come to terms with the fact of their child's disease' (Tsiantis 1990, p. 456). This can manifest as denial of the disease, such that references to it become taboo within the family – and young persons can thus struggle to find ways of expressing their feelings or finding information about their condition. Parents may also feel a sense of guilt, and respond in ways not beneficial for their children – for example, infantilising them (Atkin and Ahmad 2001) or becoming overprotective (Tsiantis 1990).

Family life can also become restricted by complicated treatment regimens, the increased workload of caring for an ill child, and recurrent trips to hospital, causing exhaustion, depression, and anxiety for parents – particularly for low-income families already living with the stresses of poverty (Lewis-Jones 2006). Many families face financial stress in caring for ill children – the costs of travel to clinics or hospitals, food for special diets, childcare for other children, and so on (Eiser 1993). These factors can lead to conflict within the family, with the illness itself the focal point (Tsiantis 1990).

Experiences of hospitals – social isolation and transitioning to adult care

The need to enter hospital recurrently can compound these problems. Hospitals can be intimidating, frightening and isolating places, especially for young people whose chronic conditions entail long and/or frequent stays or extreme treatment measures (Redfearn 2003, Bell 2007). For instance, Redfearn (2003) reports the case of one young person in an isolation ward who had not seen another young person for six weeks, and was only able to see visitors who wore appropriate sterile clothing. Burke (2002) also points out that the need for repeated trips to hospital not only disrupts school attendance, peer-group contact and social relationships in their local area, but also removes young people from sources of social support.

These negative experiences can be magnified for young people at the point of transition from paediatric to adult care. Increasing life-expectancies for diseases once thought confined to childhood make transition of care increasingly common, and culture and treatment styles vary between paediatric and adult care (Viner 1999). When adolescents make this transition, they often leave behind a familiar environment in which their conditions and histories are well understood and tolerance is shown to displays of immaturity, and in which they have forged valued and supportive relationships with carers and peers (Viner 1999, Bell 2007).

The move to adult care, by contrast, entails expectations of maturity, autonomy, punctuality and reliability. Interactions with medical staff tend to be less nurturing, briefer and more stoical in relation to discomfort (Bell 2007). Many young people find it alienating when moved to larger, crowded adult units with patients of varying ages, some in advanced stages of illness (Bell 2007). The loss of respected (even loved) carers is a difficult experience, and adult care places less emphasis on involving and making space for families (Viner 1999). Young people may also find themselves subject to extensive investigations and reassessment by new medical staff, which can also be alienating after the loss of established care relationships (Viner 1999). In addition, while diseases usually associated with childhood are well understood in paediatric settings, staff on adult wards may be more unfamiliar with them, and may especially lack knowledge of the psychosocial impact of chronic conditions and hospitalisation for young people (Por *et al.* 2004).

Despite these issues, hospitals tend to treat care transition largely as an administrative event, and to neglect the therapeutic, social and cultural changes that young people may experience at this time (Por *et al.* 2004). An abrupt or inappropriately managed transition can be an additional traumatic event for young people and further increase their feelings of alienation and discomfort. It may even be interpreted as 'a punishment and rejection by their previous carers' (Viner 1999, p. 272).

Interactions with medical staff and adherence to treatment regimens

Young people (like adults) can often be hospital–phobic and suspicious of (perceived) forms of authority. They can experience examinations and interventions by health professionals as intrusive, even confrontational (Burke 2002), and may be embarrassed at monitoring and discussing intimate details of their bodies and bodily functions (Hentinen and Kynga's 1992). These feelings can be compounded by the range of other difficult issues already discussed, and need to be handled carefully and sensitively by medical staff.

One issue here is that medical staff tend to frame their responses within a biomedical, treatment-focused model of thinking aimed at disease management, but this can be negatively perceived by young people, and limit the possibility of recognising and responding to their often varied and complex needs. This can be seen in the contestation around 'adherence' to medical treatment regimens.

Young people with conditions such as diabetes, b-thalassaemia and cystic fibrosis face frequent periods of hospitalisation and complex combinations of lifestyle restrictions and regimens of treatment. They are often considered to represent challenges in terms of compliance (e.g. Hentinen and Kynga's 1992) or, latterly, adherence (e.g. Greening *et al.* 2006, Spernak *et al.* 2007) to treatment regimens. However, such concepts have been criticised for failing to respect patients' own perspectives, their psychological and socio-cultural contexts, and their autonomy in relation to their treatment (e.g. Royal Pharmaceutical Society of Great Britain (RPSGB) 1997, Bissell *et al.* 2004).

Young people's adherence to treatment and self-care is complicated by many of the factors already mentioned. These can be magnified for young people from poorer backgrounds, who may have difficulties with travel and appointment-keeping (Fielding and Duff 1999), and those with additional background issues, such as family conflict or break-up, unhappy home lives or abuse (Redfearn 2003).

The pressure of coping with these manifold challenges can manifest itself in avoidant behaviour by some young people, in which they withdraw from medical supervision, neglect their treatment and engage in medically proscribed behaviours (Tsiantis 1990, Fielding and Duff 1999). The struggle to cope with these problems and the desire to live a 'normal' life can mean that young people hold different treatment goals from health professionals (Fielding and Duff 1999). While professionals' treatment priorities tend to focus on effective, long-term management of a condition, young people may also have priorities incorporating short-term comfort, involvement in activities with peers, and so on. There can thus be a fundamental and problematic conflict around 'compliance' with treatment. For example, the episodic nature of sickle cell disease means that young people can have 'well states' during which they are not unduly troubled by the condition and can construct a sense of 'normalcy' in their lives. Routine health-monitoring, seen as necessary for management of the condition by professionals, can undermine this, and so be perceived negatively and resisted by young people (Atkin and Ahmad 2001).

[...]

Acute and emergency cases

The focus so far has been on chronic conditions. However, there are also important challenges to consider relating to young people who present for acute and emergency treatment. Two important problems here are young people who present to hospitals with background issues that do not receive attention, and problems relating to young people's perceptions of professionals' responses to their presence in hospitals.

Some young people presenting to hospitals for emergency or acute treatment also have a variety of non-medical background problems. Although appropriate support could potentially have important medical and general benefits, they are not usually assessed or targeted for non-clinical support in hospitals. In addition, young people may be suspicious of perceived authority figures, and reticent about discussing sensitive, personal or illicit issues with hospital staff. Hospitals can be the first point of contact for some highly marginalised young people with complex social and medical needs. The ability of youth work to reach these young people in hospitals and connect them with other public services is especially congruent with the joined-up and partnership working sought for services in the Every Child Matters (ECM) measures.

For instance, Redfearn (2003) reports the case of a young woman who attended accident and emergency after taking an overdose of tablets. As a youth worker, he was able to discover that the girl was suffering stress and anxiety related to her home life and her parents' plans to take her overseas for an arranged marriage. He was able to intervene and find a refuge for the young woman. Although addressing a non-medical need, this was an important intervention that fits in with the wider welfare of the young person as defined in the ECM measures (Treasury 2003). Redfearn (2003) also notes that large numbers of adolescents go to accident and emergency departments because they have injuries from self-harming. However, even where they receive medical treatment for their injuries, they usually leave without getting the help and support that they need to address their wider welfare and reduce the likelihood of future self-harm.

Moreover, some medical responses actually have negative impacts. For instance, self-harm is usually initially a private activity and a part of an individual's coping mechanisms, and is apt to elicit misunderstandings and inappropriate and harmful responses from others (NICE 2004). Young people may feel stigmatised by the responses of carers, they may be labelled as attention-seeking or manipulative, and they may meet indifferent or even punitive responses. These responses can undermine young people's self-confidence, increase their distress and the likelihood of future banning incidents, and lead them to avoid health services in the future (NICE 2004).

One strength of youth work is the flexibility of approach that allows these problems to be handled sensitively. Its responses emphasise respect for young people's personal, social and cultural contexts; it aims to work with them holistically and facilitate their personal and social development and their engagement with decisions and choices that affect their lives (e.g. NYA 2004, Spence 2004, LLUK 2007). The principles of youth work as they have been outlined constitute a challenge to treatment-focused, 'adherence' models of intervention that see patients as largely passive. Youth work aims to enable a transactional element to such interventions, to reduce the experience of power differentials inherent in them, emphasise respect for young people's own perspectives and orientations, and encourage an engaged, responsible and active role for them.

[...]

Types of youth work in hospitals

Youth work is characterised by its flexibility of approach to young people, and often works best through processes of participative engagement tailored to the needs of each presenting situation (e.g. Spence 2004). It is therefore difficult to provide complete descriptions of exactly how it functions across various situations. In general terms, however, youth work in hospitals takes the form of one-to-one work with young people, group work, mediation, work with health-care staff and advocacy.

One-to-one work provides support, advice and guidance, and communicates information in ways that young people understand and respond to. Advice and support are not limited to health issues, but concern the whole range of young people's personal and social development, are driven by their needs and perceptions and can cover issues such as bullying, general health, drugs and alcohol, education, familial problems, and so on (Redfearn 2003). This also allows referral to other youth service agencies for short-term intensive work for example, to help improve self-esteem or re-engage young people in their communities. Referrals to other agencies are also made where appropriate – such as signposting young people to parenting projects, Women's Aid, refuges, etc.

Group work can consist of self-help groups for young people with conditions, experiences or problems in common. The NCHYWT [New Cross Hospital Youth Work Team in Central England] have used such groups with young people with diabetes, cancer and Crohn's disease, and with young people on maternity wards. They involve young people in valued joint activities and provide an environment in which group support and advice can be accessed (regarding self-care, addressing common or shared fears and anxieties, and so on). They also provide social interaction and shared social activities for young people isolated by their conditions and their presence in hospital.

Another aspect of hospital-based youth workers' partnership with health-care staff is mediation between young people and health professionals where relationships are difficult. Mediation can be, in one form, a simple translation of ideas, information, requests and so on from health staff to young people, and communication of needs, desires, discomforts and so on, from young people to health staff. It also, however, encompasses recognition of the differential forms of power that characterise the situation surrounding young people in hospitals, and takes the role of challenging this where necessary. This can involve enabling young people to exercise more control over their treatment options, and advocating support for young people's needs or the needs of specific groups of patients at a policy level (Hilton *et al.* 2004). Youth work can also provide models or direct training for hospital staff on ways of working and communicating effectively with young people.

The potential benefits of hospital-based youth work

These different youth work interventions, together, have wide-reaching potential benefits in relation to the problems discussed. A number of the issues raised concern a sense of being different from peers and experiencing discrimination, social isolation, anxiety, depression and family conflict. Youth work can have a significant positive impact with these problems. Youth workers' orientation towards young people, the voluntary nature of young people's interaction with them, their manner and mode of dress, and their skills at communicating with young people allow them to develop particular types of relationships that health professionals in positions of (real or apparent) authority cannot – relationships based on trust, voluntarism, rapport and respect for both individual and cultural and community identities that young people recognise in themselves (Davies 2005). Their role entails actively listening to the needs and views of young people that might be lost by medical staff on busy wards or overlooked in favour of medicalised conceptions of their needs.

Youth workers can provide young people with valued social contact and a trusted source of advice and support that would otherwise be lacking. As one young patient put it, 'If you are worried you can always talk it over with her' (Hilton *et al.* 2004, p. 37). The NCHYWT youth workers also discussed the value of the emotional support they offer. One commented that a young person told her: 'You're the only one that doesn't get pissed off with me ... the only one I can rely on to calm me down.' This close and trusting relationship provided much-needed emotional support, helped to foster the personal development of the young person, and allowed the discussion of 'deep and really distressing' issues between young person and youth worker.

This advice, support and social contact is beneficial in itself, and where necessary youth workers can use links with other services to obtain further support such as child and family workers for those experiencing family conflicts. Also important is the group work that youth workers can facilitate. This can combat some of the social isolation experienced on hospital wards, boost confidence, enable young people to form new social connections (Hilton *et al.* 2004), and emphasise some of the 'normal' aspects of childhood and adolescence missing from the lives of those with chronic conditions. Groups also provide a source of peer support for troubling issues, and allow the sharing and discussion of fears and anxieties. The trusted position of youth workers and their positive relationships with young people also allow groups to work as informal education sessions in which young people can talk confidentially and share information about medical and other issues that worry them (Hilton *et al.* 2004). Group work can thus help address problems of social isolation and other psychosocial problems, and reinforce young people's social development. It can also help to smooth the transition from paediatric to adult care, providing a constant point of contact and support during this period of psycho-social development.

Another important aspect of hospital-based youth work concerns young people's underlying, non-medical problems. Again, youth workers' abilities to form positive relationships with young people are crucial here. This can help to increase young people's engagement with medical services by giving personal attention to needs they experience as important, and recognising their individuality as well as their valued cultural identities. The NCHYWT fieldwork noted the recurrent problem of young people accessing health-care services in hospitals, but leaving before action is taken or treatment is completed. Feedback from young people indicated that they disengaged due to negative perceptions of their initial treatment by hospital staff. In particular, they complained that they disliked being treated as 'cases' rather than individuals. Youth workers in the team addressed this issue by forming relationships with young people who disengaged, reintroducing them to health care services, and supporting them to share important information about themselves with clinical staff to ensure that their needs inform the care they receive.

Youth workers' roles also include advocating on behalf of young people to hospital staff and management (Hilton *et al.* 2004). This includes soliciting the views of young people and presenting them to hospital staff. Clearly, this process can involve challenging the *status quo*, recognising forms of power within the social systems that young people are in, and finding a way of tipping 'the balances of power in young people's favour' (Davies 2005). There is a line to be trodden here involving being on the side of young people and advocating for them without setting them against the institution and its staff in a way that would make future relationships more difficult. This advocacy aims to change practice where necessary and contribute to the development of policy within hospitals that is informed by awareness of the broad sets of issues that most affect young people and that may underlie problems encountered in individual cases.

For instance, Hilton *et al.* (2004) report that youth worker advocacy succeeded in negotiating the setting up of a 'youth room' on the renal unit at City Hospital, Nottingham. It also saw the genesis of a 'transition project', which aimed to provide alternative ways of transferring young people from the paediatric to the adult renal unit (Hilton *et al.* 2004, p. 38), and arranged sessions in which young people, nurses and support workers from the paediatric and adult units, and those recently transferred meet to discuss important issues.

[...]

The NCHYWT fieldwork noted a number of areas of positive impact attributable to youth work in the hospital. Notable among these was a reduction in the number of aggressive incidents on wards since the establishment of the NCHYWT, as noted in the hospital's project notes and backed up by testimony from hospital staff. The evaluation also suggests that the practical support given to young people on admission and the training undertaken with medical staff has reduced readmissions of young people presenting with self-harm, overdose or other 'lifestyle' admissions. There was also evidence of personal and social development for young people, and it was reported that one senior nurse was 'unequivocal in her view' that the work of the team had contributed to increased levels of self-care by young people.

Evidence of impact also comes from discussion of specific cases in reports of hospital youth work (e.g. Redfearn 2003), and by youth workers in NCHYWT interviews. One illustrative case is cited by Redfearn (2003). This involved a young woman with cystic fibrosis who was living in a difficult, mentally abusive relationship and neglecting her self-care. She credits her youth worker with helping her to bring about a positive change in her circumstances:

> I wasn't taking my medicines properly because I was so tired and down ... My cystic fibrosis and what was happening at home really got to me.

If it wasn't for Deborah [her hospital youth worker] I would still be in that situation. Deborah didn't treat me as a patient on a piece of paper; to her I was a real person. I didn't really have anyone to talk to, so having a youth worker there really helped.

(Redfearn 2003, p. 4)

This clearly supports the positive effect that the flexibility of approach, relationship-building and individually tailored responses of youth work can have. While medical interventions did not address the issues behind her lack of self-care, the youth worker offered support that enabled her to leave her abusive relationship and relocate. She further acclaims the role of youth work and contrasts it with other interventions, by commenting, 'Deborah wasn't telling me what to do; she was just supporting me and being there for me' (Redfearn 2003, p. 4). The youth worker here enabled the young person to make informed social choices that also affected her medical care.

A somewhat similar case was encountered by the NCHYWT. One young woman was bereaved after her mother's recent death, and she was not responding to pressure from medical staff to improve her self-care. Her youth worker stated that she was 'diabolical with her care'. This youth worker went on to say that after her intervention: 'She has turned around – you could measure the improvement in her self-care.' The youth worker's account of this intervention again underscores the importance of youth work's approach to young people. She comments that positive impact was achieved 'by not bollocking the kid all the time. The specialist nurse shouts and complains: "Well, C__, why? You know, if you keep doing that, you will ... what do you think you're doing?"' By contrast, youth workers take the approach of 'talking to the young person as a young person with their own mind and full understanding of what they're doing. We have conversations where we're discussing not judging them'. The skills and experience acquired as a youth worker allowed her to 'use ... some of the conversations I had with her mother. I had to do this sensitively, knowing what lengths to go to ... finding the right thing to say at the right time comes with years of doing it'. The intervention of youth work here thus helped the young person to negotiate her own consent for treatment in a way that she did not feel able to previously.

References to 'bollocking' and 'judging' imply a specific relationship of power in which young people and hospital staff are differentially positioned. However, the voluntaristic nature of the youth worker–young person relationship, the approach of the youth worker, and the lack of authority-based sanctions mean that it is very different with respect to how power structures the relationship. The type of approach illustrated above is not simply a 'softer' form of 'bollocking', nor analogous to it, but is based upon open, reciprocal and respectful communication between youth worker and young person.

[...]

Conclusion

There are a range of potential problems and difficulties facing young people in hospitals. Although there are potential medical and general lifestyle benefits to working with these issues, hospital staff and standard clinical interventions are often not best placed to provide the support or guidance that is needed. Indeed, relationships between young people and health staff can be characterised by striking asymmetries in power that young people find challenging. Standard clinical responses may actually be negatively perceived by young people, and relationships with health-care professionals may become contested and counter-productive in terms of engaging young people and encouraging their adherence to treatment regimens.

The flexible, voluntaristic, individually tailored and relationship-based approach to intervening with young people and facilitating group work, and the skills and experience of youth workers in communicating effectively with them mean that youth work in hospitals has many potential benefits.

Youth work in hospitals encompasses individual and group-based activity, leisure-based work, supportive, therapeutic approaches, and active intervention and advocacy with medical staff. The varying approaches are unified by a concern both for the young person as an individual and an understanding of the social and institutional factors that provide context for their experiences. There is also a concern for power, and 'tipping the balances of power in favour of the young person' (Davies 2005) when power operates on them to their detriment. There is evidence that this is effective in improving relationships, communications and the consent process between young people and hospital staff, increasing levels of self-care and adherence to treatment regimens, and intervening with underlying background issues that affect young people's general and medical well-being. Being based in hospitals also allows youth workers to access large numbers of young people in real need of support that would otherwise be lost to youth services. Framed within the agency structure debate in sociology, it could perhaps be said that youth work resides within a redistributive discourse (Levitas 2005) that aims to foster interventions that increase young people's capacity for agency with respect to their own lives, and challenges discourses that situate them in one way or another as the causes of their own difficulties. These impacts of youth work also have benefits for hospital staff and the hospital itself by increasing young people's engagement, providing positive models of working with young people, and facilitating improved medical interactions in what is a busy and complex area for hospital staff.

Despite these potential positive impacts, however, hospital-based youth work remains rare in the UK. Evidence of impact and best practice in this environment is thus also scarce. The evidence discussed here presents a pressing need for a further research, possibly action research, and a broader understanding of youth work in hospital settings. Further investigation into the extent to which different aspects of youth work achieve effective impacts would be beneficial, and – potentially, at least – so would the expansion of hospital-based youth work.

References

Alvin, P. *et al.* (2002) Adolescents and emergency care. A survey conducted at the Assistance Publique-Hôpitaux de Paris. Neuropsychiatrie de l'enfance et de l'adolescence, **50**(8), 571–576.

Atkin, K. and Ahmad, W.I.U. (2000) Pumping iron: compliance with chelation therapy among young people who have thalassaemia major. *Sociology of health and illness*, **22**(4), 500–524.

Atkin, K. and Ahmad, W.I.U. (2001) Living a 'normal' life: young people coping with thalassaemia major or sickle cell disorder. *Social science and medicine*, **53**(5), 615–626.

Bell, L. (2007) Adolescents with renal disease in an adult world: meeting the challenge of transition of care. *Nephrology dialysis transplantation*, **4**(1), 988–991.

Bissell, P., May, C.R. and Noyce, P.R. (2004) From compliance to concordance: barriers to accomplishing a re-framed model of health care interactions. *Social science and medicine*, **58**(4), 851–862.

Burke, T. (2002) Awards on the ward: a youth work presence in a hospital can make a big impact. *Young people now*, **159**, 24–25.

Davies, B. (2005) Youth work: a manifesto for our times. *Youth and policy*, **88**, 5–28.

Department of Health (DH) (2000) *Framework for the assessment of children in need and their families.* London: HMSO.

Eiser, C. (1993) *Growing up with a chronic disease: the impact on children and their families.* London: Jessica Kingsley.

Fielding, D. and Duff, A. (1999) Compliance with treatment protocols: interventions for children with chronic illness. *Archives of disease in childhood*, **80**, 196–200.

Greening, L. *et al.* (2006) Child routines and youths' adherence to treatment for type 1 diabetes, *Journal of pediatric psychology*, **32**(4), 437–447.

Hentinen, M. and Kynga's, H. (1992) Compliance of young diabetics with health regimens. *Journal of advanced nursing*, **17**, 530–536.

Hilton, D. *et al.* (2004) Youth work in hospital: the impact of a youth worker on the lives of adolescents with chronic conditions is evaluated. *Paediatric nursing*, **16**(1), 36–39.

Hulse, G.K., Robertson, S.I. and Tait, R.J. (2001) Adolescent emergency department presentations with alcohol or other drug-related problems in Perth, Western Australia. *Addiction*, **96**(7), 1059–1067.

Kennedy, A. *et al.* (2007) Young people with chronic illness: the approach to transition. *Internal medicine journal*, **37**, 555–560.

Latarjet, J. and Choinere, M. (1995) Pain in burn patients. *Burns*, **21**(5), 344–348.

Levitas, R. (2005) *The inclusive society? Social exclusion and New Labour.* 2nd edn. London: Palgrave Macmillan.

Lewis-Jones, S. (2006) Quality of life and childhood atopic dermatitis: the misery of living with childhood eczema. *International journal of clinical practice*, **60**(8), 984–992.

LLUK (2007) National Occupational Standards for Youth Work. Available from: http://www. youthlink.co.uk/docs/Training%20docs/Developing%20up%20to%20date%20NOS.doc (Accessed 20 September 2008).

Marcell, A.V. *et al.* (2002) Male adolescent use of health care services: where are the boys? *Journal of adolescent health*, **30**(1), 35–43.

NICE (2004) Self-harm: the short-term physical and psychological management and secondary prevention of self-harm in primary and secondary care. London: NICE.

NYA (2004) *Ethical conduct in youth work.* Leicester: NYA.

Por, J. *et al.* (2004) Transition of care: health care professionals' view. *Journal of nursing management*, **12**, 354–361.

Redfearn, G. (2003) Hospital youth work: through the pain barrier. *Young people now.* Available from: http://www.ypnmagazine.com/news/index.cfm?fuseaction–full_ news&ID–1902 (Accessed 9 May 2007).

Royal Pharmaceutical Society of Great Britain (1997) *From compliance to concordance; achieving shared goals in medicine taking.* London: Royal Pharmaceutical Society of Great Britain.

Spence, J. (2004) Targeting, accountability and youth work practice. *Practice*, **16**(4), 261–272.

Spernak, S., Moore, P.J. and Hamm, L.F. (2007) Depression, constructive thinking and patient satisfaction in cardiac treatment adherence. *Psychology. health and medicine*, **12**(2), 172–189.

Todd, K.H. *et al.* (2006) Sickle cell disease related pain: crisis and conflict. *Journal of pain*, **7**, 453–458.

Treasury (2003) Every child matters. Norwich: Stationery Office.

Tsiantis, J. (1990) Family reactions and relationships in thalassaemia. *Annals of the New York Academy of Sciences*, **612**, 451–461.

Viner, R. (1999) Transition from paediatric to adult care: bridging gaps or passing the buck? *Archives of disease in childhood*, **81**, 271–275.

We are grateful that this chapter has provided us with an alternative approach to the standard clinical response to young people in hospital. Through exploring the use of youth work methodologies and inter-agency work it has considered how young people can become more engaged in shaping their experiences in hospital settings and become more active in making choices about their medical care.

Chapter 23

Working in the community with young people who offend

Alice Sampson and Spyros Themelis

This chapter discusses the findings of a study of four community based youth inclusion programmes (YIP) and considers how different approaches can inform and improve practice in work with young offenders. The chapter begins by comparing the 'at risk' and 'what works' approaches all too often used in the management of the youth criminal justice system. Then the authors explore a range of interventions that are meaningful to young people and which can lead to changes of behaviour which determine young people's chances of further offending.

[...]

Introduction

Two particular developments inform youth criminal justice policy making and practices in several countries including Britain, the US and Australia: an 'at risk' approach for conceptualising youth offending, and assessing young offenders' propensity to reoffend, and a 'what works' evaluation framework to assess the effectiveness of interventions to prevent further offending and to identify the most promising crime reduction and prevention programmes (Sherman *et al.* 1997, Nuttal 1998, Utting and Vernard 2000, Communities That Care (CtC) 2001, Australian Institute of Criminology (AIC) 2002).
   [...]
   [Our] purpose [...] is to discuss in more detail the gaps in our knowledge about practice that arise from the 'at risk' and 'what works' approach and to demonstrate that an alternative approach that finds out how interventions may, or may not, work produces knowledge more useful for designing interventions and for developing effective practices. To explore the value of this alternative approach, we draw on research findings from an evaluation

that took place five years ago. We make no claim that this alternative approach is either systematically or comprehensively developed; rather, our aim is to demonstrate its potential for assisting practitioners to work more effectively with young people who offend.

The Youth Inclusion Programme

The findings used to explore these issues draw on an evaluation of the Youth Inclusion Programme (YIP), a flagship intervention initiated by the Youth Justice Board (YJB). The YIP is funded by the Youth Justice Board and adheres to the 'at risk' and 'what works' framework (Brown 1998, MHB 2003). The YIP is a community-based initiative consisting of multiple interventions, initially for 133 16-year-olds at risk of offending and offenders, and more recently for 83 17-year-olds. The programme was originally set up in 70 disadvantaged neighbourhoods in England and Wales in 1998. Each YIP aims to work with the 50 most at risk offenders – also known as the 'top 50' – in an identified neighbourhood and, at the time of the research, to engage them for a minimum of 10 hours a week in constructive activities. The targets of the programme are to reduce arrest rates among the 'top 50', to reduce truancy and school exclusions, and to reduce neighbourhood crime. YIPs continue to be heralded as a success by the Youth Justice Board, and in 2008 investment in this programme was increased (YJB 2008).

YIPs offer a variety of activities including sports, music, IT courses, and one-to-one and group sessions. 'One-off' trips and outings are organised as rewards, and incentives to retain the young people's participation. YIP workers liaise with parents/carers, schoolteachers, community representatives, and staff from other agencies.

[...]

The 'at risk' framework and practice

Working with young people to understand the reasons and circumstances surrounding their offending behaviour is often a challenging process for practitioners, and having a framework within which to work can provide useful guidance. The strength of the 'at risk' framework is that it has the potential to inform practitioners about the characteristics and circumstances of young persons that may make them prone to offend.

The focus of the 'at risk' approach has been to predict anti-social behaviour and criminality at an early stage in the lives of children, before the onset of criminality (Farrington 1996). Risk factors are conceptualised as 'deficits' in young persons and their circumstances, such as inability to concentrate on tasks, forming friendships with anti-social peers, and living in poor housing (see Farrington 1996) – an approach underpinning many policies that problematises young people (Brown 2005). Some researchers have found that the accumulation of risks, rather than particular types of risks, is a strong predictor of offending (YJB 2005) or serious offending (Hawkins *et al.* 1998). Other researchers have found that particular types of risk factors are more predictive of violent criminality than others – for example, lack of social ties and anti-social peers (Lipsey and Denzon 1998).

With use of the research findings on risk and protective factors, the Asset assessment form has been devised to enable practitioners to identify a young person's risk factors, and research has found that Asset reliably predicts future criminality (Baker *et al.* 2002). However, the relationship between offending and risks lacks clarity in a number of respects. Risks are typically understood from the perspective of young people becoming criminals (CtC 2001) and the need to control problematic behaviour by reducing risks (*Smith, R.* 2006), but research also shows that many of the consequences of victimisation are predictors of offending, including poor academic performance and poor peer relationships, and that being a victim of a crime was the strongest predictor of violent offending (Wordes and Nunez 2002). These findings show that many risk factors that are expected to predict offending are associated with other outcomes as well suggesting that the predictive links between risks and offending are far from clear-cut. The same holds for other risk factors. In disadvantaged neighbourhoods, some identified risks cannot be readily linked to offending:

> A major problem, however, lies in identifying the active ingredient to be targeted. Low income and poor housing arc interrelated, but the causal chain linking these factors with offending is unclear.
>
> (Farrington 1996, p. 21)

Similarly, in a study of over 900 young teenage boys living in disadvantaged public housing areas in the US, there was no significant difference in serious offending between those with high protection scores, those with high risk scores, or those with a balance of protective risk scores (Wikström and Loeber 2000, p. 1131), a finding leading Bottoms to note that 'in certain social contexts the whole concept of "individual risk factors" might be of limited applicability' (Bottoms 2002, p. 39). [...]

'What works' and effective interventions

The 'what works' framework arose out of the reaction to the 'nothing works' thesis that was popular in the 1970s (Vennard *et al.* 1997). In 1996, Lipsey carried out a meta-analysis of 400 studies on prevention programmes for young people who offend that had used experimental or quasi-experimental research designs, and concluded, 'As a generality, treatment clearly works' (Lipsey 1996, p. 78). This and other subsequent meta-analysis studies (Sherman *et al.* 1997) brought about a new-found confidence that interventions can work, and attention turned to determining which types of interventions are 'most effective' and which might 'not work'. However, Lipsey warned against this type of data analysis:

> The inherent fuzziness of these coded categories makes futile any discussion of whether behaviour modification, or whatever your particular pet treatment might be, is universally superior to, say, family counselling.
>
> (Lipsey 1996, p. 74)

For practitioners who routinely need to decide which interventions may be effective for a young person, the knowledge arising from 'what works' research findings is not helpful in a number of respects. The same programmes 'work' in some situations, such as mentoring and truancy programmes (Utting and Vennard 2000), but not in others. Lipsey also commented on the findings of his meta-analysis study that the impact of the same interventions varies in different contexts:

> There is wide variation ranging from circumstances in which treatment actually seems to increase delinquency to those in which the reductions are quite substantial.
>
> (Lipsey 1996, p. 77)

Nevertheless, proponents of the 'at risk' perspective have argued that successful interventions are those that reduce risk factors (see, for example, CtC 2001, pp. 103–112), and that interventions should aim to maximise protective factors and minimise risk factors (Catalano and Hawkins 1996, Pollard and Hawkins 1999, YJB 2005). Protective factors include improved self-esteem and a sense of self-efficacy and the promotion of social bonding with pro-social adults and peers (CtC 2001, pp. 22–24). If interventions are going to 'implant' protective factors to mitigate adverse risk, understanding the risk–protective factors relationship is essential. However, the complexity of the interaction between risk and protective factors remains unclear (YJB 2005), the problem being that 'the relationship between risk and protective factors and the precise ways in which they interrelate and react is uncertain' (CtC 2001, p. 24).

[...]

Understanding 'the problem'

The 'problem' of offending is understood from the perspective of designing intervention. From this perspective, the 'problem' is explored with young people to find out how to intervene in a way that is meaningful to them and leads to a change in behaviour. In exploring this issue, two themes emerged from the research. The first was that 'the problem' of offending could not just be accounted for by examining risk factors. An analysis of the sample interviews found that the most common reasons for offending were as follows:

- to settle differences and maintain a presence in their area;
- boredom and to seek enjoyment and have fun ('buzz seekers');
- feelings of insecurity and vulnerability;
- for material gain – for example, food and clothing;
- to feed a drugs habit.

While some of the reasons are within the risk perspective, including stealing to obtain food and clothes or offending due to feelings of insecurity and vulnerability, other reasons for offending were not, for example those who offended to settle differences. These young people said that they should stand up for what they believe in and defend themselves to establish and maintain their credibility. These young people had a strong sense of justice that motivated them to resist being marginalised and alienated. For this reason, two young Black African women aged 15 and 13 years did not perceive their fighting as criminal. They explained:

> People are expecting us to be bad, but we're not. We're normal girls. … Sticking up for yourself and fighting if necessary.

In the YIP neighbourhoods, criminal incidents arose from tensions with adults. Young people felt aggrieved by the way adults perceived them:

> The adults? They stereotype us; they say that all young people are vandals and criminals.

As a result of these perceptions, another young man described what happened:

> If we play football they call the police and we'll get arrested for smoking drugs and making noise. Adults start fights with kids and they [the kids] get beaten.

The crimes committed by these young people were a response to a social problem, rather than a 'risk', and required a social solution. The workers on one YIP demonstrated the value of addressing the reasons for the offending and successfully initiated a community solution; they discussed the reactions of the adults with the young people, talked to the adults about the alienating consequences of their behaviour, and brought the young people and adults together. One young person commented on the effect of this intervention:

> We learnt to respect the adults. The YIP spoke to the adults and it helped a lot. They are better with us.

Second, we found that part of understanding 'the problem' included linking reasons and motives for offending to the intervention. The accounts of two young men, presented below, illustrate that when interventions address motives and reasons for offending they are more likely to be successful.

The first young man participated on the YIP for 16 months, for an average of six hours a month. He committed crime as 'something to do':

> Before I used to do crime but not any more. When you do music you enter a different world. I changed as a person ... it's the way they talk to you. They are [the YIP staff] a second parent. I made more friends. Before [joining the YIP] I used to hate every little kid. Music changed me. I performed and this gave me confidence. Before I used to get arrested. When I first came here I didn't think it would help me but it did. They [the YIP workers] talk to you. My attitude towards school has changed. I try to be good in order to come here. [Truancy] has gone down to zero.

In this example, the activity itself – the music – changed the young person, and he recognised that his relationship with the youth workers was part of the process of change. As a result of his experiences on the YIP, he acquired a better understanding of himself, grew in confidence, changed his attitude towards school and felt valued. These feelings enabled him to have the confidence to improve his skills, through participating in music and football, and going on trips and, in turn, raised his aspirations.

The second young man was involved in many activities during his three years at the YIP. He participated in football, music, internet radio, day trips, and residential courses, and was supported at his appearances in court, but one of his motives was not addressed and therefore he continued some offending. The young man explains:

When I do football I feel tired and I don't wanna go out and do bad stuff. I don't know why ... the way probably they treat us; they respect us. After music I've got the adrenaline and don't need to go out and do bad stuff. [The YIP] gives you sense of security but when you go out and don't have money ... you'll steal. I do it 'cause it's so'thin' to do. I've got money in my pocket. Nothin' can make me stop doin' it. Others do it for fun. I do it 'cause my mum doesn't have the money to buy for me and my brother for the necessary: if I wanna get a pair of trainers, she's not having that money. So, I'll steal and give her most of the money and keep the rest for myself I know I may get caught and stuff ... but I have to do it. They should give money to the parents to support their children; then we wouldn't have to do it. They don't give enough money to the parents. So I'll steal and get what I want.

The experiences of this young man illustrate how the type of activities, the amount of activities, and the length of time a young person may be engaged on a programme do not have an impact on offending behaviour where motives and reasons are not addressed.

These findings provide the basis for our contention that if interventions are to be effectively designed, it is necessary to find the reasons and motives for offending and to design a programme to address them. If reasons and motives identified by young people are not addressed through social programmes, young people are less likely to desist from further offending.

Working with young people

From the research findings, we have some indication of how practitioners can work with young people to understand their problems and to find solutions. This includes questioning, challenging and working with young persons to 'move' them on. Moving young persons 'on' is understood as intervening in ways that change their decision-making processes, assuming that this can be achieved by altering how young persons perceive their situation and circumstances. Our research findings about positive relationships illustrate how changes can occur.

Negotiating positive relationships

As in other studies, we found that creating a positive atmosphere enabled relationships to flourish (Smith 1988, Smith and Paylor 1993, Muncie *et al.* 1995, Huskins 1996), and that young people needed support and encouragement from 'significant others' to give up offending (Barry 2006). Systems of incentives, rewards and promise were integrated into activities to make young persons feel accepted and valued; certificates, meals at restaurants, and trips to the cinema were part of the activities, such as mentoring, football, and music making. In some YIPs, every effort was made to make young people feel comfortable and relaxed by providing sofas and attractive decoration, and by warmly welcoming young people. YIP workers recognised that a physically and emotionally safe environment was part of building relationships. Humour was used to build relationships, and as a way of controlling and relieving tensions. Young people responded positively to a non-judgemental approach, and to workers who were empathetic (Knight 2006). Respect, a key element in many young people's accounts of their experiences, occurred when young persons were accepted for what they really were (Sennett 2004), and this required actively listening, as well as talking, to them.

Where there was a positive and safe environment, young people were more inclined to share their feelings, and where trust and mutual respect were negotiated between a young person and a worker, more information was exchanged, particularly information that a young person considered 'private', including reasons and motives for offending. The disclosure of this information provided opportunities for YIP workers and a young person to work together to achieve change. The following comments by two young people explain how positive relationships changed how they perceived their situation. For one young man, this led to desistance from offending:

> It took me two years to learn that they [the people from the YIP] are not working for the police. Now I can trust them ... I had loads of issues [regarding his offending behaviour]. They [the YIP youth workers] helped me a lot. Then I realised there was no point getting in trouble.

For another young person, it was his positive relationship with the youth worker – and his mother – which changed how he perceived himself and led to the improvements in his school attendance:

> I have changed my attitude towards school. I try to be good in order to come to the YIP ... the youth worker, as well as my mum, has made a difference to the way I think about myself.

When young persons felt respected, they talked about becoming 'calmer', and this changed how they assessed themselves and their situation. This calmness can be achieved through participating in an activity, from advice or by talking with peers and workers. Two young men who attended different YIPs explained:

> I don't get rude to people any more ... My attitude has changed 'cause of the way they helped us. They calmed us down on trips ... When I wasn't on trips, I always used to get into trouble. Now I think I respect them [adults] more than I used to 'cause if I respect them they will respect me back ... They trust us [the young people]. It shows that they want to get us more involved.
>
> Yeah, the YIP helps you calm down. You can get advice. They can help ... I haven't been excluded after coming to the YIP. I used to have [one-to-one sessions], but not any more. It keeps you off trouble.

This 'calm' gave young people a feeling of self-confidence that motivated them to take advantage of new opportunities. The young person below took up the offer of teaching football. Being given responsibilities was confirmation of the respect accorded to him, and this gave him the social recognition that Barry (2006) found in her study on young offenders to contribute to desistance. A young man explained:

> It is also useful that all the staff are respectful and helpful. They are always there. They will try to sort you out I am really pleased that they asked me to do this job [teaching younger people football]. It's great that they trust me.

Young people who felt understood and valued were willing to learn new social skills that lead to improved relationships. One young man said:

> Yes. I met friends here and there is understanding ... [and] More respected attitude with the staff ... I don't feel bored anymore ... and it's easier to speak to girls.

In certain circumstances, fostering respect can have a direct influence on preventing crime. The following comments by young people show how the reasons for committing racially motivated crimes were removed:

> Before coming to the YIP I used to hate all people apart from Whites. In my school there were no Blacks and I was not used to them. Now we are mixed and there is more respect

Through these relationships, young people gained confidence to try new activities, acquired new skills, and used new knowledge that changed how they perceived themselves and how they interacted with others. These changes altered the reasoning and motives of young people and enabled them to reassess the 'logic' of their situation.

Identifying how to improve practices

A research approach that aims to find out how interventions make a difference has the capacity to identify how practices may be improved. Two such areas were identified in our research. First, many of the statements made by young people revealed that emotions were integral to their offending (also see Barry 2006) and to their responses to interventions.

 For each type of offender in the research sample, the main emotions varied; for those whose motive was primarily about settling differences, a sense of injustice and unfairness prevailed; for those who offended for a 'buzz', the thrill of taking risks and the excitement dominated; and for those who had many uncertainties and insecurities, anger was a motivating part of their criminal involvement.

During fieldwork observations, it was noted by researchers attending a women's group that while the youth worker was respected, she was unable to engage the young women emotionally. In a subsequent discussion with the youth worker, she felt that this was why the young women continued with much of their offending, albeit less frequently.

It appears from our research findings that engaging emotionally with young people is key to enabling them to reassess their situation and therefore to 'move on' (also see Farrall and Calverley 2006). While the importance of working with feelings and emotions has been noted elsewhere (Huskins 1996), we found that emotional work with young people was invariably neglected by YIP workers.

Second, another challenge for the YIP workers was how to work with young people so they are able to transfer improvements in their behaviour across their different social worlds. Young people talked about behaving differently at YIP activities, at home, on the streets and at school. One YIP worker was shocked by the behaviour he observed of one young person:

> At the YIP George is as good as gold, well-mannered and good fun ... I couldn't believe it when I saw him at school ... he was surly, rude and aggressive.

A Black African woman talked about her own behaviour: 'When I go through the school gates ... I just turn, I just turn nasty.' Some of the young people referred to themselves as living in 'different social worlds' and said that their attendance at a YIP had made a positive difference to some aspects of their lives, but not others. An interview with a young White woman who offended before and during her nine-month involvement with a YIP provides an example. For this young woman, her experiences on the YIP were separate from other events in her life; she continued to truant, shoplift, and enjoy drinking in pubs (she was underage), and in the last few months was involved in 'a number of fights'. She attributed positive changes in herself to her participation on the YIP: she felt more confident, but this was just in performing dance shows at festivals; she felt that she was more mature at YIP activities because she was mixing with adults, and was proud to be given responsibilities during some of the activities. Thus, the challenge for youth workers is to assist young people to make connections between their different social worlds to enable them to transfer their new skills and knowledge between each of their 'social worlds'. Unfortunately, a more detailed account of the transfer process, how it occurs, and why it occurs for some young people rather than others was outside the scope of our study. We recognise that this information would be most useful for practitioners.

Concluding comments

[...][W]e have drawn on the literature that discusses the 'at risk' approach to managing youth offending and the 'what works' approach to evaluating the effectiveness of interventions to prevent further offending, which are intended to improve the performance of youth criminal justice systems. Inadequacies are identified in the ability of this framework to explain conceptually and empirically how to design effective interventions and how to work effectively with young people who offend. Using findings from an evaluation study of a community based prevention programme, we explored the potential of an alternative approach that is more informative about how to improve practice. Our research revealed that practitioners respected by young people typically used a problem-solving approach with young people to encourage them to understand their situation and circumstances and to work with them to find solutions to their problems. The use of a problem-solving approach by practitioners underpinned our approach, and we understood interventions as solutions to problems associated with offending. In our research design, we prioritised finding out how interventions worked, and this approach has the potential to explain why an intervention may successfully reduce offending for some young people rather than others, and has the potential to generate information about how to improve practices. This is not to dismiss completely the 'at risk' management approach but to recognise that, for practitioners, it provides a framework for understanding the situations and circumstances for offending rather than the motives and reasons for offending, which is useful knowledge for those working with young people and is central to young people's decisions to offend or to desist from offending. However, we recognise that the transfer of information from research findings to actual practices, the transition from 'knowing to doing', is a complex and challenging process that also has to occur if practices are to improve (Nutley *et al.* 2003).

The research findings [...] illustrate the value of prioritising how interventions work to improve young people's experiences, and the challenges facing practitioners, centre stage, in contrast to the current marginalisation of young people's experiences and the knowledge and experience of practitioners (Garland 2001, Kemshall 2003, Case 2006). More generally, it has been argued that taking a problem-solving approach marks a 'genuine shift from punishment to problem solving [that] would produce a society that is both safer and fairer' (Allen 2006). [...]

References

Allen, R. (2006) From punishment to problem-solving. Editorial 'Community engagement'. *Criminal justice matters*, **64**, 3.

Australian Institute of Criminology (2002) What works in reducing young people's involvement in crime? Australian Capital Territory Government.

Baker, K. *et al.* (2002) *Validity and reliability of Asset: findings from the first two years of the use of Asset*, London: Youth Justice Board of England and Wales.

Barry, M. (2006) *Youth offending in transition*. London: Routledge.

Bottoms, A. (2002) Morality, crime, compliance and public policy. In: A. Bottoms and M. Tonry, (eds) *Ideology, crime and criminal justice*. Devon: Willan Publishing, 20–51.

Brown, S. (1998) Youth Works: the evaluation: a report of the external evaluation of Youth Works. Unpublished. Faculty of Law, University of Sheffield.

Brown, S. (2005) *Understanding youth and crime*. 2nd edn. Maidenhead: Open University Press.

Case, S. (2006) Youth people 'at risk' of what? Challenging risk focused early intervention as crime
prevention. *Youth justice*, **6**(3), 171–179.

Catalano, R. and Hawkins, J. (1996) The social development model: a theory of antisocial behaviour. In: J. Hawkins, (ed.) *Delinquency and crime*. Cambridge: Cambridge University Press, 149–197.

Communities That Care (CtC) (2001) *Risk and protective factors associated with youth crime and effective interventions to prevent it*. London: Youth Justice Board for England and Wales.

Farrall, S. and Calverley, A. (2006) *Understanding desistance from crime*. Maidenhead: Open University Press.

Farrington, D.P. (1996) *Understanding and preventing youth crime*. Bristol: YPS in association with Joseph Rowntree Foundation.

Garland, D. (2001) *Culture of control*. Oxford: Oxford University Press.

Hawkins, D. *et al.* (1998) A review of predictors of youth violence. In: R Loeber, and D.P. Farrington, (eds) *Serious and violent juvenile offenders: risk factors and successful interventions.* London: Sage, 106–146.

Huskins, J. (1996) *Quality work with young people: developing social skills and diversion from risk.* Bristol: Huskins.

Kemshall, H. (2003) *Understanding risk in criminal justice.* Maidenhead: Open University Press.

Knight, R. (2006) *Working with repeat users of the youth criminal justice system. Research Report 2.* University of East London: Centre for Institutional Studies.

Lipsey, M. (1996) What do we learn from 400 research studies on the effectiveness of treatment with juvenile delinquents? In: J. McGuire, (ed.) *What works: reducing re-offending.* Chichester: Wiley, 63–78.

Lipsey, M. and Derzon, J. (1998) Predictors of violent or serious delinquency in adolescence and early adulthood: a synthesis of longitudinal research. In: R Loeber and D.P. Farrington, (eds) *Serious and violent Juvenile offenders: risk factors and successful interventions.* London: Sage, 86–105.

Morgan, Harris, Burrows (MHB) (2003) Evaluation of the youth inclusion programme: end of phase one. Report 10 the Youth Justice Board of England and Wales. Available from: http:// www.youth-justice-board.gov.uk/publications (Accessed 14 January 2004).

Muncie, J., Coventry, G. and Walters, R. (1995) The politics of youth crime prevention; developments in Australia and England and Wales. In: L. Noakes, M. Levi and M. Maguire, (eds) *Contemporary issues in criminology.* Cardiff: University of Wales Press, 338–361.

Nutley, M.S., Walter, I. and Davies, H. (2003) From knowing to doing: a framework for understanding the evidence-into-practice agenda. *Evaluation,* **9**, 125–148.

Nuttal, C. (1998) Reducing offending: an assessment of research evidence on ways of dealing with offending behaviour. Research and Statistics Directorate Report 187. London: Home Office Research and Statistics Directorate.

Pollard, J. and Hawkins, D. (1999) Risk: and protection: are both necessary to understand diverse behavioural outcomes in adolescence? *Social work: research,* **23**(3), 145–158.

Sennett, R. (2004) *Respect the formation of character in an age of inequality.* London: Penguin.

Sherman, W.S. *et al.* (1997) Preventing crime: what works, what doesn't, what's promising. Report to the United States Congress, February. Washington, DC: US Department of Justice.

Smith, D. and Paylor, I. (1993) Reluctant heroes: youth workers and crime prevention. *Youth and policy,* **57**, 17–28.

Smith, M. (1988) *Developing youth work: informal education, mutual aid and popular practice.* Milton Keynes: Open University Press.

Smith, R. (2006) Actuarialism and early intervention in contemporary youth justice. In: B. Goldson and J. Muncie, eds. *Youth crime and justice: critical issues.* London: Sage, 92–109.

Utting. D. and Vennard, J. (2000) *What works with young offenders in the community?* Essex: Barnardos.

Vennard, J., Sugg, D. and Hedderman, C. (1997) Changing offenders' attitudes and' behaviour: what works? *Home Office Research Study 171.* London: Home Office.

Wikström, P.H. and Loeber, R. (2000) Do disadvantaged neighbourhoods cause well-adjusted children to become adolescent delinquents? A study of male juvenile serious offending, individual risk and protective factors, and neighbourhood risk factors. *Criminology,* **38**(4), 1109–1143.

Wordes, M. and Nunez, M. (2002) *Our vulnerable teenagers: their victimization, its consequences and directions for prevention and intervention*. National Council on Crime and Delinquency and the National Centre for Victims of Crime.

Youth Justice Board (YJB) (2005) *Role of risk and protective factors*. London: Youth Justice Board for England and Wales.

Youth Justice Board (YJB) (2008) *Youth justice magazine*. January. London: Youth Justice Board for England and Wales.

The authors in this article have suggested that the reasons and motives identified by young people for re-offending need to be addressed through social programmes, and that moving young people's experiences centre stage can reduce their marginalisation. They have also identified that a problem-solving approach towards young people can encourage young people to find solutions to their own problems. As with many of the other chapters, their findings point to enabling a more inclusive approach amongst practitioners towards young people's situations.

Index